FRANK FRIEL & JOHN GUINTHER

S0-AQI-937

BREAKING THE MOB

WARNER BOOKS

A Time Warner Company

WARNER BOOKS EDITION

This Warner Books Edition is published by arrangement with McGraw-Hill Publishing Company, 1221 Avenue of the Americas, New York, NY.

Cover design by Tom Tafuri
Cover illustration by Steven Stroud

Warner Books, Inc.
666 Fifth Avenue
New York, N.Y. 10103

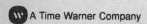 A Time Warner Company

Printed in the United States of America

First Warner Books Printing: February, 1992

10 9 8 7 6 5 4 3 2 1

For bringing the investigation of the Scarfo mob to a successful conclusion, dozens of law enforcement officers and prosecutors deserve credit. Many of them are named, and the roles they played described, in the pages ahead, and they know the high regard in which I hold them. The names of still others have been omitted, not because I value them any the less highly, but because of limitations of space, and the fact that many of them worked on cases in which I was not directly involved. To all of them, the named and the unnamed, this book is dedicated—and to the belled sheep.

—F.F.

For all their help and guidance in putting this book together, a special thank you to Elisabeth Jakab of McGraw-Hill, who served as its editor, and Elizabeth Knappman, our agent.

—F.F., J.G.

ACCLAIM FOR
LIEUTENANT FRANK FRIEL'S
EXTRAORDINARY
TRUE STORY OF
BREAKING THE MOB

"Describes the anatomy of one of the biggest and most successful investigations in Philadelphia law-enforcement history . . . It is the description of the human face of the mob—the husbands, wives, sons and daughters whose daily lives revolved around their connections to the bloody organization—that gives this book its edge."
                    —*Philadelphia Inquirer*

"A lively, entertaining adventure filled with colorful characters and an intelligent account of the American romance with organized crime."
                    —**Philip Ginsburg, author of**
                       Poisoned Blood

"What makes the book especially noteworthy are the authors' insights into the psychology of mobsters."
                    —*Publishers Weekly*

"Frank Friel is a man of stubbornness, honesty, and single-minded dedication to his goal. He is the stuff movies are made of."
                    —**Ira Rosen, senior producer,**
                       Primetime Live

"Gripping."
                                        —*Booklist*

"No detective in the history of the Philadelphia Police Department was better than Frank Friel."
                    —**Frank Rizzo, former police commissioner**
                       and former mayor of Philadelphia

"Frank Friel's unprecedented successes in battling organized crime allowed our department to assume a leadership role in nailing La Cosa Nostra's coffin shut."
                    —**Kevin M. Tucker, former**
                       Philadelphia police commissioner

OTHER BOOKS BY JOHN GUINTHER

CONTENTS

PREFACE

On a wall of his home in Atlantic City, New Jersey, Nicodemo "Little Nicky" Scarfo exhibited portraits of his three heroes. On the left was Benito Mussolini, on the right Napoleon Bonaparte, in the center a framed black-and-white photograph of Al Capone.

Scarfo—who, law enforcement authorities believe, authorized, participated in or personally committed at least twenty-six murders during his career as a criminal—reigned as don of the Philadelphia/Atlantic City Mafia between 1981 and 1989. During those years, I spent almost all of my professional life doing battle with him. I became, he told me, his principal nemesis, although he and I never came face to face until 1987.

The story I have to tell in this book is, in large part, about the law enforcement effort against Scarfo and the role I played in carrying it out. The book is also about the nature of police work as I have experienced it over thirty years. I have been a cop my entire adult life. I began with the Philadelphia Police Department as a patrol officer, was promoted to sergeant, then to lieutenant. Between 1982 and 1986, while a lieutenant, I was in charge of homicide investigations for the Philadelphia Police/FBI Organized Crime Task Force. From 1986 through 1988, as a captain, I commanded the Philadelphia Police Department's new organized crime unit and continued to work closely with the Task Force. In 1989, I retired from the police to become Director of Public Safety in Bensalem, Pennsylvania.

Thus I have, over the past three decades, been exposed to all the varieties of crime fighting, from investigating auto thefts to mob murders; I've done it on the streets in uniform, as a detective in plain clothes, and, finally, as an administrator. The conclusions I have reached from my experiences are not all happy ones. While I respect and admire the overwhelming majority of law enforcement people with whom I have worked— cops, federal agents, state troopers—I have been forced to conclude that all too often police work in this country is inefficiently and incompetently performed. The inadequacies of individuals play a role; everyone makes mistakes, and in this book I'll detail some of my own. However, the underlying problem, I am convinced, is a systemic one. It exhibits itself in unimaginative, outmoded and ineffective bureaucratic regulations, and in wrong assumptions about human psychology. The system is rife with self-defeating jealousies and prejudices that are inadvertently encouraged within police departments. Equally counterproductive rivalries occur between the police and other law enforcement bodies. Vast amounts of time are wasted on paperwork. (In Philadelphia's police department, which is typical of large metropolitan forces throughout the country, 70 percent of a detective's time is spent typing up reports.) Frequently, training is inadequate, and safeguards to assure proper performance are all too often lacking.

When safeguard protocols are absent or are not rigorously administered, a number of bad results follow; two are particularly pernicious. One is corruption. In Philadelphia, at the same time my detectives and I were working to bring the Scarfo organized crime gang to justice, within our own police department—in a situation reminiscent of Serpico and the Knapp Commission in New York some years earlier—a police-operated form of organized crime was flourishing, reaching to high levels of the administration. That shouldn't happen, but it did, and I have no reason to think it will not continue to occur as long as police departments follow their present procedures.

A second result of failure to enforce proper safeguards is the flawed investigation of crimes, which can result in the arrest and conviction of innocent people—which also means that those actually guilty of the crimes go free.

Given the system under which it must operate, what is amazing is not how often police work fails, but how often it succeeds. Nevertheless, to the extent that preventable and correctable error is allowed to go unchecked, there is only one beneficiary—the criminal.

This book is divided into four parts. In the first, I relate why I became a cop and what I learned about crime, criminals, and police procedures, both as a uniformed officer and as a lieutenant of detectives. I then go on to describe how the Philadelphia/Atlantic City bloodbath began and my own early involvement in fighting organized crime.*

Part Two focuses on "The Little Guy," as Nicodemo Scarfo was known to his henchmen, and on how a police and FBI organized crime task force was created (at least a year later than it should have been) and the work it did to fight organized crime, at last, in an organized way.

Part Three continues the bloody Scarfo story. Interwoven is another, related tale, that of my re-investigation of the particularly horrifying mob murders of two people, one of whom was an innocent woman, that took place in a South Philadelphia restaurant in 1981. The worst miscarriage of justice I ever encountered in my career as a police officer—the sentencing of an innocent man to death—took place in that case. From it, I received a lesson in how the justice system works in this country that I wish it had not been necessary for me to learn.

Part Four relates how we finally brought Scarfo

---

*During my investigation of the Mafia, I got to know scores of criminals. Some of them were so-called "made members" of the organization. That meant they were of Italian or Sicilian heritage on their father's side and that they had participated in at least one mob-authorized homicide—chillingly enough, called "making one's bones"—the prerequisites for acceptance into the Society of the Men of Honor. Others, the "associates," who are by far the most numerous, are not eligible for admission because of either ethnicity or failure to pass the murderous entrance exam.

A few of these men—like Scarfo himself and his chief executioner, Salvatore Testa—I found to be persons of virtually unadulterated evil. Others were far more complex; some had their own peculiar standards of morality, and not a few of them were charming, likable fellows whom anyone would want as a friend were it not for the fact that they were criminals.

and his gang to justice. The murders that paved the way for Scarfo's accession to power, plus the mob-related ones that took place during his reign, added up to a body toll of thirty-four by the time of the final homicide in 1985.

In the Epilogue, I discuss reforms which, if they were adopted, would, I believe, improve the quality of police work in preventing and solving all manner of crime, and at the same time make it unlikely that the innocent would be convicted, in all these ways leading to better protection of the public.

The personalities and careers of each of the individuals I dealt with is vividly implanted in my mind; however, I recognize that, because of their very number and the fact that some appear at one stage of the story and do not make a reentrance until much later, the reader might have difficulty keeping straight who is who. By way of assistance, a selected list of characters with their nicknames, if any, and a brief summary of the role each plays in the book, appears after the Epilogue, on pages 399–404.

Before beginning, a few words about what the book doesn't contain. First, like every cop, I learned about the commission of crimes largely from informants, and whenever it is safe to do so, I will give names, quote what was said to me, and describe how I developed the evidence. In some instances, however, it is necessary to allow sources to retain their anonymity, and the narration of the detection process must at times also remain vague or unstated, lest specifics inadvertently reveal the source and endanger that person's life.

There are also those—as experience has taught

me—who would like to harm the families of officers who try to catch criminals. I don't want to provide them any help. For that reason, the book contains no description of my personal life beyond my childhood years.

PART I

The Mob Murders Begin

1

The Reluctant Detective

The earliest thought I can remember was about justice.

I am three years old, maybe four, and I'm on my rocking horse, which I love more than any other possession I've ever had, and an adult (I forget who) is saying to me, "So what would you like to be when you grow up? A cowboy?" and I say, "Uh-uh, I want to be an Indian chief."

My memory of that desire is vivid in time and place, as is my accompanying belief (as I gallop along on the rocking horse) that what happened to the Indians was wrong.

I have no idea how I came upon that conclusion at such

an early age. Certainly the time—I was born in 1942—was not one in which I would have been likely to be exposed to any sympathetic portrayals of Indians. Nevertheless, the sense that they had been treated unjustly persisted in me, and I can still recall my happiness on learning, probably in the second grade, how the Indians had defeated Custer. So the chief of all the Indians I would be, and I would do battle, too, and get back for us all the lands that once were ours and had been taken from us. It was the stuff of hours and hours of childish daydreams. It would be an heroic accomplishment, too—like stopping my father from drinking.

Whenever I think of my father, one terrible memory, of a day when I was 12 years old, almost always intrudes itself first. In it, I am sitting, very stiff, very upright, next to my mother on the bus. She is still in her uniform. She works, as for many more years she would continue to work, as a waitress for Linton's, a "family-priced" chain of restaurants that was predecessor to and would eventually be driven from business by McDonald's and other fast food companies. As a little boy, I'd marvel at the dexterity of my mother and the other waitresses as they plucked the steaming plates off the conveyer belt that ran next to the counter, and marvel, too, at how they always seemed to know for which customer each dish was intended.

This day, my mother has received a phone call, hurriedly taken leave from her counter, and stopped at my school to pick me up. I am not certain why she needs to have me along. I don't ask her then, or later. I think now that mainly she didn't want to be alone.

Our destination is just outside St. Martin's parish in the northeast section of Philadelphia, where I have lived all my life. In those days, it was a safe neighborhood. At night hardly anybody bothered to lock their doors. Like my family, nearly everyone was Irish Catholic—the Jewish neighborhood began a few blocks away—an enclave of blue-collar America. The mothers, if they worked, were, like mine, likely to be waitresses, perhaps beauticians, or salesladies in the five-and-dime. The fathers might be employed in the big Sears warehouse on Roosevelt Boulevard nearby, or they might be factory workers or tavern owners or bartenders, or, like my dad, work for the public transportation company as bus drivers.

Except that my dad, by the time I am 12, is no longer a bus driver. That's why my mother works at Linton's. He'd lost his job. He lost it because some days he'd bring his bus in early and other days not show up for work at all. He'd disappear—we wouldn't know where he was—for days at a time.

I follow my mother off the bus. I wish desperately that my older brother was with us, but he, at 17, had left home to join the army, as many boys around his age in our neighborhood did around that time. The building ahead of us is of dirty red brick, with a stone entranceway and stone steps. My mother and I walk up the steps. Inside I see green walls with the paint chipping from them, the wooden floors chipped, too, long threatening splinters of wood. I know why I am there, and I feel a shame that makes me lower my head as if by not looking at anyone, somehow I can keep anyone from seeing me either. My next recollection is of an enormously high counter—it couldn't have been as high as my memory of it, and it may not have been a counter at all, perhaps a desk of some kind, but I see it as a counter with a huge man behind it, and he is peering down at us like a uniformed god. I clutch at my mother's hand or she at mine. With her free hand, she has extracted money from her purse, a wrinkled flat green offering which she makes to the god.

When my father, released on bail, comes out through the door to us, I feel a surge of love for him—he himself is a loving man—and at the same time a hatred for what has happened to him, not so much because he is here, a jailbird, but because he has made me see him here. It's a sight I don't want to have.

By the time we get home, my father humble and my mother

tight-of-lip, I am lecturing him. I seem to remember actually pointing my finger at him, wagging it. I am lecturing and then I am pleading. I want him to promise me he will never ever do what he did again. He lets me extract the promise. He may even mean to keep it.

The next time he was picked up, as I recall, he actually made it back to the house, but I don't think he knew that's where he was. If that was the second, then there was a third, and more. (And at times—I only learned this much later—it wasn't drink that made him disappear; he also gambled, and the loansharks were after him.)

I saw him in delirium tremens. I knew then that I had failed him, and that he was going to die, and he did.

(It is years later—I am somewhere in my mid-twenties— and I am standing at the foot of a narrow well of stairs. From above, I hear a man's voice: "I'm going to kill you, you bitch; I'm going to kill you." And now he knows I am there and comes out of the door and halfway down the stairs. I recognize him. I've had to arrest him before, a vicious man drunk or sober, and I know he's vowed to his street-corner pals that he'll get me. In his huge hand, deadly at that distance, is a dainty little Derringer. I hear a click. The revolver doesn't go off. I reach for his gun arm and together we roll down the stairs in a violent embrace. I get the cuffs on him. He's subdued; it's over. It's not that uncommon an occurrence. A gun this time. A knife the next. After it is over, and only after it is over, do I realize how terrified I have been. A drink, I think; I need a drink. Because my father's trembling hand is on me, I don't take it. But other officers, to expel terror, do. They have one drink, maybe two, maybe the next time, four, and then they don't need a next time for the next four. In the Department, it's known as the policeman's disease.)

By the time I reached adolescence, my wish to become an Indian chief had disappeared (and along with it my belief that I could save not only Indians but my father as well). My new goal was to become an Air Force fighter pilot, and when that wasn't engaging my fantasy life, I latched on to the idea of dropping from planes as a paratrooper. Probably around the age of 15, my airborne dreams were replaced—I don't know why—by a subterranean one: I now wanted to become a scuba diver. In my adult life, I fulfilled each of these ambitions, too, in a way. I didn't join the Air Force—being a cop is the only job I've ever had—but I did take flying lessons, and I have soloed. Once, just to say I'd done it, I tried a free fall from a plane, and I am a certified scuba diver.

Upon reaching my junior year in high school, my goal in life had taken on a more intellectual cast—I was already an omnivorous reader—and in a direction that was considerably more sedentary, too. I now saw myself, with beard and degree, as a clinical psychologist, figuring out why people do things. I suppose, in a way, I've fulfilled that ambition, too.

But even in my most adventure-minded days, the one career I never thought about for myself—perhaps because of the humiliation of that terrible day in the police station—was that of cop. My decision to become one was made for a purely practical reason. In my senior year in high school, Police Department recruiters paid a visit. They wanted to talk to the boys who were about to graduate—no girls need attend. They told us of a program they had, two years of training, starting at the police academy and followed by an assignment to non-patrol duty in district headquarters, where we would answer phones, dispatch cars, tend to paperwork. I wasn't interested at first. I became so only when the money was mentioned. We'd be paid $4,240 a year. That was a large amount for an 18-year-old boy in 1960, and with that income I figured I'd be able to save enough money to go to college. I signed on, and it was in one year, not two—the police manpower needs were mounting as the crime rate rose—that, green as I was, I went out on patrol.

The day I realized I had found my true vocation occurred

about a week—certainly not more than two—after I had been assigned to my first red patrol car. Several times on each shift I drove by a little check-cashing agency. On this occasion, I noticed a young man emerging from it. From his pace and the way he peered anxiously around, I became suspicious. I pulled my car to a stop at the curb. He noticed me, turned and ran. I jumped out of the car and dashed after him. He sprinted toward a hedge and made a graceful leap over it, only to smash his knee on an iron railing hidden by the foliage. Down he went in a sprawl. Up I went, gracefully, too, I hope, and without seeing (anymore than he had) the railing until I hit my knee on it. I went down in a sprawl on top of him. I got my cuffs out, clapped them on him. Behind me, the owner of the check-cashing place was standing in the street waving. The man had robbed him. I hauled the perpetrator back to my car, and we made quite a pair as we limped along. But I didn't think about the pain, managed not to imagine how I must have looked as I took my pratfall. I felt too good for that. I was gloriously happy. I was 19 years old.

From then on, I hated it when my shift ended, and I always looked forward to the next one's beginning.

The work was hectic, it was demanding, it was exhilarating, it could be scary—when you're out there rolling around in a police car, you can go in one minute from helping toddlers at a school crossing to responding to a report of a shooting a block away. But mostly, for me anyway, it was fun. I couldn't imagine—still can't—doing anything else with my life that would have begun to approach that pure sense of enjoyment. Excitement and fun, that was one level of my feelings.

At the next level there was a sense of fulfillment. I don't know whether or not we're born with it or it seeps into us from our earliest experiences in life, but I think all of us, one way or another, have a need to contribute to others, to believe we matter as people. Some of us work to destroy that sense, or feel we've had it beaten out of us by life, but I think it's a hardy desire that dies unwillingly if it ever really completely dies at all.

As a cop, I had that feeling of mattering. I mattered because I was taking bad people off to jail. But I also quickly discovered another sense of worthwhileness. I found it helping the children cross the street, lining them up from tallest to shortest, like a regular production number, as they laughed with me and each other, having fun. It was also found in helping look for lost children and for lost grandparents, too, who had wandered off within the corrals their minds had become. It was found in stopping by the local grocery store and knowing I was welcomed as a protector by its owner, signing the sheets next to the register to show I'd been there—the sheets that are no longer there because too much crime doesn't allow the time for the visits—to show that I, young Frank Friel, was on the watch, protecting my tribe and its territory.

There was still another level of fulfillment in the policeman's life for me. The job provided a continuing and fascinating exposure to the infinite varieties of human experience, its desperations, the myriad afflictions of being alive, and its exaltations, too. I think that no other job—not even clinical psychologist—would have given me such an opportunity so raw and rich and psychically rewarding, and certainly I would not have come upon that realization as young as I did, when my mind was at its most receptive.

Very often what I learned had nothing to do with crime or the people who were its victims. During those times when I had no shooting to respond to a block away, no one lost to be found, no children to escort, I had the chance to talk to the people on my beat—the store owner, the folks sitting on their porches. I found myself especially attracted to the older ones among them, those who were say 70 in the early 1960s, and they seemed happy to talk to me, the boy-cop, as they wouldn't have to any other stranger my age who came up to them. Through their reminiscences, I could be taken back to the previous century, and from what they told me of their parents, back further, to the Civil War or even earlier. The connection I gained in that way to living history allowed me to learn, in a way that textbooks can never teach, how people touch one another and in that fashion create the lives of others so that even when they die, they live in their effect on others. My sense of history as this endless process has, I think, in subtle ways I can't define, helped me become, when that time came, a better detective than I otherwise would have been.

But the main lesson you learn as a cop isn't at all subtle. It's about crime.

Crime—and I've never met an officer with patrol experience who doesn't agree—is caused, the overwhelming majority of the time, by just one thing: poverty. It has nothing to do, as I first thought, with people being inherently bad; some bad people never commit crimes; they wreak their destruction in other ways. Just drive around a ghetto and you'll know what leads people to rob. It is social and economic deprivation, and any theory about stopping crime that doesn't start from that premise is, I believe, totally misguided, and will fail to stop a single mugging.

In order to reduce the frequency of street crime—assuming we aren't interested in removing its cause (and we don't appear to be)—a very effective solution in the Jonathan Swift sense would be to empower the police to seize poor people's television sets so that when the last meal they've had is a bag of potato chips, they won't be able to look at people on a screen eating expensive food in candlelit restaurants. Let them instead entertain themselves by listening to the rats scurrying behind the wall, smelling the toilet that doesn't flush. If you're going to keep them poor, then you had better not let them see pictures of people living the good life; they're going to want it too, and you're going to have crime.

Criminals are most likely to prey on others like themselves. All statistical studies show that perpetrators of crimes rarely travel more than a few blocks to carry out their deeds. For them, that's a sensible decision. Like the old-time cop on the beat, they know their neighborhood and the people in it as they don't know other places and people. They know who the weak ones are, and it's on them they principally prey— and that's sensible, too. Victimizing the old, the weak, the women, the handicapped is a rational choice for the criminal to make. Such victims aren't able to fight back.

In a grim way, it is fortunate that most crime is committed for rational, economic reasons. Because it is, police often have an idea who to look for: the neighborhood person who has the motive (poverty or need for drugs or both) and who is suspected or known to have committed similar crimes. Police, therefore, can sometimes make arrests (about 20 percent of the time) that will stick. If crime were, instead, largely the work of evil people or psychotics, it would then occur in a completely unpredictable and random manner and be virtually unpreventable (other than by sheer luck), and the arrest rate would probably be a quarter of what it is. Of course, if the practical motive for crime were removed, the rate of it might be a quarter of what it is, too.

I was an ambitious young cop. I studied hard, passed the civil service exam, made sergeant at the age of 25. Two more years, another exam, and I was a newly minted lieutenant, assigned to the inner-city 26th District. I was one of four uniformed lieutenants, each of whom had his own squad of sixty patrol officers and two sergeants.

My duty each day started with roll call, but I always made it my business to arrive at least fifteen minutes ahead of time. That gave me the opportunity to pick up the hot sheets of stolen cars, glance through the wanted-person fliers, scan the summaries of complaints phoned in by citizens and businesses. I also studied the list of reported crimes since I'd last been on duty sixteen hours before. During the six years I spent in the 26th, I found this time was well spent. Just often enough, I'd be able to decipher a pattern—last night's burglary in one patrol sector similar to the one of the week before in an adjoining sector. At roll call, I'd want to alert my men to the geographic pattern that might suggest a person in the area (often one recently released from prison) who had committed such crimes in the past. But it was for my benefit, too, since I'd be out on patrol with my men and, if I was lucky, stay out for the entire shift, except to bring in someone I had arrested. I hated being confined to the precinct station as the captain was—and, for that matter, as *I* was when he was off duty and it was my turn among the lieutenants to take his place.

While on patrol, my duty theoretically was to respond exclusively to calls which, by the dispatcher's description, indicated major crimes. "Holdup in progress," "Rape in progress," "Man with gun," "Shooting with multiple hospital cases," all were phrases I've heard too many times. I still sometimes (years later) wake up at night from hearing them in a dream.

These were immediate response calls both for me and for the officers nearest the incident. The same was true of certain noncrime calls—"Report of a hospital case"—except that they were to be handled by patrol cops, not by the lieutenant. Still others—"Burned out car at Second and Dauphin"—got attended to when someone had the time. Often, depending on where I was driving when the major crime call came, I'd arrive at the scene before any of my men did.* If I was first, my job was the same as any of the men: contain the situation, make arrests if possible. When I arrived after the patrol officers, I'd stay long enough to ascertain that the problem was being controlled and give instructions on the next steps. By that time, my radio would already be announcing the next hot spot, and I'd head to it.

---

*Female cops in Philadelphia in the early 1970s were still a rarity, and I had none in my command.

Theory, as often as not, didn't conform to reality. As the number of calls mounted and the number of officers free to respond diminished, I'd take whichever call came next, the hospital case equally with the holdup in progress. There was no other option: if not me, no one. The sector concept itself was a fiction. By the time a patrol cop started out on duty, he would have backup calls waiting for him, and if he got to his sector at all during his tour, it would only be by chance.

Anyway, that's the way it was in the 26th. Our district had the highest crime rate in the city. It was largely black, but with impoverished Hispanic and white neighborhoods on its eastern perimeter. By 1975, the year I left the 26th, we were logging over 100,000 criminal incidents a year, including those we observed and those that were reported to us. That doesn't count all the calls for help—the hospital cases, the missing people, the complaints about loud parties, general rowdiness—that were either of the peacekeeping or public service nature.

Crime, as every cop knows, has a self-feeding quality. The more of it there is, the more opportunity there is for it to occur. Prior to the onslaught of street violence that began in the 1960s, police work frequently was preventive, and often successfully so.

In those days, the beat cop had the opportunity to visit retail stores and banks in his sector at different times of the day. His presence—and the uncertainty of when he would show up—discouraged robberies and thefts. Similarly, before the onslaught, the beat cop had time to get to know the folks in his sector, not only those who were likely to cause trouble, but those who needed protection. He would know, for instance, that elderly Mrs. Brown usually went out to do her shopping at a certain time on certain days, and he'd make it his business to keep an eye on her until she got safely home. By the 1970s, that same cop was so busy answering calls that such crime prevention activities were no longer ever possible. Because he was chasing Mrs. Jones's mugger, Mrs.

Brown got mugged in his absence. And the corner grocer who didn't get robbed when the cop made his periodic visits now did, because the robber knew the cop no longer had the time to drop by.

The rise in the crime rate, of course, was directly related to the rise in drug usage, itself a reflection of the hopelessness of inner-city life—a way to a moment of happiness, a way to a moment of forgetting unhappiness. During my years in the 26th, heroin was the drug of choice. Cocaine and its derivative, crack, would enter the scene in appreciable amounts only much later. While heroin addiction was particularly prevalent in the black neighborhoods, it was hardly ignored in the white and Hispanic ones. Illegal methamphetamines, often called by white users "speed" or "crank" (because of the speedy way they cranked the user up to a high) and by blacks "monster," had become popular, too, following their introduction in sizable amounts in the 1960s. (More illegal meth is manufactured in Philadelphia and its suburbs than anywhere else in the country.)

Theoretically, heroin should be a great crime-preventive, since people under its soporific spell lack the energy to go out and rob; if it were given away free, that might well be its effect. Speed, however, like cocaine, is an activity producer, creating a mental state in which judgment is distorted, and consequently is more likely to motivate crime than prevent it.

The crime-causing effect of heroin is to be found in its withdrawal symptoms, which are excruciatingly painful and are to be avoided in any way possible. One way to achieve that avoidance, many addicts found, was to pop speed on top of the receding effects of the heroin, thereby giving them the temporary energy necessary to go find money for their next heroin dosage. Since a heroin addict (unlike the person who uses only cocaine or speed) usually cannot hold a job, the only regular source of income has to be from stealing. Because the crimes are frequently committed under the pain of the withdrawal symptoms (complicated by the covering counter-prop that speed gives), the addict can have a befuddled desperate character. This often results in acts of violence that the unaddicted and purely economically motivated criminal would eschew as not worth the effort in terms of probable income.

So it was, in the drug-ridden 26th, that, year after year, I saw ever more people who had been assaulted, robbed, killed. My response was entirely a pragmatic one—try to stop the crime, catch the criminals. I don't recall pausing (I had little time to pause) to wonder where the drugs were coming from. I'd only learn that when I began to investigate the Mafia.

One day early in 1975, I was summoned to meet with Chief Police Inspector Ferdinand Spiewak. He had, he said, heard of my "fine personnel skills," and wondered if I would consider transferring to the Detective Bureau, where problems had developed in getting a full day's work out of some of the men.

To the extent I possessed the ability for which he was praising me, it was developed out of sheer necessity. When I had become a lieutenant at the age of 27, I found myself supervising men who, for the most part, were both older and more experienced than I was. The older men were resentful of me, and so were some of the fellows around my own age who hadn't advanced in rank as I had. There wasn't much I could do about my contemporaries except try to lead by example. However, I recognized that if I were going to lead at all, I'd have to bring the older cops over to my side.

To accomplish that, I made it my business to meet with the veterans, and asked for their recommendations on how to better our enforcement efforts. From my own experience as a patrolman, I knew this would be the first time a superior officer had ever asked their opinion about anything. A number of the ideas they offered were good, and when I implemented them, they had reason to want to make the changes work, since they themselves had suggested them. By the simple expediency of asking people how to improve their performance, they had improved it. I had no further leadership difficulties.

The solution I'd hit upon was, I now know, the kind of basic management technique that any halfway enlightened corporation applies as standard operating procedure. For the Police Department, with its military structure, however, it was revolutionary. If my superiors had learned how I had achieved my leadership, they probably wouldn't have approved. All they knew, judging from Spiewak's remarks to me, was that I had the reputation for getting the most out of the people who worked for me.

I had, however, no interest in becoming a detective, and I couldn't be forced to become one; as a lieutenant, I had the right to refuse the transfer. I loved patrol work, I told Spiewak, and intended to make my entire career in it. I didn't have to tell him the underlying reason; as a veteran cop, he'd know what that was. It's to be found in metropolitan police forces around the country. Uniform cops don't like detectives and detectives don't like uniforms. To the uniform—and this is a revealed truth drummed into every recruit from the first day of training at the police academy—detectives are not "plainclothes" but "soft clothes," a term of contempt. Detectives, to the uniforms, are sissies, a bunch of fags. They aren't real men, not like we uniforms are.

As our epithets suggest, macho was at the core of the uniforms' derision of the soft clothes. We were the front line. We were the ones who (as had happened to me) had bricks thrown at the windows of our cars. We were the ones who had to quell disturbances; the ones who got shot or knifed. We walked into danger every day, a point of great pride to us. Not so the detectives; they only arrived when the danger was over, and afterward sat in their offices questioning the now disarmed and no longer dangerous people we brought in.

Compounding the bad feelings the uniforms had about the detectives was the detectives' patronizing attitude toward us. To the soft clothes, the uniform is a Neanderthal, a dope, muscle unencumbered by brain, while the detective (even if a week earlier he was in uniform himself) is blessed with an advanced intellect that allows him to recognize clues and solve crimes. The detectives' sense of superiority is all-encompassing, too. I had felt it from them at every stage of my career. The only difference came when I made lieutenant; after that, it was less likely to be expressed openly.

The dislike with which the uniforms view the detectives is sincere, but there is nothing most of them would like better than to become detectives themselves. In police work, there has always been a cachet—a sense of having arrived, of prestige—attached to no longer having to wear a uniform. Thus, that which is most despised is that which is most desired.

Which brings me back to Inspector Spiewak's problem: Unlike in many other cities, in Philadelphia detective is not an assignment but a rank parallel to corporal. One can be promoted as a detective (to sergeant, lieutenant and so on) but, under our civil service rules, cannot be demoted or transferred back to uniform, except under the rarest of circumstances. Once you're in, you're in to stay.

The security created by this system can have the adverse effects that Spiewak observed. For some cops, making detective means finding a harbor safe from the dangers of the streets, where they can while away the remaining years until they are eligible for retirement. Spiewak didn't have many detectives like that, but a sufficient number that they were causing complaints among the majority who had to do not only their own work but that of the laggards as well. The morale problem was apparently most serious in the felony unit.*

I understood Spiewak's situation and sympathized with it —not all patrol officers are paragons of enthusiasm either— but I was adamant about staying where I was, or so I thought. I may have had personnel skills, but Spiewak's proved the superior. I became a lieutenant of detectives in the felony section.

When I got there I discovered the morale situation was as Spiewak had described it. Since I had no transfer disciplinary measures available to me to combat it, I decided on isolation as the best technique. I identified who the competent and eager detectives were and made clear to them and the others that they were my "in" group. I asked their advice and— just as I had the uniforms, and for the same reason—praised and encouraged them. As a result, the lazy ones were no longer resented. Where before they had been seen by the hard workers as goldbrickers who might be disliked but were clever enough to get paid for doing a minimal amount of work, now, because of the elitist view I was engendering, the laggards were perceived as failures by the favorites. Simultaneously, the favorites—actually the large majority of the detectives— had their belief in their own worthwhileness reinforced by my selection of them. Because they were eager to prove me right, they became better than they had been, the same result I had achieved with my veteran patrol officers. The solution to the detective problem was an obvious one; I was no genius in coming upon it. But I'm quite sure it would have received official disapproval if I'd let my superiors know how I was handling it: (It would have seemed wrong to them for me to let the loafers loaf. I wasn't, however, about to attempt any rehabilitative therapy with a detective who viewed his job as

---

*The Detective Bureau has two divisions, one for homicides and the second for all other crimes, principally felonies but including misdemeanors when the need to investigate them arises.

a sinecure. From my experience with patrol officers like that, I knew it would be a waste of time that properly should be given to fighting crime by those who wanted to fight it.)

Since our caseload included everything except homicides, a single day could bring an enormous variety of crimes to our attention, everything from auto thefts to robberies, from rapes to shootings and other (often drug-related) assaults.

As I recall, it took me about a month before I had forgotten entirely about the joys of patrol work. Detection became enormously interesting to me, and provided a satisfaction I hadn't been aware, until then, could exist in police work.

The satisfaction had to do with knowledge. In patrol work, I was accustomed to going to the site of a disturbance, pacifying it, maybe making an arrest, preserving the evidence for the detectives when it was necessary to bring them in. Then I'd hurry on to the next call. My life was a series of scenes, frequently very dramatic ones, but they had no connecting plot.

As a detective, however, I could follow a case from the moment it became mine until its conclusion. I had the leisure, as I'd never had before, to spend hours or days or weeks finding out everything I could about the crime. I had fewer scenes, but I had more stories.

Not all of them ended happily; many cases could never be cleared. But when I did ferret out the truth, either working alone or with my team, the feeling was one that is, I think, analogous to that of a painter upon viewing a completed canvas. The sense is not so much one of creation as it is of omnipotence. Like the painter, the detective understands each stroke—every good one and every misstroke—that went into the canvas. Just as painters know their own work as no one else can, so too do detectives understand their case—better than the victim, better than the perpetrator, better than the district attorney, the defense attorney, the judge. Only the detectives know it whole.

I am an enthusiast by nature, I suppose, and the elation I

felt on solving a crime and the desire to repeat that feeling made me always want to work the extra hour, make the extra call, knock on one more door. And that, I quickly learned, is also the secret of good detective work. In both a literal and a metaphoric sense, if you knock on enough doors, eventually someone will answer. After that, you'd better know what to do with the information you get. If you don't do enough knocking, that's not a problem you'll have. Detective laziness is the best friend a criminal has, another reason I separated out the laggards and put them to the paper-shuffling they enjoyed. They didn't do any harm that way.

In the fall of 1980, I received a call from Captain Gerald Kane, chief of the Homicide Division. He wanted me to transfer over there. I should have been pleased. In the Detective Bureau pecking order, an assignment to Homicide is considered the ultimate.

Jerry Kane was several years older than me, but we had known each other almost from the time I joined the police. A slender man with thinning dark blond hair, he possessed an incisive mind and a ruminative, thoughtful personality that I both liked and admired. Even so, I turned down his offer, for much the same reason I'd fought becoming a detective in the first place. I was happy where I was, had great pride in the team I'd put together, enjoyed their company and didn't want to desert them. I also didn't like the thought of investigating murders. In my felony division, all our victims were alive, people who could be helped if we were successful. In homicide, every time the phone rang, it was with news of a death.

Shortly after I rejected Kane's offer, a new captain was placed in charge of my division. He came in determined to reorganize. No longer would the lieutenants go out on the street to investigate. That was beneath them. Instead, they would become administrative assistants to the captain. I was appalled. The reason I'd never taken the captaincy exam myself was because if I succeeded, I'd become an administrator, taken away from the action I loved. Now the same thing was going to happen to me as a lieutenant.

I called Kane and asked if the position was still open in homicide. He said, "Come on over." I did, and that was how I happened to be the officer in charge of the Homicide Division on the morning of Sunday, March 15, 1981, the day on which, as it turned out, I embarked on my career as an investigator of organized crime.

2
Blowing Up Phil Testa

My shift had begun at midnight, and how long it would last beyond the regular eight hours depended on who got killed and under what circumstances. So far no one had, but someone would. I could count on that. Saturday night and the dark hours of Sunday morning are violence time in the city.

On my arrival that night, the first thing I did, as usual, was to look for a place to sit. Captain Kane had an office—so small you could take only one step inside it before being confronted by his desk—but the lieutenants didn't. After grabbing a free desk, I spent the next two-and-a-half hours studying reports of ongoing murder investigations and making calls. You can find some surprising people up and about in those dark hours. Those tasks completed, I decided to get a cup of coffee at one of the 24-hour joints that surround Philadelphia's central police headquarters. A need for coffee had nothing to do with my going out; getting away from noise did.

Prisoners often talk about going stir-crazy, and at the heart of their complaint is the shouting, the moaning, the cursing, the clanging of doors, the playing of the boom boxes, day after day, year after year—the never-ending clamor of jail. The noise of the Detective Bureau had a similar relentless quality. The office was a huge arched enclave with the walls cunningly designed so that each voice, regardless of its pitch, bounced right into others: into the voices of detectives questioning witnesses; into the voices of other waiting witnesses huddled on wooden benches, demanding to know how much longer before they'd be called; and into the alternating whines and screams of unseen suspects of all kinds of crimes being held in detention in the holding rooms along one wall. To the babble was added the electronic stirring of the senses brought about by the ringing, over and over, of the phones. When you can get away from all that for twenty minutes, you do.

I was on my way back from my coffee break, just a few minutes shy of 3 a.m., when I heard the explosion. I looked to the south, from where it seemed to have emanated, but saw nothing out of order, and so I reentered the Police Administration Building, a three-story circular fortress that everyone called the Roundhouse. It was built twenty years earlier in the then-heart of Philadelphia's tenderloin district; gentrification was now creeping toward it. Just a few blocks away, houses which, when I was a boy, could be bought in Society Hill for a thousand dollars were going for six hundred thousand. Along with the rich people had come a burgeoning nightlife. Expensive restaurants, some with good food and entertainment, others tourist traps, had opened, one, it seemed, with each new day. Of them, a restaurant called Virgilio's, was of particular interest to the police.

At about the same time I had headed out for my coffee, the owner of Virgilio's was locking its doors for the night. Following a careful look around—life had taught him always to be careful—he got into his car and started the twenty-minute drive to his home on the Girard Estates, a section of South Philadelphia consisting of a fine grassy park surrounded by middle-class, semidetached homes.

Named after Stephen Girard, the venomous one-eyed opium merchant who had become Philadelphia's first millionaire in the early nineteenth century, the Estates was something of an anomaly in South Philadelphia, an area otherwise consisting largely of little red-brick row houses with white stoops that the wives scrubbed every Saturday morning. Frank Rizzo, who would become Philadelphia's police commissioner and then its mayor for two terms in the 1970s, was an Italian-American from the row houses, his father a cop before him.

The people who lived on the Estates (I never knew why the plural) were, for the most part, themselves South Philadelphians from working-class origins. When they made good in life, rather than moving east to Society Hill or out to the suburbs, they bought a home on the Estates so that they could remain visible to their old neighbors who hadn't succeeded. They enjoyed the envy and respect their new addresses brought them. Judges and lawyers and doctors lived there, as well as men of respect of a different kind, men like the owner of Virgilio's. His name was Philip Testa.* He was somewhere in his mid-fifties, a heavyset, squat man, about

---

*For the reader's convenience, a selected list of characters, with their nicknames, if any, and a brief summary of the role each plays in the book, can be found on pages 399–404.

5'8" with narrow-set eyes, a brush moustache, and a pock-marked face. His restaurant was a success, and he himself was a success in another way, too: He was the chief of organized crime in Philadelphia, the local Mafia don. People called him the Chicken Man (but never where he could hear them) because his father had owned a poultry shop.

At 2:55 a.m., Testa turned his car east onto Porter Street, intending, as was his habit, to make a stop at his house at 2117 before continuing his late-night tour. His wife had died six months before, and he now shared his home with his 25-year-old son, Salvatore, but Salvy, he knew, wouldn't be there. Along with Frank Monte, who was in charge of a large gambling operation, Salvy would be waiting for him to show up at the nearby Melrose Diner, a chrome-plated relic from an earlier and more innocent era. There the three men planned, as usual, to go over the day's receipts. The Virgilio's take was part of that, a small part, the legal part.

Two hundred yards away, on the other side of the park, two young men were seated in a black panel van. They watched Testa as he left his car and walked up the sidewalk. They had an unobstructed view of him, their line of vision along a walkway that came to an end directly across the street from Testa's house.

Testa mounted the steps to his porch. In the dark, he didn't notice—even though he was a careful man—the thin antenna wire that ran along the porch to the retaining wall. Testa took out his key, placed it in the lock, turned it. As he did, the man in the driver's seat of the van pressed his finger on the button of his radio transmitter. It was 2:58 a.m. The bomb exploded with such force that Testa was flung feet first through the door, which followed him into the living room.

The noise of the bomb even penetrated through the clatter in the Detective Bureau. "What do you think, lieutenant?" my sergeant asked me as I came back in. "Oil refinery?" From the general direction of the sound, it could have been the Arco plant on the way to International Airport, I figured. We'd had a catastrophe there a few years earlier—victims burned, victims killed.

But if that's what it was, it now occurred to me, I should have seen the sky illuminated by fire while I was still outside. I hadn't. "Maybe," I said. If it was, we'd hear the sirens in another minute or two. We didn't.

The first call came from one of Testa's neighbors. A lieutenant in a patrol car responded. As he did, he passed the van, obtaining a glimpse of the youth in the passenger seat. When the lieutenant arrived at the site, Testa was still alive, moaning, his clothes smoldering, his body now as pockmarked as his face, pocked by the bee-bee shots and long nails that had been inserted in the bomb.

The victim was difficult to recognize, but the lieutenant knew the house as Testa's. He put the call out on the police radio; the dispatcher notified us. "Saddle up," I said. I sent the sergeant and five of the detectives to the Girard Estates, and taking several other men with me, I headed for St. Agnes Hospital where, we were told, Testa had been taken. Within an hour, I had called in detectives from every division in the police force to the crime scene; I had them sweeping the neighborhood, knocking on doors, trying to find someone who had seen something.

I got to the hospital about 3:15. An FBI agent, Gary Scalf, had also been notified and arrived about the same time I did. The lobby was already becoming crowded. I have never figured out how the South Philadelphia communications system works, but it does, as speedily as that of the police or more so.

Among those on hand—I made a note of their presence as I rushed by them—were the stocky Monte and, just behind him, the fleshy, dark-haired, heavy-lidded Salvy Testa. I couldn't read Salvy's expression as he looked at me. Hate, maybe.

Scalf and I identified ourselves to a nurse and followed her into the emergency room, leaving behind us the assorted criminals and curious neighbors who had decided St. Agnes's was the place to be at three o'clock on a Sunday morning.

Testa was lying on a table, naked. The lower half of his body had turned black. His face was black. The only white I could see was the exposed bone of one leg. The attending physician looked back at me. He shook his head.

Even though I had been a cop for more than twenty years by the time of Testa's murder, his death was only the second instance in which I had any direct investigatory involvement with organized crime. The killing of a low-level mob enforcer, Frankie Stillitano, had come my way, a month earlier, for the same reason as the Testa assassination—I happened to be the lieutenant in charge when the body was discovered.

With Stillitano, I'd had my first experience—many more were to come—in the frustrations of working on a mob hit. I learned from informants why the killing had been ordered and who had carried it out, but didn't have a scintilla of hard evidence to take into court. (To this day, the Stillitano case remains on the books of the Philadelphia Police Department as an open homicide.)

Prior to Stillitano and Testa, however, my comprehension of the workings of organized crime was pretty much that of the average citizen. I knew, as most everybody else did, that the mob went by different names at different times in its history: the Honored Society; the Mafia (a word of obscure origins but which may come from the Tuscan *maffia*, meaning misery or distress); the Black Hand (from the practice of sending extortionate letters signed with the black ink impression of a hand); the Syndicate; and La Cosa Nostra ("This Thing of Ours"), which led to law enforcement's acronym for the mob, LCN.

From reading and from watching movies, I had also learned that each crime family was vertically structured with the don, or boss, at the top, followed by the underboss, or the consigliere (who serves as an arbiter to resolve disputes within the gang that can't be taken care of at lower levels), the capos, or captains, and finally the criminal "crews" consisting of "soldiers," some of whom are mob members but the majority of whom are not. I knew there was a national commission that presumably coordinates the Syndicate's activities, and I'd heard that gambling was the financial keystone of the mob. "It makes everything go around," as one Mafia associate put it, specifically referring to "numbers" or "policy." This game, which had been widely played by the folks in my neighborhood when I was a boy, is the simplest of all forms of gambling: Pick the right three-digit number for that day and you win. (Until recent years, the number was the last numeral of the amount bet on each of the first three horse races of that day; now, most places, a state lottery daily number is the one used.) The profit from a numbers bank can be quite sizable—a decent-sized one will net its operator more than $100,000 a year, and even the runners who pick up the bets can make $25,000.

Finally, I was aware, as most people are, that the Mafia runs a "tribute" system in which the proceeds from crimes are shared by the perpetrators with their superiors, who, in turn, forward a portion of their share to their superiors, with the residue eventually reaching the don. Some of the "tribute" money is accumulated from payment of "street tax" to enforcers by independent criminals as the price for being allowed to stay in business.

As I subsequently learned, when investigating the Mafia became my life's work, both the tribute and street tax systems work quite well despite the fact that there are no rules governing the amounts to be paid. Street tax extortionists simply demand the amount they figure the traffic will bear, and similarly, the size of tribute payments is a matter of choice by the payers. Cheating occurs. The extortionist claims he collected less street tax than he did; an authorized numbers banker skims money off the top before paying tribute on the remainder. However, a carrot and stick is always effectively at work. The stick is the cheater's awareness that if he gets caught, he'll likely be killed. But the carrot is the main reason for the arrangement's success. Good things come to those known to their chieftains as generating large amounts of income—their gambling territory will be extended, or if they're into robberies and burglaries, they find themselves participating in the jobs with the biggest hauls. The tribute system, therefore, is the major fulcrum of the power of a crime family: By receiving, it gives.

Regardless of the gaps in my knowledge of the Mafia, I fully comprehended that I had a hot case on my hands as I stared down at Phil Testa's blackened body. The murder of any Mafia boss would be considered a major crime, but Testa's took on an added importance as the latest in a series of mob killings that had already proved an embarrassment to law enforcement. Probably it was an embarrassment, most of all, to the Philadelphia Police Department, but also to the FBI, the U.S. Justice Department, the local district attorney. All—even before Testa was blown up—were under a barrage of ridiculing criticism from the media, and justifiably so. Testa's was the seventh mob murder in a year and no one in law enforcement, local or federal, had come close to arresting anyone for any of the homicides. Later on, by which time the body count had reached the twenties, a columnist would refer to us as the New Untouchables: We weren't able to touch anybody.

As I quickly learned when I began to investigate the Testa case, everybody had a good idea why the mob warfare had started and also had a fix on who the generals were on each side, although generals, in this kind of war, sometimes change sides depending on who seems to be winning.

At stake was control of one of the nation's largest organized crime territories and—more to the point—a highly lucrative one. The home base of it was my city of Philadelphia (with its multimillion-dollar annual illegal methamphetamine trade); the boundary extended north through New Jersey to Newark, with Atlantic City the easternmost outpost. Until three years before Testa's death, Atlantic City had been a nickel-and-dime crime operation, its capo, the 5'5" Nick Scarfo, having to hustle every day to turn a dishonest dollar. Now all that had changed. The glittering gambling casinos, which began to be built in 1978, beckoned not only to the Philadelphia mobsters but to the powerful New York crime families as well. They all foresaw their own private new Las Vegas. There was one other thing everyone knew: The turf war had begun with the death of Angelo Bruno.

3
The Ungentle Death
of the Gentle Don

Sometime in 1972, three years before I transferred to the Detective Bureau, I happened to read a newspaper article in which Angelo Bruno, in his thirteenth year as don of Philadelphia's LCN family, was quoted as saying, "All we do is let people gamble." I recall how impressed I was by the eloquent and sorrowful way he then went on to describe the drug addiction plague that had visited the city, the consequences of which I had to deal with every day. His people —the "men of honor"—would never, he said, engage in so loathsome an enterprise as narcotics sales. He forbade it. And since neither he nor any of his men were being arrested for dope dealing, apparently he was telling the truth.

By the time of his death in 1980, a month short of his seventieth birthday, Bruno looked to be an old man; his complexion was gray, his gait shuffling, and a pouch of unneeded weight hung from his 5'9" frame. He suffered, he said, from bleeding ulcers, a condition that had led to his furlough from a prison in New Jersey in 1973, where he'd been incarcerated for refusal to answer questions about his activities. When, a year after Bruno's death, my investigations caused me to look into his background, I uncovered photos of him in his youth. His eyes then were dark and dancing, his black hair combed back George Raft style, and he sported a pencil moustache. Several old associates mentioned to me how fond he used to be of playing the violin and piano, and that he loved to sing, his voice a pleasing tenor.

He also seemed to enjoy talking to the press, which, in response, doted on him, almost invariably referring to him as the Gentle Don. There was a measure of truth to the label. His reign had generally been a nonviolent one, and he personally was a quiet and rather charming man who displayed all the little courtesies. Neighbors who had not the remotest connection to organized crime came to him for advice about life's problems; and like them, he was patriotic, never failing to hang out his flag on the Fourth of July. (Most mafiosos are great believers in America and its free enterprise system.)

Unlike his successor, Phil Testa, Bruno never moved to the showy grandeur of the Girard Estates but rather remained in his little row house on Snyder Avenue. There he lived with his wife Sue, whom he had married in 1932. I was told they were a devoted couple, and that he was a good father to his son and daughter. He bought his clothes off the rack; no $200 shoes for him. He died a multimillionaire.

Bruno's own career running gambling operations—I don't think he ever placed a bet on anything himself—probably began in the late 1920s, shortly after his arrival in Philadelphia from Sicily. At that time, he also became involved in the bootlegging operation begun by the family's founder, Salvatore Sabella, who was not a member of the Mafia when he arrived in the United States from Sicily in 1911. For that matter, few if any of the Italian and Sicilian chieftains made the trek to America, where the streets were supposed to be paved with gold; they had plenty of gold on their own streets to pick up. However, the immigrants in the Little Italys of America's big cities were well aware of the might of the Mafia; they considered it a secret government to be dreaded more than the real government. Recognizing the fear, young hoodlums like Sabella styled themselves as mafiosos, thereby extracting obedience to their rule. Few of these early American mafiosos had connections with their cohorts in other cities until the coming of Prohibition made banding together profitable.

I have never learned when Bruno committed his first murder, and he may never have actually pulled the trigger on anyone. (That's not necessary to become a made member; participation at any stage of the proceedings—the plotting, the shooting, the disposal of the corpse—will do to make one's bones.) Bruno's sponsor for entrance to the Honored Society, probably sometime in the early 1930s, was an older man named Michael Maggio. About that time, Bruno began to appear as a salesman on the books of a cheese company Maggio owned, in order to give him a legitimate source of earnings for income tax purposes.

A much more important alliance for Bruno, and one which affected the history of organized crime in Philadelphia and Atlantic City in a major way, was struck somewhere around 1934 when Bruno became partners in a profitable Florida land deal with Carlo Gambino, a fellow Sicilian about his own age. Gambino was to go on to become the dominant figure in La Cosa Nostra during the 1960s and 1970s, and may have been more responsible than any other individual for the heroin epidemic that seized America during that era.

In manner mild and meek, Gambino, by the 1950s, had become underboss to Albert Anastasia, head of Murder, Inc. Anastasia, cruel and violent even by Mafia standards, treated Gambino as his flunky, made jokes about him, once even spat in his face. Gambino bided his time. He believed in the three basic principles of the Men of Honor, one of which is *omertà* (the rule of silence about all Mafia activities), the second of which is *umiltà* (the concept that a man of honor must expect to suffer and endure persecution, to which he turns the other cheek), and the third of which is *vendetta*. He believed in the last the most.

Gambino's opportunity came in 1957 when Vito Genovese, a New York City rival of Anastasia, approached him with a plot to murder Anastasia. Genovese had frequently ridiculed Gambino, too; even so, Gambino agreed to participate in the assassination, after which, Genovese promised, Gambino would be allowed to take over the Anastasia mob and report to Genovese, who would replace Anastasia as *capo dei capi* (boss of bosses).

By helping murder Anastasia, Gambino gained vendetta for one cause of his umiltà. He now turned to the second. Conveniently forgetting omertà, he secretly provided evidence of Genovese's drug trafficking to New York City police.* Genovese was duly convicted and died in prison in 1969, never knowing Gambino had turned him in. Although Genovese continued to operate his gang from behind bars, Gambino was on the scene, the new boss of bosses. No one laughed at him or spat in his face anymore.

Gambino's succession to power saved Bruno's life. In 1959, the new head of the Philadelphia crime family was 67-

---

*It would never have occurred to Gambino to go to J. Edgar Hoover's FBI, not in those days. In the late 1950s, Hoover had exactly four agents assigned to surveil the Mafia—that wasn't four in New York City, that was four for the entire country—with 400 agents, by comparison, doing loyalty investigations. Not until after Hoover's death in 1972 did the FBI try, in any meaningful way, to combat the Mafia.

year-old Antonio Dominick Pollina, another of Maggio's "salesmen." The Italian-born Pollina had been named don by his predecessor, Giuseppe Idda, just before Idda fled to his native Italy to escape indictment. Pollina apparently considered the Sicilian Bruno as a rival and ordered his underboss, Sicilian Ignazio Denaro, to kill Bruno. Denaro, however, went to Bruno and warned him of the plot. Upon hearing that, Bruno immediately headed for New York to meet with his good friend and fellow Sicilian, Carlo Gambino.

The ethnic heritage that Bruno and Gambino shared may have been more important to Gambino than their old friendship when Bruno came to him for help. From as far back as the days of the Roman Empire, Sicilians hated Italians as a conquering race that despoiled their land and raped their women. For their part, the Italians looked down on Sicilians as loutish peasants. When the Honored Society, which had its origins as a terrorist organization against the Romans, expanded to southern Italy in the mid-nineteenth century, the alliances that developed between Sicilian and Italian gangsters did not allay the prejudice with which they viewed one another. The animosity, which frequently led to outbreaks of internecine warfare, has also marked the history of the Mafia in the United States. Thus, when Denaro informed Bruno that the Italian Pollina planned to kill him, it was a case of one Sicilian protecting another, and it was that same ethnic-based protection that Bruno now expected to receive from Gambino.

At their meeting, Gambino promised Bruno his support and said he would take the matter up with the National Commission, which had been formed by New York mobster Salvatore "Lucky" Luciano in 1933 as a board to arbitrate disputes within and between crime families. In a "national" commission sense, it has never worked out that way. The membership was too heavily biased in favor of New York City for Mafia families beyond the East Coast to pay much attention to it, and the bosses themselves were too treacherous and greedy to ever permit an effective national governing body.*

From Bruno's view, however, in 1959—as from Scarfo's twenty-two years later in 1981—support from the National Commission was vital for survival. The Philadelphia crime family, then and later, was like a client state to the New York gangs that dominated the Commission. Often they paid no attention to Philadelphia, but when they did, they had the numbers, as a group or individually, to impose their law. If New York said the boss in Philadelphia was to be Pollina, then Pollina it would be. If New York said Bruno, then Bruno it would be.

Bruno recognized that the heads of the various New York families, including the Genoveses, who were second in number to Gambino's gang, might, on certain matters, try to cross Gambino. But Bruno also knew it was highly unlikely that any dispute would occur over Philadelphia, which was the weakest of the East Coast families, its outpost in Atlantic City still years from becoming a potential mob bonanza. They'd leave that decision to Gambino.

Gambino almost immediately got back to Bruno with the news he expected to hear. The Commission, Gambino said, had approved him as don in place of Pollina, and he had its authority to kill Pollina.

The 49-year-old Bruno must have been tempted to make use of that fiat, but he was a man who believed in thinking things out before he acted, a trait that his successor Scarfo never shared. Bruno's decision was to let Pollina live. If he had Pollina killed, he reckoned, the ex-boss's followers might feel honor-bound to avenge their patron's death, and the result would be a gang war. With Pollina alive, his men would

---

*"Organized" crime in this country is principally local, with the families in one city organized much the same way as those elsewhere. Coalitions among them form and disintegrate as needs and opportunities arise.

have no such motive and, recognizing where the power now lay, might come over to him. And that is what happened.*

When Bruno proclaimed to the newspaper reporter in 1972 how much he loathed narcotics and decried the great harm they did the young, he may have been expressing his true feelings. He had a strong moralistic bent, which had shown itself when he ordered his gang out of the prostitution business.

When, however, he further assured the reporter that he and his "friends" would never engage in the loathsome dope peddling, he was lying. It was he who was responsible for bringing heroin into my inner-city 26th District.

Bruno opened Philadelphia to large-scale heroin trafficking in the early 1960s at the behest of his protector Gambino who, by then, was flooding New York City's Harlem with the drug. (There, the colorful Leroy "Big Bad Leroy Brown" Barnes became one of the Mafia's first black associates.)

Gambino recognized Bruno's wish not to become a heroin dealer personally. Although he probably could have forced him to, he produced a face-saving plan whereby Bruno could remain aloof from the actual sales and still profit by them (as he already was doing in meth trafficking).

By this scheme, which Bruno accepted, Gambino's "salesmen" (Genovese's only became involved later) would supply heroin to interested Bruno lieutenants. The price varied, but at the time of the 1972 newspaper interview, the New Yorkers were paying $5,000 a kilo and selling it to the Philadelphians for $20,000. The Bruno men, in turn, sold it to independent dealers, all of them white, whose customers were inner-city dealers, almost all of them—like *their* customers—black. A

---

*In the end, Pollina survived Bruno (and nearly everybody else). I interviewed him in 1986 when he was 94 years old. He denied being a mafioso, denied heading the Philadelphia mob, would only admit—just as Bruno always only admitted—to being a "gambler."

$5,000 kilo eventually, through its various transactions, generated about $250,000. The inner-city dealers got the largest share, but because there were so many of them, and so many were themselves addicts, the net profit per street pusher was minuscule compared to that reaped by the mobsters who never set foot in the ghettos for which the product was always intended.

Bruno made his profit by putting out money for his lieutenants to use to buy from the New York "salesmen." The lieutenants then repaid Bruno by collecting his interest charges (and more) on the money they lent to the dealers to buy the product from them. It didn't matter how much capital of his own a participant in the scheme might have. The only way he could get the heroin was by borrowing the purchase price at the loanshark rates.

By the mid-1970s, signs were developing of a growing restiveness toward Bruno in the Philadelphia family. The principal complaint was that Bruno had failed to exploit the narcotics business to its full potential. (Bruno feared that too rapid an expansion might let undercover cops into the fold.) Bruno's conservatism on the drug issue had led to talk he was becoming a "Moustachio Pete," a Mafia term of derision for a boss who doesn't keep up with the times.

Bruno's next decision led to his death. Following the passage of the gambling casino act in New Jersey in 1977, Bruno, assuring his gang there'd be plenty for everyone, announced that Atlantic City was to be considered "open" to any LCN family that wanted to do business there. In so doing, Bruno was acting with his usual realism. He knew that the New York families, led by the Gambinos and Genoveses (who were growing in strength following Carlo Gambino's death of natural causes in 1976), had their eyes set on Atlantic City, too. They vastly outnumbered his forces, and he couldn't have stopped them if he tried.

However, Bruno's underlings, not having to face up to

facts as their boss did, responded in a predictable macho fashion. Atlantic City was theirs by territorial right, they grumbled among themselves, and if they could control the fantastic riches the new gambling industry seemed to promise, would they not become equal in power to the hated New Yorkers? Particularly voluble on the subject was the new consigliere Antonio Caponigro, a major crime figure in northern New Jersey. The dissidents also included underboss Phil Testa and Testa's close ally, Scarfo.

Angelo Bruno had his last supper on the evening of March 21, 1980. That afternoon, as he had so many times in the past, he dropped by to see his long-time lawyer and friend, Jake Kossman. A big and balding man about Bruno's age, Kossman, who once represented Jimmy Hoffa, wore wildly clashing bright and rumpled clothes that would have been rejected by K-Mart as unfashionable. His seedy haberdashery was a calculated part of his courtroom persona when defending mobsters. He once asked a jury, "If the things [the prosecutor says] about my client were true and he made all this money, why would he go out and hire some bum like me?"

During his and Bruno's get-togethers, Kossman would sit behind his desk in his dark office, staring reflectively at the remains of ancient half-eaten corned beef sandwiches, now and then passing a plate of peanuts to Bruno, as the two men listened to the classical music of which they were both devotees. On this occasion, arriving at Kossman's office to pick them up for dinner was 53-year-old Raymond "Long John" Martorano, a co-owner of John's Vending Company, which had replaced Maggio Cheese as Bruno's source of supposedly legitimate income. Bruno's salary was $50,000 a year, and he was a valuable employee for Martorano even if he never showed up for work. The mention of his name was sufficient to shift business Martorano's way, as happened in Atlantic City shortly after the casinos opened. At that time, Martorano's company took over a $500,000 account for cigarette machines that had for years been held by a competitor.

Martorano drove the two men to Cous' Little Italy Restaurant in the heart of South Philadelphia. On their arrival, the doorman greeted the Gentle Don with due deference, and the bartender—probably Ronald "Cuddles" DiCaprio—waved a greeting. That alerted the men at the bar, who turned around, each hoping that Bruno might favor him with a nod or a word, a recognition that would quickly spread through the neighborhood, proving that the person who was the recipient of the greeting was himself a man of importance and to be honored.

A bowing waiter showed Bruno to his own table where, in addition to Martorano and Kossman, he was joined by several members of his organization, including Mario Riccobene and Joseph Scalleat. The 47-year-old Riccobene was a younger half-brother of Bruno's lifelong ally, Harry "The Hunchback" Riccobene. Scalleat, in his late sixties, was a dress manufacturer from Hazleton in upstate Pennsylvania, who was alleged by Pennsylvania law enforcement sources to be an associate of Russell Bufalino, the purported Mafia chieftain of the state's anthracite coal regions.

For dinner, Bruno had chicken Sicilian, a chicken and vegetable dish that has hot cherry peppers as a principal ingredient, an odd culinary choice for someone presumably in failing health due to his bleeding ulcers. In fact, Bruno's autopsy revealed he was in excellent health, had never had ulcers, bleeding or otherwise. He had lied about that. He lied often.

An informant of mine once told me, not too helpfully, that the dinner table conversation was on matters of "mutual interest," but considering Kossman, it was probably dominated by him. A gifted raconteur of his many courtroom battles, Kossman could hold an audience enthralled—and appalled—as he bellowed away, all the while scooping up spaghetti into his mouth with his fingers and then wiping those fingers clean on his necktie.

As the dinner was breaking up around 9:30, the question arose of who would drive Kossman and Bruno home. For reasons he didn't make clear, Martorano said he couldn't do it. Offering to drive Bruno was Mario Riccobene. Kossman, however, was eager to get going—he had an opera broadcast on the radio he wanted to hear—and Mario, who adored Bruno, agreed to take him instead, to his everlasting regret. A patron at the bar, John Stanfa, was asked to serve as Bruno's driver; he had done so before. (My informant wasn't certain who did the asking.) The Sicilian-born Stanfa had come to the United States in the early 1970s, possessed of excellent credentials provided by the men of honor there. Because of that sponsorship, he had been accepted immediately as a friend of the Philadelphia family. He owned a contracting business and had done some work on Bruno's house.

Shortly after Kossman and Riccobene departed, Bruno left with Stanfa, driving off in Stanfa's battered 1969 Chevrolet. They made a stop at Broad Street and Snyder Avenue, where Bruno got out to purchase a newspaper. They then drove five blocks east to Bruno's house. Bruno, however, did not get out of the car as he and Stanfa continued with a conversation.

While they were talking, either Bruno or Stanfa lowered the window on Bruno's side—why is unclear—and a moment later a double-barreled shotgun was poked into the window and pressed against the back of Bruno's right ear. The gunman emptied both barrels; Bruno was killed instantly. Pellets that passed through Bruno's head embedded themselves in the arm and leg of John Stanfa, who was already on his way out of the car. The gunman, who may have had an accomplice —the reports on that are conflicting—fled into the night.

When Bruno was shot, his body pitched forward and his

head hit the dashboard of the car. But that is not what the police photos of his body show. On hearing the gunshots, Bruno's wife of 48 years came out of the house and in her last tribute to her dying husband, she cupped his bleeding head in her hands and laid him gently back in his seat, his eyes closed, mouth open in the grimace of death.

Bruno's murder provided publicity for Cous' Little Italy.* The accompanying stories, which described Cous' as a mob hangout, flushed out tourists and the city's young professionals, many of whom had already begun to move into South Philadelphia, gentrifying it, but who had hitherto ignored the restaurant as just another neighborhood tavern. Now they came in droves, people who had never been any closer to danger than watching mayhem on a movie screen. They went to gawk at the men of honor lined at the bar, whispering about them, pointing them out, speculating if this one was a consigliere, that one a capo. It was all very exciting, and the supposed men of honor preened themselves under all the attention they were getting.

Less than a month after Bruno's death, consigliere Caponigro met his, and along with him went his brother-in-law and driver, Alfred Salerno. Their bodies were found in separate places in New York City.

For the Gentle Don, respect, as the mob understands that word, had been shown in his dispatching. It was a clean hit, without warning, and without terrorizing the victim before slaying him. Not so for either Caponigro or Salerno. Each man was beaten, stabbed and tortured before being shot; their mouths and anuses were stuffed with $20 bills.* So savage were the executions that the bodies couldn't be identified until fingerprint matches were made three days later.

---

*The restaurant was named after its chef, who had no crime connections. It no longer exists under that name.

*The torturing was the traditional mob way of showing contempt for the victim; the money symbolized that the victim was greedy.

The timing of the murders indicated they were related to Bruno's; the location, that they were authorized by the Commission. The why, however, wasn't clear. Had Caponigro killed Bruno without authorization, so that his and his brother-in-law's deaths were retaliatory? Or did the murders signify that a general housecleaning of the Bruno organization was underway from New York?

The housecleaning theory seemed to gain support a month later when John Simone, Bruno's cousin and a capo, was murdered—no torture in his case—in northern New Jersey. The site again suggested a Commission-ordered hit, but (from a later investigation which I helped lead) we now know Simone's death was the work of Phil Testa. He had been named by the Commission as Bruno's successor, presumably because, as underboss, he was next in line.

In consolidating control of his new empire, the surly and violent Testa had a potential rival in fiftyish Frank Sindone, a hulking legbreaker who loved big cars and fancy clothes. Bruno had always disapproved of such displays of wealth—he thought they would attract police attention—but Sindone, despite his flamboyance, had remained closely allied to Bruno and was the choice of the capos, including Simone, to succeed him. That doomed him in Testa's eyes. A few months after Simone's death, Sindone's body was found in a parking lot in South Philadelphia.

Now Phil Testa, the new don, was dead, and it was my case to solve.

4

The Mafia's Christmas Murder

At the beginning of the Testa investigation, my team had one of those pieces of luck that you get when you knock on enough doors. Behind one of these doors, we found a man who said that immediately prior to the explosion, as he was driving home, he noticed a black panel truck parked on Shunk Street, right across the park from Testa's home. That matched up with the description provided by the passing patrol lieutenant. More importantly—and here is where the luck came in—the civilian who observed the truck happened to be one of those rare people who memorize license plate numbers, or try to. When we ran the numbers he gave us through the Bureau of Motor Vehicles, he turned out not to be quite as good as he thought he was, but good enough. The first three license digits matched those for a black panel truck belonging to 29-year-old mob associate Rocco Marinucci. He was the driver for Peter Casella, Phil Testa's underboss. In his seventies, Casella had recently completed a 17-year prison sentence on narcotics charges and, according to an informant, believed that in return for doing all that hard time he had deserved to be named don instead of Testa after Bruno's death. Testa's appointment of Casella as underboss had been an apparent—and apparently unsuccessful—attempt to buy the old gangster's loyalty. Casella, who was famed in mob circles for his expertise in making bombs, had disappeared within a week after Testa's death. That meant that he might be dead, too, or that he was in hiding from the wrath of Testa loyalists—including Testa's son, Salvy, who would almost certainly have revenge on his mind.

In high hopes, I obtained a court order to seize Marinucci's van. We took it to the police garage. I let my experts loose on it. They went over every inch and found—nothing. No trace of a bomb. No trace of a bomb component.

Even so, I decided to bring Marinucci in for questioning. I got into my '78 Chrysler, drove to South Philadelphia, parked near his house, and waited for him. There'd be no point knocking at his door; he'd look out, recognize me from the time I had his van seized, and not answer. When, an hour or so later, I saw him leave his house, I walked up behind him, put my hand on his shoulder, and said, "Rocco, I want to talk to you." He was a slender little man with a neatly trimmed black moustache, a tic at his right eye. "I got nothin' to say," he said, but he got into the car with me. At headquarters, I took him into an interrogation room. "You got the wrong guy. I ain't no killer. My truck was home. You prove it wasn't." We couldn't. The man who'd given us the license plate numbers was too terrified to testify.

The longer I questioned Marinucci, the more pronounced his eye tic was. "Don't bother me," he said. I was fascinated by his eyes. If you have ever seen a cobra, elegantly coiled, head lifted, watching you, ready to swallow you whole: those eyes. They didn't go with his dandyish features or his build. "You got nothin' on me. You got somethin' on me, you arrest me. If not, I'm walkin'." If Rocco Marinucci had been a laughing man (he wasn't), he would have been laughing at me. He had a right to. I had nothing except what we both knew, and I couldn't prove that he'd blown Phil Testa to pieces.

Our only other lead in the case didn't pan out either. Based on the patrol lieutenant's description, a police artist had constructed a sketch of the young man in the passenger seat of Marinucci's truck. My detectives showed the drawing around. Nobody recognized the person depicted, or if they did, they weren't saying.

The investigation, which had begun so promisingly, was now completely stymied. I'd eventually solve the Testa murder, but the way proved to be a circuitous one. It began about a week after my unsuccessful interrogation of Rocco Marinucci, when Captain Jerry Kane, who had recruited me for the Homicide Bureau, asked me to drop by and see him. As I inserted myself into his tiny office, he asked, "How would you like to head up Special Investigations?"

The twelve detectives of the Special Investigations Unit (SIU), whose desks were crowded into an alcove next to Kane's office, had as their duty to solve so-called "back shelf" homicides. As the name suggests, these were murders for which the detectives originally assigned had been unable to make an arrest, and which, as new cases came their way, they lacked the time to continue to investigate.

I told Jerry I didn't want the assignment. Other lieutenants in homicide, I pointed out, were much more experienced than I was, and by rights the post, which was considered a plush one, should go to one of them. "Uh-uh," said Jerry. "You're the guy. It's a small unit and we need another investigator in there like you, not someone who sits on his rear and answers phone calls."

My real reason for turning him down, which I'd papered over with my pious suggestion that the job go to someone senior, paralleled my patrol officer's bias against detectives. After five years in the Detective Bureau, I knew that detectives weren't sissies, as I'd been taught, but I held to another belief, this one considered gospel by the detectives with whom I worked: The SIUs were sissies. They were, to us, the softest of the soft clothes. They worked regular hours—even (I'd heard) had weekends off!—whereas I and the other homicide and felony detectives often worked around the clock. That proved we were real men.

I thanked Jerry for thinking about me and, smug in my macho pride, I marched out of the office. Almost immediately, I stopped. You are an idiot, I advised myself firmly. Here you are, a cop for twenty-one years, with never a weekend off, and this guy's handing you that opportunity, and you're turning it down? I executed one of my finer military pirouettes and strode right back into Jerry's office. He was laughing. "You want that job?" he asked. I managed to laugh, too.

When I took on the SIU command at the beginning of April 1981, I had no choice but to let the Testa case ride for a while. My assignment was to take charge of the investigation of still another organized crime killing in which the victim was one of Philadelphia's leading citizens.

It had occurred on December 16, 1980, three months before Testa's death. Around 5:30 that evening, John McCullough, the business agent for Roofers Union Local 30B, was on the phone to his wife, Audrey. His evening meeting, he told her, had been postponed, so he was going to leave the office in a few minutes and head right home. Audrey said that was good news; she'd get the dinner on. Recently, John had seen Audrey through a serious illness, but she was recovering now, and they both thanked God for that. Her improvement was the present that would make this Christmas a happy one.

At the age of 60, John McCullough was still a physically imposing man, big and burly, his brush haircut hearkening back to his days as a marine in World War II. Advancing age hadn't slowed him down a bit. He could still drink guys half his age under the table, and his laugh was a roar, his smile warm and engaging. His men in the union adored him, would follow him, as one said, through the fires of hell itself. He was tough, all right, and they liked that; roofing's a tough job. But he was also the kindest of men, and they liked that, too. Go to Big John when you needed a few dollars to tide you over. Go to Big John with a problem —didn't matter if you were a union member—and he'd try to solve it, whether it meant putting a free roof on the parish church or going to bat with the judge for a neighbor's boy who'd gotten into trouble with the law.

Big John was evenhanded in his generosity, willing to help both cops and robbers. If you were in the slammer and could get out only if you had a job, John McCullough would see to it that you got one on a roofing crew; and working right next to you in the heat and the smell of the tar might be an off-duty policeman to whom John had given the work because he needed extra money for his family.

McCullough was also one of the most politically powerful men in Philadelphia. His success in organizing the Roofers, his personality, his ability to get along with people, had paved the way for his rise in the Building Trades Council of the AFL-CIO, and with that ascendancy came a growing influence on Philadelphia's dominant Democratic Party. Candidates for office, from state legislator to judge, were more than likely to make one of their stops a meeting with Big

John. His blessing would usually mean an endorsement from the party bosses, and it would definitely mean a cash contribution from the Roofers Union Political Action Committee, the purse of which was in Big John's pocket.

Soon after speaking with his wife, McCullough left the Roofers headquarters. Twenty minutes later, about 5:55 p.m., he parked his car in the driveway in front of his home, a modest brick twin at 2005 Foster Street in the city's nearly all-white Great Northeast, not far from the neighborhood in which I was raised. He probably didn't notice, had no reason to notice, the white panel van that was just then pulling to the curb halfway down the block.

He entered his house through the kitchen. Audrey was talking on the kitchen phone. As he came in, she said, "It's for you," and without removing his overcoat, he took the receiver from her. It was one of his men; he had a problem for Big John to solve.

As Audrey turned from the phone, she heard a rap at the kitchen door. Opening it, she saw a tall young man with his cap pulled down over his forehead. He was carrying an oblong box covered with green plastic. She could see the leaves of a poinsettia plant peeping out from the wrapping. "Is this the residence of John McCullough?" the young man inquired.

"Yes, come in," said Audrey, and he did. He glanced around before placing the box on the kitchen table next to a Christmas wreath. "I have another package," he said with a polite smile.

John put his hand over the receiver and instructed Audrey, "Be sure to give him a good tip." The man left and a minute or so later returned with a second poinsettia, packaged like the first one. Audrey glanced around for her purse, John continued to talk on the phone, and the man reached inside the top of the box.

He lifted his hand. In it was a gun equipped with a silencer. He pulled the trigger. It went "pop." The bullet went through

John McCullough's head. He fell, dragging with him from the table several little plastic snowmen intended for the Christmas tree.

Kicking one of the toy snowmen aside, the man leaned over John and fired five more bullets into his brain.

The murder had taken only a few seconds, during which Audrey stood still, unable to move, unable to speak. Now, she screamed. She ran out of the house. Making sure he had his second weapon, a .38, handy, the young man strode after her. He found her in the driveway. She was trembling, weeping hysterically. He put his arm around her shoulder as if he were comforting her and walked her back into the kitchen. At that moment, she may not even have been sure who was escorting her. While in the kitchen with her, he hesitated a moment, studying her, apparently trying to decide whether he should murder her, too. Then he turned on his heel, left the house, strolled down the street to his van, got in and drove off. The vehicle was found by police in the parking lot of a shopping mall a few blocks away.

The McCullough killing led off all the TV news broadcasts that Tuesday evening and was the headline story in the newspapers the next day. McCullough was the most prominent Philadelphian murdered in the 300-year history of the city.

Thousands of mourners turned up for his viewing and funeral—members of his union, average citizens whose lives had been touched by his kindnesses, politicians great and small whose careers he had helped make, judges, policemen, leaders of other unions. Anecdotes about his countless acts of generosity appeared in the press, so that even people who hadn't known who he was were outraged by his murder. The coldbloodedness of the crime—shooting him down in his own house in front of his wife—added to the horror, as did the little Christmas touches—the poinsettia plants, the tree ornaments found next to his body.

But within a day or two, the newspapers were retracting

some of their praise of McCullough. Stories now carried accounts of past violence on the part of the Roofers. The most famous instance had occurred nearly twenty years before in the Philadelphia suburbs. A contractor, Leon Altemose, had hired nonunion labor for a major construction site, and the Roofers, led by McCullough, had come out in force. By the time the Roofers were done, Altemose's equipment and the property had suffered $400,000 worth of damage.

This and other stories of Roofer goon squads beating up nonunion roofing contractors and their men were bitterly assailed by the men of Local 30B (the vast majority of whom are honest and hardworking), who accused the press of smearing their fallen leader.

Pervading the case from the beginning was the realization—not only by reporters and law enforcement officials but by the public as well—that the shooting had all the earmarks of a gangland hit. There had been no robbery, not even an attempt to make the slaying look like a robbery. Whoever was responsible seemed to want to leave no doubt about the motive.

The apparent Mafia involvement gave the case an ominous cast in the public mind. McCullough's was the sixth such assassination of the year. The other five—those of Bruno, Caponigro, Salerno, Simone, Sindone—all had an intramural character; they were gangsters killing gangsters, and good riddance. But McCullough's was different. It was as if the mob, after honing its killing skills on its own, was now branching out into public murder. McCullough might not have been the saint of the early stories, but he was a mover and shaker, a philanthropist, one of the mighty and a friend of the mighty. If they could murder him, who might not be next?

It was, as we say in the department, a high-profile killing.

It was treated that way, too—cosmetically. With great fanfare, the case was assigned to the Special Investigations Unit, apparently solely because the unit's title gave the public the impression that it comprised the city's best detectives who were assigned only to the most important cases. Nothing could have been further from the truth. Not only did the SIU detectives work old cases, rather than hot-breaking ones like McCullough, but no one in the Department had ever pretended they were the best detectives. A number of them were first-rate, but then again, so were many of those assigned to regular homicide and felony investigations.

The immediate result of sending the McCullough case to SIU with instructions that the entire squad work on it full-time was that hundreds of unsolved homicides which the squad had under active investigation had to be shoved onto the back shelf until McCullough was solved or until the public concern about it had sufficiently abated that it could be back-shelfed, too.

At the time the McCullough homicide reached the SIU, cases were allocated by the lieutenant in charge on a rotation system. Whoever came next on the wheel was assigned the next case regardless of the detective's ability, or the difficulty of the case, or the difficulty and size of the caseload the detective was already carrying. (I subsequently changed the system. I made it my business to review all the unit's cases and assign each the detective or detectives I thought most capable of handling it.)

For the McCullough case, by good luck, the name that came up on the wheel as lead detective was one of the unit's best, John Main. Big and round, Main liked to work with the highly capable Jimmy Jackson, who was short and round. Not that they were officially partners—the Philadelphia Police Department has a policy against that—but in practice they often were, and they made a good team. Main was a straight-ahead sort, individualistic, something of a loner—Jackson was the only one he was close to—and with a detective's typical strong ego. Jackson, intelligent like Main, was more self-effacing, willing to plod through the kind of boring routine that detectives like Main hated but did (and that the slackers simply avoided while claiming they did it). The scut work entailed going from house to house in the crime area on the off chance someone might have seen something; it meant spending hour after hour patiently locating truck and service-vehicle drivers who may have been at or near the scene of the crime and interviewing them. In the overwhelming majority of cases, scut work has no payoff, but when it does it can be the key that leads to an arrest.

The SIU wasn't the only agency investigating the McCullough murder. The FBI was also investigating, not its Organized Crime Unit as might have been expected, but rather its Labor Squad, which had been surveilling McCullough's activities before his death.

During the initial stage of the investigation, our SIU and the FBI's Labor Squad had maintained contact with each other, but the relationship had quickly deteriorated to the point that by the time I took SIU command, neither side was talking to the other. The surprise was not that communication had ceased, but that it had ever occurred. It rarely does. Police everywhere dislike and mistrust the FBI; the FBI dislikes and mistrusts police. Historically, the two bodies have viewed each other as rivals, not as allies. The standard procedure has been noncooperation.

Even my failure to make a quick arrest in the Testa case could be laid in part to the mutual failure to cooperate. As I was conducting my investigation, FBI agents were busy on a parallel one of their own. They (as I later learned) picked up some information we didn't have, just as we had some they didn't have. But I, who bought into the police view of the FBI, never talked to their agents, they never talked to me, and Rocco Marinucci remained untouched—by either of us. Marinucci, I'm sure, didn't know about the rivalry, but if he had, he would have had more cause to laugh at me than he already did.

The police distaste for the FBI is analogous to the uniforms' hatred of soft clothes. To the cops (detectives as well as uniforms), FBI agents are a bunch of three-piece suits who drink their tea with a pinky finger extended and have Harvard accents, who pump the local cops for information but never explain why (just as the police detective soft suit never explains the why of anything to the uniform), and who, after being in town for a few weeks, consider themselves the world's greatest experts. They act as if we cops don't know our own city; only they do. It's insulting; it's aggravating. And it's so delightful when the FBI agents stumble over their own well-shod feet while we supposedly inferior flatfeet bumble ahead and break the case they can't figure out.

The FBI arrogance is institutional. Agents, from the time they enter its academy, are taught they are members of the nation's elite justice agency, superior in intelligence, superior in resources, superior in integrity, to everyone else in law enforcement. (That includes other federal agencies; the FBI looks down on the Drug Enforcement Administration with almost the same amount of disdain as it does local cops, and I've never heard Treasury agents speak warmly of the FBI, either.)

The FBI's traditional unwillingness to cooperate with local law enforcement authorities has, however, more than arrogance as a reason. Unlike the FBI, many police departments, including Philadelphia's, have long histories of corruption. Cops have been known to be in gangsters' pockets, help them commit crimes, tip them off. As the FBI sees it, therefore, the less cops know about what it knows, the more likely it is to solve crimes and protect the safety of its informants.

The FBI has another reason to fear sharing information with local authorities: politics. It's not that the cops themselves are perceived as creatures of political favor. I doubt if there is a single city in the country any longer where police appointments are made by ward leaders (as they were in Philadelphia until 1951). However, police report to the district attorney, and the district attorney is an elected official who usually wants to get elected again; when pressure is on to solve a high-profile case, favorable information about its progress sometimes unofficially reaches the press.

That happened in the McCullough investigation just before I took over the command, when an item appeared in the *Philadelphia Inquirer* stating that an arrest in the case was imminent. (The source was a member of DA Ed Rendell's staff, but I have no reason to think Rendell authorized the leak.) According to the story, a father-and-son hit team was responsible for the killing.

While the article had a certain flavor to it—father-and-son hit teams make for tantalizing breakfast-table reading—its publication at that time could have compromised the entire investigation and led to the death of the person who was its source, as the FBI quickly pointed out. To the FBI, the affair was just one more proof that cops weren't to be trusted. My detectives were every bit as upset as the FBI. It had never occurred to them that anyone in the DA's office could be irresponsible enough to release such sensitive, confidential, *unevaluated* material.

In fact, by the beginning of April an arrest was in the offing in the McCullough case, but not of any father and son. As I learned in studying the file, Main and the other SIU investigators had been making solid progress, and they figured the FBI was headed in the same direction as they were. Whoever got to the goal line first would win all the publicity.

Our investigation had started with the truck that the lethal deliveryman had been driving and that was found a few blocks from the murder site, linked to the crime by the poinsettia leaves discovered inside it. Through the license plates, Main and Jackson traced the vehicle to Rice & Holman, an auto leasing firm in New Jersey. The clerks on duty at the time recalled that two men had rented it. Their descriptions of the men were vague, but even so, composite drawings were made. The sketches, which turned out not to resemble either man, had caused a lot of time-wasting. When they were shown to street informants, sure enough—informants never like to appear ignorant—they "recognized" the nonexistent persons in the drawings, different identifications from each informant, leading the detectives on a series of wild goose chases.

The Rice & Holman clerks were, however, useful in producing a contract indicating that the rental was for business use by Aladdin Carpets, a New Jersey rug-cleaning firm. The contract was signed by Jan Mullaney.

A check with the National Crime Information Center of the FBI revealed that across the United States just three individuals named Jan Mullaney held driver's licenses. One lived in Buffalo, another on Long Island, the third in Florida. The Florida Mullaney had been issued his license on December 9, 1980, just seven days before McCullough's murder. He gave his address as 2107 Orange Grove Drive, Tampa. If he had ever lived there, he no longer did.

The Buffalo and Long Island Mullaneys were eliminated as suspects, but the one on Long Island offered a promising lead when he revealed that his license was missing, possibly stolen. If so, it might have been presented as the basis for issuance of the Florida permit, which could then have been used in that state for identification purposes in making weapons purchases.

That apparently was what had happened. A check with Florida authorities revealed that on December 9, a person using the Mullaney Florida permit had bought two .22 Ruger automatics.

The SIU detectives had also been following the Aladdin Carpet lead. They went through the company's personnel files and discovered that a part-time employee named Howard Dale Young had given 2107 Orange Grove Drive in Tampa as his previous address. Young had a criminal record, all nonviolent offenses.

A search and seizure warrant to go through Young's New Jersey home was obtained by the SIU. There, detectives discovered a copy of the truck rental agreement as well as paperwork relating to the weapons purchase in Florida. The knot tightened further around Young when his fingerprints were discovered on the Mullaney driver permit.

All this had been accomplished within a month or so following the McCullough murder, but neither the SIU nor the FBI—conducting its parallel investigation and no doubt coming up with much the same information—was in any hurry to arrest Young. The mutual hope was that he might lead investigators to the person or persons who had hired him to buy the weapons.

As this chronology indicates, the killer or killers had made a series of glaring mistakes. The pivotal error was leaving the van a few blocks from the murder site, making it easy to locate and therefore readily traceable. Howard Dale Young further helped by giving the name of his real employer when signing the lease in Mullaney's name. Had he not done that, we might never have learned his identity. Even then he could have been safe had he not, while in Florida, given the same Tampa address as on the Aladdin records.

To a psychologist, this kind of easily followed trail might indicate someone who wants to be caught. Such criminals do exist, but in my experience, they are few and far between. Rather, fortunately for cops and the public, crooks constantly make mistakes of this kind, very often out of plain stupidity.*

---

*As one example among many, I recall a robber who took a cab to a bank he was going to hold up. Asking the driver to wait for him, he left behind his briefcase containing his name and address and a series of ''This is a stickup'' notes he'd been practicing. When the cabbie saw his fare running out of the bank brandishing a gun, not surprisingly he drove off and turned the briefcase over to the first cop he encountered. When the robber was arrested forty-five minutes later, he seemed genuinely surprised we had caught up with him.

* * *

Throughout the first few months of 1981, Howard Dale Young found himself repeatedly questioned by the SIU and the FBI. I assume he figured the two agencies were coming at him in well-orchestrated relays, and had no idea that neither knew what the other was doing.

The cumulative effect, however, was positive. Continuing to deny he had any knowledge of the murder itself but realizing he was in serious trouble, he began to make overtures to both investigating teams, dropping little bits of information formulated in vague and evasive terms. Each statement we got was checked, and several turned out to be completely false. Many, however, could be neither proved nor disproved. Among them were references to a "cousin" who might have knowledge of the murder. At other times, Young talked about "Junior," who at times seemed to be the same person as the "cousin."

At one point, Young agreed to take a lie detector test from the FBI. His responses indicated deception when he continued to assert he hadn't killed McCullough. That by itself did not prove he was the gunman, since the polygraph, even assuming it can detect deception, can never tell *why* the subject is lying. (Most suspects fail to recognize the limitations of the polygraph, and when told they have failed it, they often immediately confess.)

Finally, around the middle of March 1981, the pressure on Young led him to identify the "cousin" (who turned out not to be a cousin) as Willard Moran, Jr., a minor drug dealer. Moran had been convicted of killing a man in a barroom brawl in 1974 and had served about three years. His father had a peripheral involvement in the crime, and was convicted and sentenced to 364 days of county time. Young was now indicating he believed the father and son might have acted together to kill McCullough. That was the flimsy basis for the story leaked to the press by the DA's office.

If either Moran were part of the conspiracy, the father-son hit team story would endanger Young if he was believed to be its source. That meant it was no longer safe to let him remain out on the street. He was brought in and charged with first-degree murder.

5

The Atlantic City Connection

After studying the progress of the McCullough investigation, I decided, for the time being, to leave Young to detectives Main and Jackson. I got on the phone. Over the years I'd developed a stable of informants, many of them nighttime characters I'd frequently meet in after-hours clubs; some of them moved within and around the edges of that ugly world where organized crime and labor union racketeering met. It was one of these men that I called first.

Me: "Hey, listen, I got this case here, the brush-hair guy,

and it's driving me crazy. We're developing information about who whacked him, and I need to tap your brain."

Him: "Oh, look, I don't wanta get involved in that, man; big people involved in that. I can't help ya on that."

Me: (You never take that kind of "no" for a "no"): "Well, just meet me for a drink."

We did, and he did help.

I never brought informants in for questioning, didn't meet them at their homes,* but rather at some neutral place like an out-of-the-way bar, sometimes an out-of-the-way town, where no one would recognize them or me.

I had originally met my best informant for the McCullough investigation—the one I called first—in the 1960s when I was a patrol officer. Over the years, he had provided tips that, for the most part, proved reliable, and I knew he had contacts with the Roofers Union. Drinks, yes, meals, yes, but I never paid him cash; that wasn't what he was in it for. Not that his motives were pure. From time to time I'd hear from him, asking me about a case. One that I recall involved a breaking and entering into a warehouse. "Hey, Frank," he said, "what's the word? What they going for?" Because of the favors he'd done me, I called the DA's office to learn their posture in the prosecution (nothing wrong in my doing

---

*There is one exception: when I've been stood up. For example, during the course of the McCullough investigation, an informant arranged to meet me at a bar in New Brunswick in northern New Jersey, a good couple of hours drive from Philadelphia. I waited at the bar for more than an hour. When he didn't arrive—I've spent more time than I like to remember sitting in a scrofulous bar nursing a beer waiting for someone who never appears—I returned to Philadelphia, and a couple of nights later, when I had the time, I showed up at his house—at three in the morning. I didn't knock, either. I started kicking at his door. Two stories up, a window was raised: "Whatta ya want?" "Come on down here." Recognizing me: "Oh, shit, sorry, man, I missed ya. My car broke down. . . ." "Come on down here." He did, and *then* we had our talk. He never stood me up again.

that) and then got back to him. "It's nickel and dime," I told him. "If he pleads, they'll ask for 11½ to 23 months probation."

That was exactly what my man wanted to hear. I found out later that he went back to the guy who was in trouble, told him he'd fixed the case, and got him probation. The guy gratefully paid him for his help.

He now filled me in on the details of who was who in the Roofers Union, which was helpful, but his meatiest offering came when he said, "Ya wanta find out why John was killed, look to Angelo Bruno," and added some details. He wasn't right about everything, but enough—he sent me in the right direction.

That Bruno and McCullough knew each other didn't surprise me. A man like McCullough who had the capacity to bring out several hundred strong-arm men on a moment's notice, as he had in the Altemose fracas, was someone the mob would find worth cultivating.

Extortion of real estate developers is the game a corrupt union leader can help a mafioso like Bruno play. The scheme typically works this way: At an initial stage of a project, the developer receives a visit from mob emissaries—rarely just one; two or three are much more threatening. He is told that if he wants his project to be concluded on time, without strikes, without delayed deliveries by Teamsters, without sabotage by workers, it will be prudent for him to hand out construction contracts to named companies, all of which either are mob-owned or pay commissions to the mob for jobs they get. The developer who agrees to the emissaries' demands seals the bargain by paying them a "finder's" or "management consultant" fee. Those who don't agree get the trouble that was forecast for them—at least, until they do agree.

Just as is in street tax collections, the size of the fee is based on how much the extortionists figure the traffic will bear. It can be quite a large amount. In one well-documented

Philadelphia case, the demand was for one percent of a $100 million budget.

The FBI Labor Squad had information that McCullough was receiving portions of the finder's fees. My own investigation did not confirm that allegation, but even if it wasn't true, the blackmail schemes he and Bruno worked against developers were to McCullough's interest in several ways.

To begin with, in acceding to the mobsters' demands, developers had to guarantee they would use only union labor, including racketeer-influenced unions like McCullough's and the Teamsters, with whom he maintained a close working relationship. The employment of union help meant jobs for McCullough's men, which kept his members happy with his leadership. More significant to McCullough, however, were the health and welfare benefits that employers are required to pay to unions working on their projects. McCullough siphoned portions of these payments intended for the workers into the union's Political Action Committee. It was this transfer of funds that gave him the financial muscle to influence nominations and elections to political office. And for him— if my reading of him is correct—power, not money, was the great intoxicant.

I found all this information interesting, but it was not taking me anywhere in finding a motive for McCullough's murder. On the contrary, it suggested a good reason for the mob *not* to kill him. He had proved reliable in the developer extortions—who could say if his successor would be as adept or as cooperative? Or have the influence McCullough did in causing other unions to call strikes when that was in the mob's interest? Moreover, his insider position in the Democratic Party gave the Mafia an insider position, too, something not easily come by, nor to be lightly discarded. Even if his successor was every bit as corrupt, it would take that person years before he could command the central political role McCullough held. So—why was McCullough killed?

Another of my sources said, "Look to Atlantic City."
That's where I turned my attention next.

My knowledge of mob activities in Atlantic City was sketchy in 1981. However, I was aware that the New Jersey Gaming Commission, with the grim lesson of Las Vegas in front of it, had attempted to prevent mob infiltration of casino ownership. Already, several would-be entrepreneurs had been rejected because of alleged organized crime connections.

Mafiosos like Bruno in Philadelphia, his Atlantic City capo Scarfo, and the Gambinos and Genoveses in New York had other ways to go. Atlantic City construction contracts were extorted in the same manner Bruno had used in Philadelphia. (Scarfo owned a cement company, a symbolically fitting business for any mafioso to be in and a great one in the Atlantic City boom economy. The same office housed another construction company owned by Scarfo allies.)

Once the casinos were built, however, that source of income would cease. Since continuing influence was the goal, the attention of mobsters—the Philadelphians and the New Yorkers—focused on industries that served the casinos, and on the employees who worked for them.

New Jersey and federal law enforcement agencies believe, and I agree, that the service businesses, in conjunction with the casino unions, have produced tens of millions of dollars in profits for La Cosa Nostra. Since everyone involved in these shakedowns has good reason not to talk, indictable evidence has been hard to come by.

The Poultry King scam (which I investigated subsequent to the McCullough case) was typical. The Poultry King* did not start out as royalty. He had only a modest-sized butchering business when, according to my information, he was approached by an acquaintance who had connections with the

*To protect a source, I cannot name names and must change a few of the facts.

Philadelphia/Atlantic City LCN. The butcher's meetings with this individual allegedly led to a $10 million contract for him as the exclusive provisioner of poultry to several casinos. In return, the newly minted Poultry King kicked back a million dollars a year to the mob.

The Poultry King's chickens were no better than those the casinos had been getting from a previous supplier and were also more expensive (to cover the cost of the kickback). Nevertheless, casino managers allegedly agreed to the deal without protest.

They did so—and here is where the control of unions dovetails with that of concessions and suppliers—because a mob-allied union official asked them to. In each instance, the union representative remarked that he would consider it a personal favor if the Poultry King was given the chicken concession. He made no threats of what could happen if the casino didn't agree; that wasn't necessary. The casino management assumed that if it didn't go along, the union would find an excuse to call a strike. Even if the walkout lasted only one day, a good-sized casino could lose a million dollars in revenue. Expensive chicken (the extra cost of which could be passed on to customers by increasing the menu price) was a sensible trade-off to prevent that kind of financial loss.

Apparently, sometime in 1979 (or possibly earlier) Bruno and McCullough hit on a similar scheme. A reading of the Gaming Commission regulations revealed to them that in order to remain open, a casino was required to have a complement of security guards on duty. McCullough immediately got to work organizing the guards. He didn't think it would ever be necessary to call them out on strike; the casinos would understand who had to be paid to prevent that.

McCullough was the ideal front man for the job. The Commission knew all about Bruno, and if it had gotten even a whiff of his involvement in the unionizing activities, the plan would have been stymied. McCullough, however, as far as New Jersey knew, was a highly respected, politically wired union leader; no reason to stop him from doing what he did for a living, organizing workers.

Once I was aware of the security guard scheme, I figured I had the motive for McCullough's murder. As long as Bruno was alive, McCullough was protected; with Bruno gone, I figured, Testa and his allies, including the rapidly rising Scarfo, decided to eliminate McCullough and grab the newly formed union for themselves.

My theory, however, had a hole. The same reasons that made it sound business to keep McCullough alive and functioning in Philadelphia held true in Atlantic City as well. Bruno's death didn't change that. McCullough would still be the mob's ideal front man for organizing the guards—and other unions, too, for that matter. Logic dictated he be kept on the scene.

Yet if I was right about the motive—and it struck me as compelling—logic hadn't prevailed as it ordinarily does in the execution of an economic crime. To try to find out why, I went back to my sources, now focusing my inquiries on McCullough's relationships with his gangster cohorts. Perhaps it wasn't business; perhaps it was personal.

McCullough and Bruno, I learned, had not only been partners in crime; they genuinely liked one another. I am not sure what it was in Bruno that appealed to McCullough, but I suspect Bruno was entranced by McCullough's riproaring, drinking-with-the-boys robustness, which may have represented to him, Sicilian-born, an all-American quality that he envied and found neither in himself nor in his crime family.

He may also have admired McCullough's generosity. Bruno himself enjoyed playing the godfather role, judiciously handing out wisdom and sometimes cash to those in need. But there was a meditated, controlled quality to everything he did, and he may have wished he could act in McCullough's impulsive, heart-on-the-sleeve manner.

The next piece of information that I picked up brought me nearer to my goal. Bruno's lieutenants, I was told, resented

the closeness that had developed between Bruno and Mc-
Cullough, much as natural children might resent it if their
father favored an adopted son. They had the feeling they were
being squeezed out, and they weren't entirely wrong about
that, either. Apparently, the lieutenants—including the on-
the-scene capo, Scarfo—did not hear about the security guard
scheme in Atlantic City until it was well under way, and
perhaps not until after Bruno's death.

The men around Bruno, however, not only were jealous
of McCullough's influence with him but also disliked the
union boss for the very qualities that Bruno admired.

Everything about McCullough irritated them, from his
gruff and jovial ways to his open enjoyment of his political
power (theirs were the ways of stealth) to his marine's brush
haircut (they wore their hair pomaded and slicked back). But
for them, perhaps McCullough's worst trait was that he acted
toward them as if he were their equal, nay, their superior;
was there not even an edge of contempt in his treatment of
them? That was insupportable.

Once I learned this, I was pretty sure of what must have
happened. Now able to ask better questions, I got better and
more detailed answers from my sometimes evasive (and fearful) sources.

When I put all my information together—it took me about
three weeks—it was apparent that the decision to kill
McCullough hadn't been made immediately. As I'd assumed,
Testa and his advisers recognized McCullough's stature in
Philadelphia. With that in mind, Testa first tried nonviolent
means to eliminate McCullough. During the early fall of
1980, he had two—by one account, three—meetings with
Big John in which he advised him that it would be to everyone's interest if he backed off from his Atlantic City activities.

McCullough refused. He may have thought Testa was bluff-
ing, may have thought, because of his strength in the union
movement and politics, that he was safe from an attempt on
his life. He may also have felt his masculinity challenged by

Testa—he'd lose face with himself and his henchmen who were helping with the organizing if he backed down. Whatever his reasons, he told Testa he would not be scared off; he and his boys were going ahead. After the final meeting, Testa put out the word that McCullough "was no longer to be considered an associate" of the Philadelphia family. That was his way of announcing McCullough's death warrant.

Once I knew why McCullough was killed, I decided the time had come to interview Young, who was being held without bail in the Camden County, New Jersey jail.

When I arrived at the jail, I was accompanied by detectives John Main and Jimmy Jackson, who had interviewed Young about a dozen times before arresting him.

Young was a big plump country boy in his late twenties with a decided southern drawl. He had, I observed, the tightness of fear around his eyes, but he seemed genuinely glad to see Main and Jackson. I think it was John who cracked the first joke; Young laughed, responded in kind. Jimmy said something, more laughter. It was apparent to me that the two detectives had developed a rapport with Young, which meant there was no need for me to do so.

Good detectives understand the value of rapport and go to great efforts to create this kind of zone of trust in which the suspect feels comfortable with the interrogator. With Howard Dale Young, John and Jimmy had made use of good-ole-boy, man-to-man stuff, just as regular guys together, a technique that is often quite effective. Since the detectives are easygoing sorts, it is easier for the suspect to talk to them—often not realizing how much he is revealing in the relaxed atmosphere that has been created.

My favorite method is to begin an interrogation—and this phase can go on for hours—by delving into areas the suspect will see as nonthreatening. Very frequently, his family offers that opportunity. I ask him about his wife, children, parents, by so doing getting him into the habit of answering questions (which is good in itself) and also allowing him to offer a "decency" response. That is, by telling me how much he loves his dear old mother, he is expressing to me that no matter what I think he has done (or what he knows he has done), he also has the capacity for normal feelings just like any decent person. By responding to his decency expressions sympathetically and understandingly, I move from being the Grand Inquisitor of his fears to someone who has responded to him as a fellow human being who, like everyone else, has good qualities. I am now someone to whom he can talk if he sees it to his interest to talk. (The discussion doesn't have to be about family either; with one suspect, I established this zone of trust when I finally discovered we had favorite authors in common.)

Regardless of how the rapport is created, the goal is always to use it to encourage a confession. However, not all detectives, by any means, use the trust technique to obtain statements. Some prefer to scare them out of the suspect. It is relatively easy to do that. Threats may do it, banging on the table may do it, insults may do it, or a combination of all three—"You're scum," (bang, bang) "and I'm going to put your ass in jail for the rest of your life" (bang, bang). Sometimes the bangs go further, and the suspect is beaten. Quite apart from the fact that this technique is redolent of the torture chamber, it has the potential to cause two problems: First, it may scare a confession out of an innocent person who, as a result, is convicted of a crime he didn't commit while the real perpetrator goes free. Second, it is much less likely than the trust technique to produce a full confession.

Truth, despite the confessions we encounter in crime fiction and movies, has never, in my experience, come in one spontaneous outburst from a guilty person. Truth from the guilty, rather, arrives on the installment plan. A phrase is added to this day's interrogation that wasn't in yesterday's, a nuance tomorrow, a sudden ability to remember a fact on the next day. When a zone of trust rather than one of terror exists between interrogator and criminal, the number of installments, in my experience, multiplies.

The extra installments can be important, too. Truthful information about accomplices is much more likely in the trust confession. (In the terrorized one, the confessing suspect, upon being given names of people the detective thinks are accomplices, will agree they were involved in the crime even if they weren't, because at this point the suspect is going to give the threatening detective anything he thinks the detective wants.) The trust confession is also much more likely to develop information about other crimes than the terrorized confession, since an atmosphere has been created in which the suspect feels willing to confide. I've also encountered instances in which the complete story lessens the suspect's degree of culpability—some people think they're more guilty than they are legally—and that's an important, if often overlooked, aspect of the detective's job. Our duty is to prepare evidence as accurately as we can. When we do that competently, we make fair trials and proper sentencing more likely.

I am not suggesting that the detective try to make an interrogation a pleasant experience for the subject. Quite the contrary; one does play on fears. But the goal is primarily to give the suspect, if he is guilty, a reason to confess, even if it does not go beyond relieving his conscience. Once the chatter about family is over, the jokes are over, the discussions of favorite authors or football teams is over, an interrogation is a very serious business, and it is important that the suspect then be plunged right into it. The contrast with the pleasantries that went before is itself helpful.

With Young, I initiated the serious stage by physically separating myself from the two joking detectives. I stood to one side of them, unsmiling. They had already introduced me as their lieutenant—a useful distancing right there—and now, as the you-all convivialities went on, I noted Young peeping over at me, taking in my stern expression with growing anxiety. My first words were: "I don't understand all this joking in a murder investigation."

At that, John and Jimmy fell silent. They looked at each other with guilty expressions; they shuffled their feet. Jimmy, I think it was, shot Young a raised eyebrow that said, "Look at this hard-ass we have to put up with." They were splendid. The smile faded from Young's face. He wiped his hands along the sides of his trousers.

He was psychologically all alone with me now, much more than he would have been if they had actually left the room. As it was, their abashed and silent presence constantly reminded him of their powerlessness to help him and, by implication, my power over him.

While John and Jimmy continued to hover in the background, ghosts of good times past, I pointed Young to a seat and took my place directly across from him. He didn't know what to expect from me, but must have assumed I was going to ask him questions. That, however, was not what he was going to get from me. I was, instead, about to become his consulting physician. The specialist called in by the general practitioners, I, having given due study to his case, was about to analyze his symptoms to him and proffer my diagnosis.

From the gravity of my demeanor and matching tone of my voice, he could tell, even before I got into the details, that the news wasn't going to be good. In adopting this role, I had a goal that went beyond scaring him. He had been pawed over by us and by the FBI for more than two months. He had tried to make a deal, but because he'd now failed two polygraph tests, neither we nor the FBI was willing to enter into an agreement with him. He was facing a first-degree murder charge. His life was spinning out of control. It was my job, as his physician, to prescribe the medicine that would allow him to regain control.

To accomplish that, my diagnosis had to replicate as much as possible his thoughts about his situation, and more than that: to bring out into the open the fears he would be most desperately trying not to admit to himself. His dilemma was a simple, exquisitely terrible one. He was scared of us and what we could do to him, but he was equally fearful of the mob, which, he must have heard, had a long arm that could reach right into prison and kill him if it believed—if it even suspected—he had talked. (The newspaper story, in that sense, had inadvertently helped us; its mention of a father-son hit team strongly suggested someone was talking, and who more likely than he, the one person who was under arrest? That contributed to his fear, too.) But because his fears conflicted with one another, and he didn't know how to handle them, he took refuge in half-truths and lies, providing no concrete evidence, merely inference. He was pointing at "cousin" Willard Moran, Jr., and his father, but he wasn't telling us enough to bring either of them in for questioning. I didn't know what the final installment would be— an admission he was the gunman himself?—but I knew we had not gotten past the first one.

I don't recall everything I said to Howard Dale Young in the hour or more I spent with him that day, but I can recount the key comments I made to him and describe the reasons for them. I started out, as I always do in such situations, by establishing the control-of-one's-own-destiny motif, one that I would then drop and get back to later. My outset remarks, therefore, went like this: "Howard, you're not going to like what I'm about to say to you, because no matter what you decide to do, life is not going to be any bed of roses for you. You aren't going to decide on anything because it serves our interests; I know that and so do you. But you are going to have to decide, and if you do decide to cooperate, it has to be because somewhere down the line you see it as being beneficial to you."

With the groundwork laid for the cure, I proceeded to the diagnosis: "The way things are going now, Howard," I went on, "it's very possible you're going to be convicted of killing a very prominent figure in the City of Philadelphia, and if you are convicted, the likelihood of your going to death row and ultimately being executed looms very strongly.''

Predictably, he interrupted to say, as he had so often, that he hadn't killed McCullough, didn't know anything about the actual murder. I shook my head. "No, Howard," I replied, "this homicide is a classic death penalty case under Pennsylvania law. It involves lying in wait and malice aforethought, so it doesn't matter whether you pulled the trigger or not. Your participation in the conspiracy makes you as guilty as the actual gunman. Don't take my word for it. Ask your lawyer if I'm right or not.''*

That seemed to come as a shock to him, I noted. Until now, he must have believed that the most we could get him for was buying guns, an accessory-before-the-fact charge. I don't know if he ever asked his lawyer about my description of his degree of culpability—assuming he wasn't the gunman—but, for the moment anyway, he obviously believed me.

I now continued the diagnosis with a control sub-theme, by opening up the area he had almost certainly been trying not to think about: "Howard, I think the real question for you is this: Who is going to get you? Will it be us or will it be your friends? You're an intelligent man, Howard, and you know that all your friends have to do is eliminate the weak link in the chain and the chain is ended. You're the weak link, Howard. So you have to come to your own conclusion, which way you'll be better off, with them or us, Howard.'' Back to diagnosis: "But let's talk about your friends a minute, Howard. Where are they now? The reality is you have to pay for your own defense. They aren't doing that for you. And

*Following his arrest, he'd been advised, as is standard procedure, that if he couldn't afford an attorney, one would be provided for him. We had also warned him that while he could engage anyone he wanted with his own money, if his attorney represented the mob, he could forget about any deal with us. That did not turn out to be a problem; Young's lawyer had no organized crime connections.

we know you're worried about your mom. You're afraid she's going to meet with an accident, or your sister will, as a lesson to you. Now you know law enforcement is not going to be precipitating these accidents. Your friends are. We're not your friends, as you know full well, but are they?"

The next switch was from that which could happen to that which would. Looking around the room thoughtfully, I remarked, "I guess you know that you're practically living in country club conditions here in this Camden jail, Howard." I shook my head sadly. "But I don't know how it is going to be for you when we transfer you to a Philadelphia prison. You might be big on the streets with all your mob friends, you might be a tough guy, but when you get in there, Howard, all those black prisoners we have over there, you know what you'll be? Just another fat white boy, Howard. The blacks love white boys who think they're tough guys, and they especially love them when they have a southern white-boy accent like you have, Howard. They're going to love you, Howard."

Switch to the longer future: "So when you're lying in a prison cell over there, when your new lovers are done with you for the day, and you're in that cell twenty-two hours a day, looking up at the ceiling, thinking about things, and I know you will be, think of where your friends are. Think of who's out and living well, and who's eating steak while you eat gray eggs, and think how you'd like to be in this position twenty years down the line while your friends are laughing about you, how you were the one who maintained the code of silence. That is, if you survive twenty years in there, and aren't killed by one of them or put to death by the state."

Back to control: "Yes, think about that, Howard, about how fine it is for you to have friends like that, as opposed to doing things that are in your best interest." Pause. "I can't make that decision for you, Howard. Only you, only you can do that. That's the decision you can make, Howard."

I arose as if to leave. He said he'd like to say something,

which is how we got the next installment. By the time several more interviews had passed, we had the final one.

Howard Dale Young's revised and completed version of his involvement in the McCullough murder featured Willard Moran, Jr. (He had been misleading us about the father; *he* played no role in the crime.)

Howard first got to know Junior as a customer at the Admiral, a girly joint on the porno stretch of Admiral Wilson Boulevard where Howard worked part-time as a bartender. Moran, he said, was about his own age and height, but powerfully built—he lifted weights as a hobby. "I'm on the fast track to go up in the mob," he allegedly informed Young, bragging that Raymond "Long John" Martorano had promised to let him be his driver, a position of great honor and trust. But Martorano's wasn't the only organized crime name Moran mentioned, according to Young; he also spoke frequently of his "cousin," Al Daidone, whom Moran described as a behind-the-scenes power.

The pivotal event in his relationship with Moran, Young said, occurred probably sometime in November 1980, when Moran said to him, "If you'll be in my crew, Dale, good things'll happen for you."

Young found Moran's offer attractive. (He apparently felt much as a hoodlum named Thomas DelGiorno did, who offered this explanation for wanting to become a member of the Mafia: "It's the difference between being in the major leagues and minor leagues as far as gangsters are concerned.")

After obtaining Young's enthusiastic assent to come on board Moran's crime wagon, Moran purportedly confided to him that certain people were to be "eliminated from the mob," and it was necessary to gather the tools to do so. That was to be Young's job. He was given the Mullaney driver's license, which Moran allegedly had stolen while visiting friends on Long Island; with it Young traveled to Florida to get the permit which he used for identification in making the weapons purchase. When I asked him why he had given his own former address in Tampa, he explained, "I got flustered; I couldn't think of no place else to say."

He bought four guns, two .22 Rugers and two semiautomatic rifles. On his return from Florida, around December 10, he explained, he delivered the weapons to a drug-dealer associate of Moran's, David Kupets, who had once been a West Point cadet. The following day, he and Moran went to Rice & Holman, where they rented the white panel van. With Moran following him in his car, Young continued, he drove the van to Camden, where they parked by a building in which Local 54 of the Bartenders Union had its office. Moran told Young to wait for him. "I got to see Cousin Albert," was how Young recalled his words and "drop the keys off with him," a reference to the keys for the rented truck.

When Moran returned from the building—Young said he did not see any meeting between the two men—he and Moran then drove to Edelman's, a gun shop, where Young purchased a box of .22 ammunition which, he said, he handed over to Moran, who was waiting outside.

Sometime during the next several days, Young added, test firings of the weapons took place in a house in Camden that Moran shared with a mutual friend. This man, who was never charged (and so I will not use his name),* allegedly shaved the barrel of one of the Rugers and fixed a silencer over it.

His own participation, Young asserted, ended with the purchase of the ammunition. He assumed at least one murder was to be committed with the weapons he'd bought—there was no other conceivable reason for their out-of-state purchase or for fitting one of them with a silencer—but, he said,

---

*Young had never wanted to bring the man into the case. He liked him; the man had done him favors, had a family, a legitimate job. It seems at least possible that Young's reluctance to involve his friend was one reason he tested deceptive in his responses when polygraphed by the FBI.

he had never asked nor been told who was to be killed or why.

Young concluded his confession by recalling events that took place at the Admiral Wilson Bar on the evening of December 16, 1980. When he reported for duty, he said, a man he knew was already there drinking. At some later point—Young couldn't pinpoint the time—Moran arrived, said hello to Young, and then joined Young's friend at the bar. Moran, Young recalled, was wearing a dark leather jacket, was smiling and happy-looking: "pumped up," as Young described it. Moran ordered three shots of whiskey. He and the friend each drank one. Moran then picked up the third shot glass and flung it. It bounced against the wall, the contents splashing on the floor. As Young explained, he later figured out that was the victim's last drink. Just as he was leaving, Moran turned and said, "Watch the eleven o'clock news." Young did, and that's how he learned who the victim was.

The arrangement tentatively worked out for Young by his lawyer was that he plead guilty to third-degree murder and be placed in the Federal Witness Protection Program, both while he was in prison and afterward, providing he gave complete and truthful testimony at the trial of the McCullough killer or killers.

Before signing any deal, we wanted to corroborate as much of Young's story as possible. That included eliminating the possibility of cross-role playing. That is, it was conceivable that everything Young was claiming Moran did, he himself had done. He might have been banking on Moran's previous history of violence—and his own lack of it—to make us believe him when he fingered Moran.

I doubted that. By the time I got the final installment from Young, his story, unlike its earlier versions, had, I thought, the ring of truth to it. The part about turning the weapons over to the drug dealing ex-cadet Kupets rather than Moran moved strongly in that direction. If Young were trying to frame Moran, he would have said he had given the weapons directly to him. He also would have had Moran admitting the killing to him. Instead, the only "admission" he had was Moran's throwing the shot glass in the bar and his parting comment about watching the eleven o'clock news. The shot glass business was so bizarre that I didn't think many people could have made it up, much less a Howard Dale Young.

As credible as Young's final installment was, it did not, however, literally put a smoking gun in Moran's hand. (On the witness stand, Young would be able neither to place Moran on the murder scene nor in possession of the murder weapon at any time.)

Since I didn't yet have sufficient grounds to arrest Moran, I decided the best thing to do was to give him some rope. Even if he wasn't aware of the father-son story, which could only apply to him, he would have heard by now that Young had been arrested, which meant Young might be talking. Good. I wanted him worried, but I also figured the longer we let him alone, didn't even visit him to question him, the more his confidence would grow, leading him to make a mistake that would lead us to his employer.

I'd like to say we kept Moran under 24-hour surveillance; in the world of fiction, we would have, but in reality police lack the money and manpower to do that. Fortunately, most criminals don't realize how underfunded the police are; they think they are being observed when they aren't. Several years later, when I was talking to Moran informally, I asked him why it was, when both he and Howard Dale Young were free, he hadn't tried to kill Young; he must have realized Young was not exactly a rock of Gibraltar. "I wanted to," Moran replied, "but you guys was watching me all the time, and I didn't get the chance." During that period, Moran wasn't under observation by either us or the FBI.

The possible confederate mentioned by Young who most interested me was Al Daidone. He wasn't Moran's cousin—

we quickly established they weren't related at all—nor did any of our information indicate Daidone was any behind-the-scenes power in the mob world. As far as we knew, he wasn't even a made member.

According to police and FBI information, some officers of the New Jersey bartenders union for which Daidone worked had LCN connections, as did Daidone, a stocky man in his mid-forties who wore tinted glasses. Our intelligence reports showed a meeting at which Harry Riccobene and Martorano advised Bruno that Albert Daidone was the ideal choice to be the mob's new representative in the New Jersey branch of the union.

Albert, who may actually have worked as a bartender at one time—he had gotten a union card somehow—was forth-with named business agent of Local 54 in Camden, and within a month after McCullough's murder was promoted to vice president and placed in charge of organizing a bartenders local in Atlantic City.

For the moment, however, the background information concerning Daidone and the bartenders remained just that. All we had against Daidone was Young's assertion that Moran said he delivered the keys to the van to Daidone. Perhaps if Young had seen the exchange we'd have something, but he said he hadn't—inconvenient for us, but another indication he was telling the truth. If Daidone did have possession of the keys to the van, it was certainly possible that he and not Moran was the shooter. (The problem with that speculation was that Daidone didn't meet Audrey McCullough's sketchy description of the killer; Moran more nearly did.)

I had sent Jimmy Jackson to Florida to check out the details of Young's descriptions of his activities there, and Jimmy came up with enough evidence to make us conclude Young wasn't holding back anything there. The ex-cadet Kupets, a ruggedly built, good-looking and well-spoken fellow, proved a dead end; he wasn't admitting to anything at that time. (He later confessed to his role.) Others whom Young named (but

I can't), however, filled in parts of the story. It was holding together admirably.

All these little pieces of corroboration would be valuable if we were able to bring Moran to trial. Juries are understandably reluctant to take the word of an admitted criminal like Young when he is implicating another criminal. But if enough of his story can be shown to be true through independent police evidence, then the jury is likely to believe the parts that are based on the informant's unsupported word, such as Young's account of his conversations with Moran.

Perhaps the single most important lead that Young had given us was his recollection that the weapons he bought in Florida were test-fired in the Camden house. (That such testing might have taken place didn't surprise me. Anyone familiar with guns knows that automatic weapons, and particularly new ones—unlike mechanically operated ones—frequently jam, so it is prudent to test them before they are used.) We obtained a search warrant for the Camden house. There, in the basement, we found what we were looking for. Moran, or whoever had done the test firing, hadn't bothered to clean up afterward. From the floor, we picked up shell casings.

We turned our evidence over to ballistics. The answer came back: The casings had been fired from the .22 Ruger that killed John McCullough, and no other gun in the world.

That was the clincher. I now had enough to arrest Moran for first-degree murder. Since, however, I still had hopes he would lead us to his leader, I decided to let him run free for a while longer. If, after a reasonable period of time, nothing new turned up, we could then move to have him indicted by a grand jury empaneled by the district attorney.

On my other mob murder front, the Testa killing, the news continued to be no news. I remember, at that point, feeling as gloomy about Testa as I felt happy about solving the McCullough case, which is how it all too often goes in detective work. Success is balanced by failure, elation by frustration, and the frustration is always at its worst when you know, as I did in the Testa murder, who had committed the crime (Rocco Marinucci) and who had ordered it (the still-vanished Petey Casella) but you have no evidence for an arrest. While keeping an eye on Moran and hoping for a new lead in the Testa case, I turned my attention to the SIU's bulging back shelf of non-mob unsolved homicides. I became increasingly engrossed as my team and I began making break-throughs in those cases, some of them horrible murders, but none of them a part of this story. Testa was now sitting on the back shelf himself.

6
Long John Watches Two Murders Committed

By the time I had Moran in my sights for the McCullough murder, it was mid-May of 1981, and the rumor had already reached me that Nicodemo Scarfo had been chosen by the New York Commission as the new don of the Philadelphia crime family. I had first come across his name when investigating the Atlantic City connection in the McCullough murder. I learned he was the capo there, that he and Phil Testa were supposed to have been close friends; but other than that, the only piece of information I had about him came from one of my New Jersey snitches, who described him as "violent" and "emotional," by which I surmised the source believed he was unstable.

More interesting to me than Scarfo at the moment, from the perspective of the McCullough murder, was the middle-aged Raymond "Long John" Martorano, the man who had driven Angelo Bruno to his last dinner but who—for some unknown reason—had avoided driving him home. Martorano had now made two appearances in the McCullough case. His name first surfaced when an informant told me that Martorano had urged Phil Testa to force McCullough out of his Atlantic City security guard unionizing activities. He had next turned up, according to Howard Dale Young, as the high-ranking mobster Willard Moran was claiming as his patron. The two pieces of information together suggested to me that Martorano, as well as Daidone, had an interest in Atlantic City, and that Martorano might have hired Moran to kill McCullough. "Might," however, is not proof. I doubled back on my informants. Nothing.

On May 27, 1981—about three weeks after I got my final installment from Howard Dale Young about the McCullough murder—Long John Martorano appeared again, this time as a witness to a double homicide at the Meletis, a Greek restaurant in South Philadelphia.

This case, to which I was not assigned and to which I paid little attention at the time of its occurrence, was to become of consuming importance to me three years later. My life was threatened over it, and because of it I came close to ruining my career as a police officer.

The first person in the Meletis Restaurant to glimpse the killers on that warm May night of 1981 was 36-year-old Marcella Kohler, the barmaid. She was on her break at 9:30 p.m., having a cup of coffee, when she noted two bulky male figures through the curtain that covered the restaurant's door. Thinking they were late-arriving diners, she motioned to the maitre d' to call his attention to them, but as the men entered she drew back. They were wearing parkas and their faces were masked.

As she watched in mounting terror, the men drew guns from inside their jackets. "Don't nobody move," yelled one as he fired two bullets into the ceiling. He and his companion by now were facing a table a few feet from the door at which a party of nine was just finishing dinner. The second masked man pumped off five shots. Four of the bullets entered the head of a beefy middle-aged man, and the fifth went through the forehead of the woman seated next to him.

The killers turned and ran out of the restaurant into the headlights of a car that was about to park. Glancing back at the restaurant, one of them tore off his mask, then dashed after his companion. They turned the corner onto Fulton Street, climbed into a car where a confederate was at the wheel, drove off.

The man who had been shot died immediately, gracefully sliding out of his chair and onto the floor. Crawling toward him under the table was his bodyguard, Joseph "Joey Eye" Inadi, a former Philadelphia cop. Joey Eye wasn't taking his little subterranean journey to offer his master any help. Instead, with a singular presence of mind, he began to strip the body of its $20,000 diamond ring and $10,000 diamond watch.

Still in her chair, her head thrown back, her eyes appearing to be studying the holes in the ceiling above her, was the second victim. A sobbing woman, who had been sitting next to her, placed a napkin over her face.

The dead man was well known to local and federal law enforcement. He was 50-year-old Steve Booras, one-time strong-arm man for the Teamsters Local 107. I had previously run across his name as an associate of John McCullough.

The dead woman was Janette Curro, who was in her mid-fifties. She was the first innocent victim of the mob murders.

Seated across from Booras at the table had been Long John

Martorano, his host for the evening. Martorano had brought his wife, Evelyn, who in turn had invited three of her best girlfriends, all sisters, one of whom, the dead woman, Janette Curro, had met Booras a month before at his birthday party (also hosted by his good friend Long John). The remaining people at the table were the disc jockey Jerry Blavat (''The Geater with the Heater,'' as he styled himself), and his date for the evening. Blavat had been an usher at Angelo Bruno's funeral a year before.

Within minutes after Marcella Kohler dialed her 911 call, uniformed police were on the scene. An ambulance was summoned; the bodies were taken away. By then, detectives had arrived. Several officers remained inside the restaurant to take statements from patrons and employees. But not from Raymond Martorano and his wife: Apparently they had left through the back of the building immediately after the shooting. Meanwhile, other officers were questioning passersby and neighbors. A man on Fulton Street gave a description of the getaway vehicle that was immediately put out on police radio. But too late. The killers had vanished into the night. Their car was never found.

The best police lead on the murders came from Mr. and Mrs. John Egan, who were in the car in front of which the killers passed as they fled the restaurant. Both Egans said they had seen the features of the gunman who removed his mask, and the next morning they went to the Police Administration Building to help an artist make a sketch of that person.

The Meletis murders were headline news. This time the victims weren't prominent, as McCullough had been, and the story itself lacked the human interest angle of a horrified wife watching her husband being shot down in cold blood. However, the public nature of the Meletis killings struck a chord that prompted outrage tinged with terror. ''They'' were now killing people in restaurants; where next? a crowded theater? And nobody doing anything to stop it? cops? FBI? What was

Philadelphia becoming (editorialists thundered), Capone's Chicago of the 1920s?

Under the lash of that criticism, the police moved quickly. On June 8, eleven days after the shooting, Neil Ferber, a 35-year-old unemployed furniture salesman, was charged with the murders of Booras and Curro. At a press conference to announce the arrest, a police spokesperson told reporters that the identity of the second gunman was known and that he would be arrested shortly. DA Rendell announced he would seek the death penalty for Ferber. The congratulatory stories that followed emphasized that Ferber's arrest marked the first time a mob contract killer had been brought to justice in the history of Philadelphia.

Receiving most of the plaudits was the investigating team led by Sergeant Danny Rosenstein and Detective Mike Chitwood. Both were media favorites from previous acts of derring-do that had earned them the nicknames of the Batman and Robin of the Philadelphia police. The tall, wiry, moustachioed and charismatic Chitwood was Batman, the heavier Rosenstein, Robin, which did not sit particularly well with him, since he was Chitwood's superior officer.

The apparent solving of the Meletis murders, however, did nothing to forward the investigations of the preceding mob hits. To the contrary, the Police Department announced that the shooting of Booras—everyone agreed Curro had been hit by a stray bullet—was entirely unrelated to the other killings. Rather, Booras's murder, police believed, had its origin in another homicide a few days earlier in which the victim was a Booras associate, Harry Peetros. By the time of Booras's death, police had information that fingered a criminal named Barry Saltzburg as the Peetros killer; the assumption was that Saltzburg had decided to murder Booras in a preemptive strike before Booras could get to him for slaying his pal, Peetros. According to this theory, Saltzburg was the one who shot Booras and Curro, with Ferber's role limited to firing the warning shots in the ceiling which, even so, under the law, was sufficient to put him in the electric chair.

The Meletis murders, therefore, were a gang killing only in the sense that they involved members of the self-styled Greek Mob, a tiny and loosely organized cadre of criminals who shared a Greek heritage. Allegedly, the Greeks were involved in narcotics and loan-sharking (Peetros's speciality): They paid street tax to the Mafia but were not directly associated with it. For that matter, neither was Saltzburg, save in a fringe way; this seemed to be true of Ferber as well. It was also far from certain that Ferber could properly be labeled the "first contract killer" to be arrested, since he may not have been paid by Saltzburg to help him. The two of them, I heard somewhere, had known each other since they were boys and had participated together in previous crimes.

I remember taking note that Martorano, who (according to Howard Dale Young) seemed so fond of Willard Moran, was seated at the table. But it was just a passing thought. I assumed—since I considered him an excellent detective—that Danny Rosenstein and his squad had solved the case.

About a month after Ferber's arrest, Raymond Martorano made yet another crime appearance when he met in Philadelphia's fashionable Rittenhouse Square with a drug dealer named Ronald Raiton. As the two men sat on a bench watching little children at play nearby, Martorano slid over an envelope containing $104,000 to Raiton who, in return, handed him the keys to a truck that contained fifty-two gallons of phenyl-2-propanone (P2P), the chemical necessary to manufacture methamphetamines. The exchange between Martorano and Raiton led to a series of arrests in which I played no role (nor did anyone in the police; it was an FBI operation), but the circumstances surrounding the case were to help me when I later tried to find out what had really happened at the Meletis Restaurant that fatal night.

As I shall relate when I describe my own investigation of

the Meletis murders, Raiton, the man to whom Martorano handed all that cash, had information about Booras's death which should have, but didn't, affected the course of the original investigation. Quite apart from that, Raiton was a significant figure—during his brief period of ascendancy*—in the history of organized crime in Philadelphia and elsewhere. His tentacles reached as far west as Los Angeles, and he had connections going back to the 1970s with the Columbian cocaine cartel.

By around 1980, in tribute to his many nefarious ways, Raiton was being described by the federal Drug Enforcement Administration (DEA) as the single most dangerous criminal in America. Whether that was true or not, he was certainly one of its most successful ever.

He was also the most intelligent criminal I've ever met—I've interrogated him at least a dozen times—and a likable one, too. A portly fellow of middle years with a bushy white beard, Ronald Raiton makes for an interesting dinner companion, well educated, well read, interested in the arts and quite capable of discoursing knowledgeably on almost any subject, although I have observed that his favorite topic is money.

Raiton's goal in life had always been to become not just a millionaire but a multimillionaire. "I have no great interest in material possessions," he once explained. "It's just that I don't like to have to think about the price of anything I want to buy." By the time the late 1970s arrived, and Raiton was in his early forties, he was comfortably fixed—nice suburban home, big car—principally due to his success in running commercial frauds. However, he had not yet accumulated even his first million, and that was a source of annoyance to him.

---

*And afterward, indirectly: His principal scheme was copied (as I shall describe in Chapter 15) by members of the Scarfo gang, to their and Scarfo's considerable enrichment.

The United States government inadvertently showed Raiton—and later, the Scarfo gang—the way to the fortune he was about to make and keep. His opportunity came in 1978 when federal law enforcement officials, alarmed by the growing trafficking in meth, moved to stop distribution by placing P2P, the crucial ingredient, which smells like cat urine, on its restricted chemical list.

That order meant that P2P now could only be sold to pharmaceutical companies for their use in manufacturing amphetamines for prescription purposes. The regulation permitted the DEA to put all the chemical companies that made P2P under surveillance. As a result, thefts from these companies (sometimes by their own employees, who sold the P2P to the drug dealers) began to result in arrests. The embargo, it appeared, was going to work. It might have, too, were it not for Raiton. Drawing on his knowledge of the import-export business gained during one of his few legitimate jobs, Raiton located a company in West Germany where P2P manufacture was legal and unrestricted. He bought the product for $40 a gallon, had it shipped from Germany through Gambia, then across the Atlantic to the Bahamas, from which he brought it into Miami (and later, Fort Lauderdale) by yacht. On its arrival, he and his confederates, several of whom were beautiful young women—his chief lieutenant, Bebe Papantonio, was a fashion model—arranged to deliver the product by car to Philadelphia, where Raiton sold it usually at $3,500 a gallon.

Even when overhead was taken into account, his profits were extraordinary. He soon added to them by branching out into selling marijuana, Quaaludes (the latter, he once observed, "to keep me in Dom Perignon") and cocaine, for which his principal courier was also a handsome young woman. His cocaine business, however, was infiltrated by a federal agent, he and his accomplices were arrested, and he was convicted.

Out on bail while an appeal was pending, in the fall of

1980 Raiton hied himself to the DEA with an offer to provide complete information on his P2P business if, in return, a deal could be made on the cocaine conviction and any P2P charges. The DEA advised him that he, no one else, was its target. He was bade a cool farewell.

Undaunted by this rebuff, Raiton turned to the FBI, which he had all along considered a target more promising for his purposes. As he had remarked at one point to a lawyer: "I have a scheme, the greatest scheme in the world. I'll make millions selling P2P and when they're ready to close in on me"—as they were by early 1981—"I'll hand the FBI some mafiosos and some crooked lawyers and they'll let me go."

With that providential thought in mind—very few criminals are sharp enough, as Raiton was, to make plans for when they are caught—he began dealing directly with the Mafia, instead of through intermediaries as he had in the past.

He was proved right about the FBI, which (to the outrage of the DEA) accepted him as an informant. Soon thereafter —just prior to the Meletis murders—Raiton set up a series of meetings with Raymond Martorano, culminating in the one in Rittenhouse Square, for which Raiton wore a body wire.

The FBI was delighted to get Martorano and other meth dealers, mob or not, whom Raiton named and against whom he helped compile evidence both at person-to-person meetings and during phone conversations bugged by the FBI. While he was at it, Raiton testified against every member of his own crew, which, as promised, included lawyers whom he had enticed into illegal activities. Most of the members of his gang were convicted, including the beauteous Bebe, with whom he had been living.

Raiton, however, did not, as he'd planned, walk away scott free. The deal he worked out with the United States Justice Department saw him accepting a 6½-year sentence with the guarantee he'd only have to serve a third of it, and at the prison of his choice. As part of the arrangement, Raiton promised to turn over to the IRS all the records of the corporations—some twenty of them—that he had set up to expedite his illegal activities. Any money the IRS accumulated by seizing the assets of these companies would go toward paying off the $5 million tax lien it had filed against him. (The IRS estimated his profits at between $10 and $20 million between 1978 and 1981.) In return for that cooperation, Raiton asked for, and received, only one small favor: When he'd served his two-year-and-two-month term, he was to be given a passport.

On completing his sentence in January 1984, Raiton, who once described drug dealing as "the last vestige of pure capitalism in America" (you don't need much start-up cash, don't have to keep records for the government or pay taxes), headed straight for Europe on the passport the government had provided him. There, Raiton visited Luxembourg, Lichtenstein and Gibraltar—the friendly bankers in those places apparently never ask a question no matter how much cash a customer has to deposit—where he happily called upon his various million-dollar Eurodollar certificates of deposit. (Raiton has always denied he made anything like $20 million, but he is hardly poor; by his own admission, his interest income alone is in excess of $21,000 a *month*.)

Meanwhile, the IRS was pursuing the corporate trail that Raiton had helpfully left behind him. When the revenuers reached the end of it, they discovered Raiton had left them zero dollars in assets to seize. Raiton's snookering of the IRS—to this date, it has yet to get a penny out of him—no doubt makes him something of a folk hero to millions of Americans. More pertinently perhaps, his career suggests how fortunate are Americans, civilians and cops alike, that most criminals are on Howard Dale Young's end of the intelligence scale and very few on Ronald Raiton's.

The arrest of Martorano that Raiton helped bring about had an ironic twist. A day or two before Long John was due to be taken into custody, a story appeared in the *Philadelphia*

Inquirer announcing that indictments were pending against him and two of his associates, Frank Vadino and John Berkery. Martorano and Vadino did not get away, but Berkery read the story and left immediately for Ireland, where he had associations with the Irish Republican Army, to which he allegedly had been selling guns.

The only place the *Inquirer* reporter could have gotten his story was from sources in the federal government, either in the U.S. Attorney's Office or the FBI. Apparently, it isn't just the Philadelphia police or the Philadelphia DA who can't keep secrets.

Berkery, who, like Raiton, would play a role in the eventual unraveling of the Meletis murders, was no minor hoodlum either. Intelligent and personable—he was like Raiton that way—his criminal career went back to the late 1950s, when he was a member of the fabled Lillian ("Tiger Lil") Reis gang.

Lil, who was in her twenties then and quite pretty, made national headlines when she and a merry band of mostly Irish rogues (Lil was Jewish) broke into a safe in the home of elderly John Rich, an anthracite coal baron who lived in Pottsville, Pennsylvania. The gang had a tip that Rich kept considerable amounts of cash—around $25,000—in his safe. To their amazement, the burglars found not $25,000 but nearer $2,500,000.

The Sicilian-born Rich, whose real name was Giovanni Riccione, played down the size of the theft to the police, putting it at $3,500. While he was making these protestations, Rich contacted the Philadelphia family. Soon after (my information comes from Raiton, who says Martorano told him the story) Lil Reis and John Berkery were paid a visit by Martorano, who was then about 30 years old. The money they had stolen, Martorano informed them, was to be returned to the Philadelphia mob, in which event no harm would come to them. Two members of the gang refused to go along. One was murdered when his car exploded; the other's body was fished out of the Atlantic Ocean laden with chains. Soon after, Tiger Lil, who apparently had acceded to Martorano's demands, opened a nightclub in downtown Philadelphia called the Celebrity Room. During its brief existence, it was well favored with trade from members of Philadelphia's LCN.

John Berkery's cooperation paid off well for him. Over the years that followed, he became a leg-breaker for the mob, a successful loan shark, and my chief suspect in the Frankie Stillitano murder. The charming Berkery may have been one of the few people the self-centered and suspicious Raymond Martorano actually liked, much as Angelo Bruno enjoyed the company of his Irish friend, John McCullough.

By 1980, Berkery was buying P2P from Raiton, both for himself and, as a front, for Martorano. As Raiton later recalled it: ''We would meet for dinner. We'd take care of our business first and then simply talk. Berkery, at the time, was taking courses in Irish poetry at the University of Pennsylvania and we'd discuss that and literature in general.''

By the early months of 1981, just before he became an informant, Raiton had developed another excellent customer for his P2P. His name was Steve Booras, the murder target at the Meletis.

That I paid virtually no attention to Booras's murder at the time of its occurrence, despite the fact that one of my suspects in the McCullough hit, Martorano, was at the table when Booras was killed, may seem odd, but not to anyone who was trained as a Philadelphia police officer. From the time we entered the force, we were taught to concentrate on our own cases, not anyone else's. Consequently, even if it had occurred to me, as it didn't then, that Martorano's presence in the Meletis Restaurant deserved more attention than it apparently had been given, I had no right to make my view known, regardless of the fact that I was a lieutenant and the detective in charge of the case, Rosenstein, was a sergeant.

If I had concrete evidence, I would be expected to pass on the information, but nothing more than that. Hand it over.

Bow out again. The result was that cases such as mob killings that were frequently related to one another were invariably investigated as entirely separate entities. Why this policy of noninterference was ever formulated, I have no idea. It had been in existence long before I joined the police, and I don't think anyone questioned it. I know I didn't, anymore than I questioned that we weren't supposed to help the FBI. It was just the way things were done—or not done.

In any event, with Ferber's arrest, the Meletis case was marked "solved," and I was as happy as everyone else about that. Busy as I was with wrapping up the McCullough investigation, it escaped my attention that the promised arrest of Ferber's alleged confederate, Barry Saltzburg, never took place.

7

Arrest of a Wiseguy

On September 8, 1981, I left my house around 5:30 a.m. and drove across the Benjamin Franklin Bridge into New Jersey. Since becoming a detective, I rarely carried a gun, but for this occasion I did. I was on my way to arrest Willard Moran, Jr., for the murder of John McCullough.

We had presented our case against Moran (we didn't have trialworthy evidence against anyone else, other than Howard Dale Young) to the Philadelphia grand jury. The formal indictment was about to be issued, and John Main would phone me through the New Jersey state police as soon as he got it.

The previous evening, cooperating New Jersey troopers had followed Moran to his home in Gloucester, a town along the Delaware River a few miles south of Camden. He lived in one of a series of small two-story apartments in a development. He was staked out there overnight.

When I arrived at 6 a.m., one of the New Jersey troopers advised me that Moran was still safely in place. I had the house surrounded, and deployed the remaining officers to keep watch nearby in unmarked cars. Our complement consisted of nineteen New Jersey troopers wearing armor, and six Philadelphia homicide detectives, including me.

Sitting in my car, sipping coffee, I watched the house. I felt edgy. The day, I knew, could go very wrong. Our surveillance reports placed Moran's wife Debbie and her 6-year-old son from a previous marriage in the house with him. Moran might hold them as hostages, I feared, in an effort to bargain his way to freedom. Alternatively, he might decide to shoot it out with us, and the woman and child might be injured in the battle, no matter how carefully our sharpshooters tried to avoid them. All it would take would be a sudden move and they'd be cut down.

The safety of innocent people outside the Moran house worried me, too. We had the area cordoned off, but that was no guarantee no one would be hurt. When people see a bunch of cops in bullet-proof vests carrying rifles enter their neighborhood, they're going to be frightened but also curious. As I waited for news of the indictment, I observed faces at neighbors' windows, doors cautiously opened, people peeking out. At the corner, behind the secured area, a handful of gapers had already arrived, and I knew from past experience that more would come as the day came alive and word spread about the excitement.

As more time passed the danger would mount. As a scene like ours continues with nothing apparently happening, fear among the spectators recedes and curiosity begins to dominate. I dreaded the possibility of someone—probably a kid on a dare—breaking the cordon and dashing into the street just as the shooting began.

And time was passing. I hadn't expected to hear from Main much before eight o'clock, but it went by, and so did nine, and ten, and eleven. We were giving Moran altogether too much time to make escape plans. I kept looking back to our command post, as if my gaze would make the message come across its radio. Every once in a while, a window blind moved in Moran's apartment, usually from the second floor, but nothing beyond that. I thought about the little boy. Was his mother saying to him, "No, dear, you can't go out to play"?

Shortly after eleven, the New Jersey State Police barracks in nearby Belmont radioed. John Main had called. We had the warrant.

I ordered the men to take their places, guns out, leveled. I motioned to four of the New Jersey officers, including the biggest one I saw, to join me. I marched up to the front of the house, the four officers on either side of me. I cupped my hands to my mouth. I called: "Willard Moran!" The blind moved. "Philadelphia Police Department. I have a warrant for your arrest." Another blind moved. "Open the door! You have thirty seconds!"

I took out my weapon. When the thirty seconds was over and the door hadn't opened, I nodded to the big trooper. As we crowded around him, he kicked the door off its hinges. In we rushed. Moran was coming down the stairs. He was dressed only in a bathrobe, unarmed. From the floor above him, I heard a woman screaming. Suddenly, standing right in front of me in the living room—I've no idea where he came from—was the little boy. His eyes were wide; his thumb had fled to his mouth. In the moment of hearing his mother's cry, his little body convulsed with shuddering; he began to cry. We had given him a lifetime memory.

Two of my men grabbed Moran, hustled him back up the stairs, ordered him to get dressed, watched as he did. (It was only much later that I learned why Moran was in his robe.

When he realized we were out there, rather than trying to escape, he told me, he had sex with Debbie. "I knew I was going to be in jail for a while," he explained, "and I decided to have one for the road.")

He was brought back down the stairs, his hands cuffed behind him. He was snapping his fingers. He was grinning. He was sneering. "You got the wrong guy. What's this all about?" he asked. "Come on. Come on. Why you after me? It's that fuckin' Dale, that's who it is, that fuckin' Dale, he ratted me out."

I put him in the back of a car. We drove him to the Belmont Barracks, where he was fingerprinted, photographed, read his rights. Howard Dale Young, I noted, was right about him; he was well built, with weight-lifter muscles; his complexion was ruddy, forehead high, hair dyed red. During the processing, he moved into the second stage of his role playing. He held himself stiffly erect as if on parade drill. While he did, he glanced about, assessing how his audience was responding to his performance.

I'd seen his act maybe hundreds of times before, had come to expect it. Wiseguys—their name for themselves—perform that way, a male ritualistic dance (I never have seen a woman do it). They'll do it for their admiring buddies on the corner, do it for their girlfriends, and when they are caught, they do it for the cops who have arrested them. Especially for the cops. As long as they are permitted to continue to do it, as long as they can remain the center of attention, they aren't alone with their fear.

I cut him off in mid-strut. With a nod I had him brought to a room I liked because of its small size. I wanted him now to feel hemmed in, just him and me together in its narrow confines. I closed the door behind us. I pointed to a chair behind a table. He sat. He looked up at me. His posture, I observed, wasn't quite so Marine-Corps as it had been thirty seconds before.

I wasted no time on preliminaries. With wiseguys you

don't, not until they've given up on their act. I was, however, polite as always. Good manners, I've discovered, can be as threatening as rudeness would not be for wiseguys. They are mentally equipped to handle rough verbal treatment—that's part of their own mechanism for dealing with life—so they are on familiar ground when they get it from the police. Cold courtesy (and mine at such moments is frigid) is, on the contrary, disorienting, and the person who employs it creates a forbidding distance psychologically. Formal English, which is foreign to the wiseguy's speech patterns, compounds the effect, and has an added benefit: When it is suddenly abandoned—and I try to do this no more than once during an interrogation—the vulgarity that replaces it has a dramatic impact it wouldn't have if such language had been used all along.

So, calmly and dispassionately, much as I had in my interview with Howard Dale Young, using some of the same phrases (favorites because I knew they worked), I informed Moran solemnly of the charges against him. I told him he had been under investigation since the night of McCullough's murder (that was scary for him, and also technically true; we just didn't know who he was then) and that we were now going to proceed to bring him to trial in Philadelphia and that we were going to convict him and—pause; here comes the vulgarity—"we are then going to fry your ass in the electric chair."

My tone now was positively lugubrious, as if telling him all this made me feel sad for his sake. I outlined some of the evidence we had on him. "I . . . I don't know . . . th-that f-fuckin' Dale," he mumbled. He had not before stammered.

Switching to a more ruminative mode, I went on to remark that it might take a few days to arrange his extradition to Philadelphia and that he ought to enjoy himself while in Belmont, which allowed me to segue into my white-boy-in-the-Philadelphia-prisons routine.

By now I was seated quite close to him, never letting my

attention waver from his face, so that even when he looked away—maybe especially when he looked away—he knew my gaze was there. At one point, somewhere in my prison lecture, he said, "I-I'm glad I was arrested. Now I get a chance . . . chance to t-tell my story 'cause I know you guys been there . . . followin' me."

"I'd be delighted to hear the truth from you, Willard," I replied.

I'm not sure if it was his use of the word "story" or mine of "truth," but whichever—he knew the truth of the story he could tell—at that moment he began to sweat. Forehead sweat. I'd rarely seen it come that suddenly. Beads of it. He didn't seem aware of it. "Nah, nah!" He pulled back. "I wanta lawyer," and under his breath the mantra he'd discovered to comfort himself: "That . . . that . . . that . . . fuckin', fuckin' Dale."

I arose. "If you have nothing to worry about, as you have indicated, Willard, you don't need a lawyer, but since you've asked for one, we'll stop talking. But keep in mind, if there's anything you want to say, I'll always be eager to listen to you, have you tell your side of the story."

He shook his head. He seemed incapable of even saying his mantra anymore.

As I left the little room, I was pleased. My perception was that this person one day would be ours. Whether it would be before trial or after, that I couldn't foretell, but I knew he knew that while it might be played out a while longer, his game was over.

PART II

The Scarfo-Riccobene Wars

8
Nicky Scarfo
Takes Over

Whatever good will the police engendered by the arrest of Ferber for the Meletis murders and Moran for McCullough's was quickly dissipated as a new rash of mob hits broke out. The Philadelphia police, we soon learned from the media, had only one discernible talent: carrying dead bodies out of parking lots in plastic bags.

All the new killings, we believed, had been ordered by the new don, Little Nicky Scarfo, either to eliminate potential rivals or to punish those who refused to pay him tribute, or both. The first to go was Johnny Calabrese, a gambler and drug dealer who was an old-time Angelo Bruno associate. He was shot in the back five times by two men on October 6, 1981, as he was leaving Cous' Little Italy, the restaurant in which Bruno had his last meal.

Next was a more important figure, Frank "Chickie" Narducci, Sr., on January 7, 1982. Capo in charge of gambling operations under Bruno, Narducci was, according to our street information, a conspirator with the still-vanished Pete Casella in the Phil Testa murder. I learned several years later that his killer was Phil Testa's son, Salvy, who reportedly told a friend, "Chickie was just coming out of his car. I yelled at him, so he'd look around and know it was me who was about to kill him."

The body of the next victim, drug dealer Peter Inzarella, was found in the trunk of his car.

A particularly horrible double murder followed less than a month later, on February 3. In one way, it was even more outrageous than the Meletis shootings. There, the innocent victim, Janette Curro, had apparently been killed accidentally. Not so this one.

The target was 60-year-old Vincent "Tippy" Panetta, who probably wasn't a made member but was a long-time LCN associate. He was discovered strangled in his apartment in Cheltenham, a Philadelphia suburb; slain in the same lingering fashion was his 19-year-old girlfriend Rochelle Podraza who, except for the fact that she knew Tippy, had no known crime connections. Because there was no sign of forced entry, Tippy must have allowed the killers (evidence suggested two of them) into his apartment; they were probably friends or business associates of his. Rochelle apparently had been murdered because she happened to be there and could have identified the killers.

Three weeks later, the body of the handsome, riverboat-style gambler Mickey Diamond was discovered in the trunk of his car at Ninth and Bainbridge streets in South Philadelphia, only a few blocks from the site of Philadelphia's first gangland rubout on Memorial Day, 1927.

And on March 15, 1982, a year to the day after Phil Testa's bombing death, my suspect in that murder, Rocco Marinucci, was murdered. The scheme against Rocco's life, according to information I was to receive four years later, had its inception in late 1981 or early 1982 when he was paid a visit by the chubby Salvy Testa.

In his visit to Rocco, Salvy was neither armed nor the least bit threatening. On the contrary, he was in a friendly and generous mood. He asked if Rocco would like to take on a numbers territory—one of those Salvy had inherited from his father—for which Salvy would pay him $500 a week. Rocco, fearful that Salvy was setting him up, declined. "I ain't interested in doin' numbers," he explained; his specialty, he said, was burglaries. Salvy didn't press the matter, wished Rocco well and left.

A few weeks later, around the time Salvy killed Chickie Narducci, Rocco had two more visitors he recognized as friends of Salvy's. The two men told Rocco they had located a great place to burgle and would like his help. Rocco went along with the scheme; the job was pulled off successfully and the $12,000 take was divided among Rocco and Salvy's two pals.

The happy Rocco paid off some debts, bought himself a couple of new suits. Ever since his mentor, Petey Casella, had departed the scene, the going had been a little tough for Rocco. But now things were looking up for him, and it was about time. The best news was that he had apparently been wrong to worry about Salvy; the dumb kid seemed to have no inkling that he'd murdered his father.

In that relieved frame of mind, Rocco readily agreed to participate in the next burglary Salvy's pals proposed. This, they said, was to be the big haul. When John Berkery fled to Ireland, they explained, he had left behind him a million dollars in drug profits, and they were going to get it. Staggered by the sum, Rocco told the pals he sure appreciated them letting him in on it.

Late on the night of March 14, the three men met. The plan, Rocco had been told, was to drive to a jewelry store in northeast Philadelphia, where Berkery allegedly had his fortune stashed. Within moments of getting into the car, the trusting Rocco found himself facing a gun pointed at his head. He was taken to a mob-owned private club, the Buckeye, in South Philadelphia. It was well past midnight when the trio arrived. Greeting them at the door was Salvy.

He and the pals proceeded to tie Rocco with ropes. They then beat him. Savagely. Repeatedly. When they finally tired of that sport, they sat him on a chair. He was conscious. They pried his mouth open. Into it, they stuffed nine cherry bombs, the kind used for Fourth of July fireworks. One lodged in his throat. Salvy bent over him with a lighted match, intending to blow Rocco up just as Rocco had blown up his father.

To Salvy's keen disappointment, the bombs wouldn't ignite, moistened as they were by Rocco's saliva. Eventually, Salvy had to satisfy himself by blowing off a part of Rocco's head with his gun.

News of the Marinucci hit spread with a gush of excitement throughout the South Philadelphia neighborhoods. Even old-time mobsters were impressed. The kid had shown style, had shown patience. Killing Narducci in the way Salvy had was mildly impressive, but waiting for the anniversary of his father's death and then waiting until almost the exact minute—that indicated a rising new star in the art of cold-blooded killing. From Atlantic City, the new don, Nicky Scarfo, the man who had been Salvy's father's best friend, was equally impressed. He named Salvy his capo in charge of murder. The new don was a good patron to have and, as Salvy would subsequently learn, a terrible enemy.

* * *

Nicodemo Scarfo was born in Brooklyn on March 8, 1929. During his early childhood his parents moved to Philadelphia, where they had relatives. Among them were Nicky's uncles, the Piccolo brothers. The eldest, Nicholas, was born in Calabria, Italy, in 1905; a year younger was Joseph, born in Philadelphia, with Michael, also a Philadelphian, coming along in 1911. All three brothers, according to law enforcement sources, were made-members of the Mafia and came to be considered major players in the Bruno family.

Just as some little boys dream of growing up to be baseball players or cowboys—or Indians—Nicky, from the time he was about seven or eight, had only one ambition: He wanted to become a gangster.

He served his apprenticeship at the corner of Hutchinson and Catherine streets in the heart of South Philadelphia's Little Italy, where the men of respect, including his uncles, would gather and dispatch likely youths such as Nicky on errands and eventually, if they showed promise, move them up to act as couriers for their numbers business.

Nicky might have been considered promising by the men on the corner, but among his peers he was detested. Tiny and cocky, he regularly invoked the names of his uncles in an attempt to impress and intimidate his classmates. They were neither impressed nor intimidated. Instead, they regularly beat Nicky to the ground, gleefully taunting him as a gangster's kid. (Many years later, Scarfo's own 16-year-old son, taunted because of his father's reputation, hanged himself; he was cut down by his horrified mother in time to save his life, but not before he suffered irreversible brain damage.)

We have only sketchy knowledge of Scarfo's criminal career during his young adult years. Prior to the age of 34, he had just two minor contacts with the law, but that's not surprising: during his youth, as for many years later, arrests of Mafia figures were extremely rare, largely due to the traditional fear law-abiding folks had of them. Scarfo's pugnaciousness resulted in his first arrest at age 19 on assault charges (which were dropped), apparently the aftermath of a street brawl. His second arrest, two years later, was on bookmaking charges; he was fined $75 and given a year's probation. Reason exists to believe he also added to his income from burglaries, perhaps from truck hijackings. He was, in any event, well placed in mob circles through his three redoubtable uncles, the Piccolo brothers.

At one point, when Scarfo was either in his late teens or early twenties, he was enamored of a young lady but lost her (assuming she was ever interested in him) to a taller, more handsome rival, Anthony DeVito, who later adopted the name of Mickey Diamond. When DeVito was murdered by Scarfo hitmen in 1982, his body was found outside the former home of the girl that Nicky thought Mickey had taken from him.

Scarfo made his first headline one day in 1963, when he strolled into the Oregon Diner in South Philadelphia and demanded that a beefy man seated on a stool give up his seat to him. When the man refused, Scarfo snarled, "You know who I am?" The man, Joseph Dugan, gave Scarfo a scornful look, saying, "And do you know who I am? I'm a longshoreman," and proceeded, as so many had before him, to punch Nicky in the jaw and knock him to the floor. Regaining his feet, Scarfo drew out a knife, leaped forward, and plunged it into Dugan, killing him.

Scarfo was arrested, and found himself before a remarkably understanding judge, who sentenced him to just 3 years for the homicide. Although Scarfo was already a made-member of the Mafia by then, which meant he had at least one previous murder in his background, the current one did not please the Gentle Don, Angelo Bruno. In a kid maybe it could be forgiven, but this was a hotheaded, purposeless act of violence by a 34-year-old man. Such a person, Bruno realized, might be likely to do something equally stupid in the future and thereby call unwanted attention to the activities of Bruno and his stealthy cohorts.

Scarfo, therefore, had to be gotten rid of. But not through murder. Bruno had nothing against murder, but killing Scarfo would incur the wrath of the three uncles. The solution to his problem he hit upon was vintage Bruno: He'd get rid of Nicky by promoting him. That would allow the Piccolos, as well as Nicky, to save face, and at the same time everybody in the family would know what had happened and why—a show of leadership through statecraft by Bruno. So off Nicky went, banished from Philadelphia but also named the capo in charge of the farthest flung and least profitable outpost of Bruno's empire, Atlantic City.

By the late 1960s, when Scarfo arrived in Atlantic City, the elegant old hotels like the Marlborough-Blenheim and Chalfonte-Haddon Hall were just beginning their long descent into seedy decay. The boardwalk throngs were diminishing; the amusement palaces like Steel Pier, which had once brought to town the biggest names in show business, seemed to be in a race to see which would happen first, bankruptcy or the crumbling of their splintering wooden piers into the ocean. The bars were emptying, the downtown was deserted, and the hookers had nobody left to hook.

According to police intelligence reports from the late 1960s to the mid-1970s, Scarfo, nevertheless, did the best with what he had. He put together a skeleton crew that worked hard to squeeze extortion money out of saloon keepers; he got involved in gambling, narcotics and, if Ronald Raiton is to be believed, burglaries. (Raiton, who was then operating a credit card swindle in Atlantic City, says he principally knew Scarfo circa 1970 as a second-story man.)

In 1973, the New Jersey Crime Commission was investigating the Mafia, and one of the witnesses it called was Scarfo. When he refused to testify, he was cited for contempt and jailed at the Yardville Prison in the central part of the state, where Bruno was already incarcerated for the same reason.

Playing the role of acolyte, Scarfo sought out his don. Although Bruno detested him, he could hardly snub him; after all, Scarfo's uncles were still Bruno's allies. Among the inmates at Yardville, present because they also refused to testify, were a number of New York mobsters, including the highly placed Jerry Catena. Bruno, with the nondescript Scarfo hanging around him, had no choice but to introduce Nicky to the New Yorkers as "a friend of ours," the code phrase to indicate a made-member. These meetings were to prove helpful to Scarfo a few years later.

Scarfo's banishment to Atlantic City had, with the passage of the casino act in 1977, turned out to be for him a stroke of the greatest good fortune. He might only be a capo, but he was at the center of the new action, with a gang in place, all ready to go. Probably closest to Scarfo at that time was a supposedly retired Teamsters Union boss, Frank Lentino. He acted as a "consultant" to the Bartenders Union, where Scarfo soon also had on board Al Daidone and another mob associate, Frank Gerace. Then there were the Merlino brothers, the elder of whom, Salvatore ("Chuckie") had been with Scarfo the day in 1963 when Scarfo knifed the longshoreman Dugan to death. A somewhat more recent adviser was Saul Kane, a shakedown artist who was about to move onto bigger things. The inner circle was rounded out by Scarfo's good-looking but erratic and lethal nephew, Philip "Crazy Phil" Leonetti.

In 1978, in recognition of Scarfo's new importance, Phil Testa urged Don Bruno to appoint Little Nicky to the vacant post of consigliere. Bruno refused. Not only did he continue to have the same low opinion of Scarfo as before, but he also saw no need to promote him. Bruno's own friends, the Gambinos, were already moving in on the casino business full-bore and had made it clear they considered Bruno, not the likes of Scarfo, as the one person they were counting on for help to keep the Genoveses at bay in the new gambling mecca.*

In the face of the Gambino support of Bruno, Scarfo could do all the strutting about he wanted as the self-styled boss of the casinos, but he'd be easy for Bruno—and the Gambinos—to slap down if he got out of line.

When his mentor (and successor to Bruno as don) Phil Testa was killed in March of 1981, Scarfo (who had nothing to do with that assassination) believed himself positioned to become the new boss. As part of his preparations, he had honed his skills in murder. During the late 1970s, he had been responsible for four deaths, but present only at one.

Three of these early murders by Scarfo took place in or near Atlantic City, and were heavily played in the media as connected with the newly minted casino business. Much shaking of heads and many I-told-you-so's were voiced by those who had opposed the gambling legislation for fear it would cause what it apparently now had, a rash of mob homicides. In fact, none of these early Scarfo murders had anything to do with the casinos.

They began on February 17, 1978, when a masked gunman entered the Flamingo Restaurant near Atlantic City, proceeded to the table where former Judge Edwin Helfant was dining, and shot him dead. The gunman ran from the restaurant, got into a getaway car, and he and its driver sped off. That crime remained unsolved for ten years. We know now that the killer was "Nick the Blade" Virgilio, and the getaway driver was his boss, Nicky Scarfo, who had given his permission for the murder. Virgilio had paid good money to Helfant to get a lenient sentence on a crime for which he'd

---

*Just so there'd be no doubt about Bruno's premier position, Big Pauly Castellano, Carlo Gambino's successor (and himself murdered a few years later, allegedly by John Gotti) sent Carlo's nephews, Giuseppe and Manny, to pay homage to the Gentle Don at a 1978 mob conclave at Valentino's Restaurant in Cherry Hill, New Jersey.

been convicted, but Helfant hadn't come through. This was sufficient reason in Scarfo's mind—and in Virgilio's—to murder him.

The next murder, also authorized by Scarfo, was that of small-time crook Pepe Leva, who had failed to pay back loanshark money to Phil Leonetti, Scarfo's nephew. Leonetti was arrested on the basis of a statement given by a truck driver who had witnessed the killing. When the case came to trial, the truck driver lost his memory, and the 26-year-old Leonetti walked.

The victim of Scarfo's third murder, which took place in a South Philadelphia restaurant late in 1979, was Michael "Coco" Cifelli, a drug dealer. The killers were Chuckie Merlino, Scarfo's Atlantic City pal, and Salvy Testa. Merlino subsequently told one of our informants: "Salvy [whose first murder it was] was shooting like a crazy man. I thought he was trying to kill me." Scarfo remarked to the same informant, "That was another one I had to set up."

The next murder—the one Scarfo was on hand to watch —took place on December 16, 1979, a year to the day before McCullough was assassinated. The victim this time was a long-time Scarfo crime associate, Vincent Falcone. The relationship between Scarfo and Falcone had recently soured. Falcone had allegedly described Scarfo as "crazy," and his insult apparently got back to Scarfo. On the evening of the murder, a Christmas celebration was scheduled, and three of Falcone's friends stopped by to pick him up, presumably to take him with them to the party. One friend was Leonetti, another Chuckie Merlino's younger brother Larry, who was in his mid-thirties; the third man, who rented an apartment in the building in which Scarfo lived, was Joseph Salerno, Jr. (He was no relation to Alfred Salerno, who had been tortured to death, along with his brother-in-law Antonio Caponigro, following Bruno's death.) This Salerno, rather, was known to New Jersey police as an inconsequential mob hanger-on who gloried in his association with Little Nicky. As he later said, "If you went somewhere with him, the people would just cater to him, look up to him. It was a good feeling to me." Salerno, however, had begun to perceive Scarfo as emotionally volatile—"people were scared to death of him"—and dreaded that he himself might inadvertently say something (or be accused of saying something) that would turn Scarfo against him, as had just happened with Falcone.

Rather than going to the party, the three men drove Falcone to an apartment in Margate, just outside Atlantic City. Scarfo was waiting there for them. Many years later, Salerno, by then in the Federal Witness Protection Program, testified: "Philip [Leonetti] pulled a gun out of his jacket and reached over and shot Vincent Falcone in the head. That's what he did. He [Philip] turned and looked at me immediately"— Salerno hadn't known the murder was to take place—"and said, 'Joe, this guy was a no-good mother-fucker.'"

Scarfo, Salerno said, began supervising the removal of the body. "Here's what I want you to do," he said, "tie him up like a cowboy. . . . Tie this blanket around him." At that point, Scarfo broke off and, leaning down over the body, staring at the mangled head of the victim, he said to no one in particular, "I love this. I love it." No words Scarfo ever uttered, I think, could have better expressed his character.

The bombing death of Phil Testa fifteen months later had left the Philadelphia/Atlantic City mob in disarray. Two bosses had been killed within a year, and Testa's underboss, Petey Casella, who presumably was next in line, had disappeared. The members of the mob were confused, suspicious of one another, uncertain of whom to talk to, whom to follow.

Scarfo, who had been Testa's consigliere, moved swiftly to fill the vacuum. Within a week of Testa's death, he put out the word he was going to New York. Everyone knew what that meant. He was seeking the Commission's blessing, which probably meant he was certain of getting it. At the least, it could be dangerous to assume otherwise. Just as had been true twenty-two years earlier when Bruno paid his call on Gambino, whoever New York said was boss *was* boss, and the locals knew that.

In going before the Commission, Scarfo had good cards to play. Thanks to his introduction to Commission members by Bruno eight years before when they were in prison together in Yardville, Scarfo was a known quantity to them, a "friend of ours," vouched for by none other than the Gentle Don himself, the legendary Carlo Gambino's great good friend.

That Scarfo was situated in Atlantic City was significant, too, not only to the Gambinos and Genoveses but to the three lesser New York families as well—the Luccheses, Bonnanos, and Columbos—all of whom had their own expansionist plans afoot there. It would be better all around that Scarfo, with an organization in place and valuable knowledge of which government and union officials were corrupt, was a help rather than a hindrance. Aware of that, Scarfo made promises. He'd be willing to work with everybody, he declared. And that seems to be one promise he actually kept. Four years later, in 1986, he flew to New York on a Resorts International helicopter to meet with the incumbent boss of bosses, John Gotti of the Gambino family. According to our surveillance of their meetings, Scarfo apparently was trusted by Gotti, which meant he'd upheld his end of the bargain. (And according to law enforcement sources, committed a couple of murders at Gotti's request while he was at it. On November 10, 1983, the body of a hoodlum named Salvatore Sollena was found in New Jersey stuffed into the trunk of his car, and nine days later Salvatore's brother, Matte, was discovered dead in the trunk of *his* car. My sources believe the murders were carried out on Scarfo's orders at the behest of the Gambino mob, which the Sollena brothers had crossed in some manner. No one to date has been charged for these murders.)

Scarfo's accession in April of 1981 as don had some of the qualities of a revolution. The line of succession, which had been upheld when Testa replaced Bruno as don, had now been disrupted, much to the dismay of the old guard in Philadelphia, many of whom felt, as the late Angelo Bruno had, that Scarfo was wild-eyed, untrustworthy, and unnecessarily violent. (The second round of murders that began in the fall of 1981 were principally of those who refused to pay cash tribute to Scarfo as they had obediently to Bruno and Testa.) Even the capital of the empire had been removed. It was now no longer, in effect, the Philadelphia mob but the Atlantic City mob, another bitter pill for the Philadelphians to swallow.

The new leadership also meant there might be room for new blood. Perhaps, unlike in the Bruno days, a gangster would no longer have to wait in line for some Moustachio Pete to die or be murdered before he could move ahead. Philadelphians like Salvy Testa and a hitherto small-time gambler named Thomas DelGiorno were quick to recognize that possibility. They were among the many who came to Atlantic City to pay homage to "the Little Guy," as Scarfo began to be called. Another Philadelphian who easily slithered his way into power was the indefatigable Raymond Martorano; courtier to Bruno and to Testa, he was soon playing the same role with Scarfo. But the Philadelphians who found power under Scarfo were the exceptions. It was now the Atlantic City gangsters, long considered outcasts, who were in charge. Their triumph was officially marked when Scarfo named the heavy-drinking Chuckie Merlino as underboss.

Conspicuous by his failure to make any trip to pay obeisance to Scarfo was one major player in the Philadelphia mob, the ancient and ferocious Harry "The Hunchback" Riccobene. His absence led Scarfo to believe that Riccobene, who had a gang of his own, was planning to oppose him. The stage was thus set for the next outbreak of mob murders, which began in the spring of 1982.

By then, the tally of known Philadelphia/Atlantic City organized crime murders—not counting the Meletis killings, which were still believed not to be mob-related—had reached nineteen: Bruno, Caponigro, Salerno, Simone, Sindone, Stillitano, McCullough, Falcone, Testa, Narducci, Marinucci, Cifelli, Calabrese, Inzarella, Helfant, Leva, Panetta, Podraza and Diamond. In the face of all that mayhem, law enforcement, federal and local, had produced no convictions and only one promising arrest, my squad's of Willard Moran for the McCullough homicide.

The Testa case would be next to be cleared by arrest, but only after a revolutionary change in law enforcement took place, brought about by a Philadelphia cop of Italian ancestry named Scafidi.

9
The Organized Crime Task Force

In late March of 1982, John Hogan, the special agent in charge (SAC) of the Philadelphia FBI office, and Dennis O'Callaghan, the supervisor of its Organized Crime Squad, paid a visit to Philadelphia Police Commissioner Morton Solomon. The FBI, Hogan admitted to Solomon, was making no headway on its own in bringing the gang murders to an end. Would the Philadelphia police be interested in cooperating? he asked. The solemn-faced Solomon didn't commit himself. Instead, he turned the FBI men over to his Chief of Detectives Frank Scafidi.

Tough-minded and analytical, Scafidi had been a detective most of his professional life, which dated back to the early 1950s. He had long recognized (as I came to understand during the McCullough investigation) that the turf battles between our departments and the secrets we kept from each other had only one predictable outcome: We helped organized crime.

Scafidi, therefore, was pleased by Hogan's approach. But he was not pleased by his terms. Hogan made clear that his idea of cooperation was that the two sides would exchange verbal updates on investigations. He also hoped, he said, that Scafidi would allow his agents access to police files; he didn't offer to make his own available. Scafidi replied, "The hell with that. Why don't we actually work with each other for a change?"

What Scafidi had in mind was not informal cooperation. He suggested, instead, a permanent joint task force focused on solving the gang murders. The surprised Hogan declared that Scafidi's idea was "beyond all our expectations." It may have been beyond all their desires, too, but since they had come to us to get help—not to offer it—they were not in a good position to refuse.

Soon after, Scafidi went to Captain Jerry Kane to recommend someone to head up our participation. With my success in the McCullough case in mind, Kane suggested me.

As the negotiations were being completed to establish the Task Force, Neil Ferber was going on trial for the murders of the Greek Mob boss Steve Booras and the woman, Janette Curro. No arrest had yet been made of the other gunman or of the getaway driver. Barry Saltzburg, originally believed to be the one who fired the fatal bullets, had been eliminated as a suspect, and attention was now focused on another associate of Ferber's, Anthony "Mad Dog" DiPasquale, who years earlier used to punch out Scarfo when they were hoodlums together on the streets of South Philadelphia.

During the course of his trial, Ferber was offered a chance to plead guilty to third-degree murder if he would name his accomplices, presumably thereby giving up DiPasquale. Ferber, who had pleaded not guilty, turned down the deal. The jury convicted him of both homicides and made the binding recommendation he be electrocuted. The feeling in the Homicide Bureau was one of elation. Ferber was perceived as a weakling, under DiPasquale's domination, and it was assumed he'd soon talk to save his life.

By now I was reduced to hoping that's what would also happen with Willard Moran. I knew from experience that the day I questioned him, he had been close to talking. But I never had a chance to follow up; he was now guarded from us by his lawyer, and had resumed his tough-guy demeanor.

If Moran was eventually going to confess, it was still a long way off. The usual delays had set in. By the spring of 1982, when I was offered the codirector post of the new Organized Crime Task Force, six months had passed since Moran's indictment and his trial wasn't even scheduled yet.

I was reluctant to leave the SIU. I had found working the back-shelf murders to be not only challenging but ego-gratifying, too, when—often years after the crime was committed—we were able to bring a killer to justice. (One man we got had murdered twelve people.) But the satisfaction went beyond a personal sense of accomplishment. Typically the victims were innocent people. The fact that their murders had remained unsolved often had had a devastating emotional impact on their survivors, who couldn't let go of the death; they were haunted by the incompleteness. Only when we found the killer were they finally able to deal with their grief. I felt good on such occasions; I knew I had given something valuable to people who desperately needed it, and I didn't think that going after gangsters who killed other gangsters had the same importance.

While my reaction was sincere, I was also aware, somewhere in the back of my mind, that my unwillingness to accept the Task Force post had a familiar psychological ring to it. I didn't want this new job just as I had not wanted to shift from patrol lieutenant to detective lieutenant in felony cases, hadn't wanted to shift from felony to homicide, hadn't wanted to shift from homicide to SIU, each time because I was happy and felt fulfilled by what I was doing. Yet each time I had shifted and then found the new job even more satisfying than the previous one. Wasn't there a good chance that would happen this time, too?

Maybe. But I also had other reasons for being leery of the Task Force. I knew Frank Scafidi and had absolutely no doubt that he meant every word he said, but I had also noticed that his idea just happened to get approved precisely at the time that media questions concerning the competence of law enforcement, both local and federal, had reached a new height of intensity, and rightly so—we were awash in gang murders, and with no expectation that the next day wouldn't bring more. Under those circumstances, the Task Force had the worst kind of smell to me, that of a public relations gimmick. Its formation had already been announced with maximum hoopla. I feared that the principal (maybe sole) purpose was to get reporters off our backs for a while.

My second reservation was a deeper one, born out of pessimism. Even if formation of the Task Force was seriously intended, even if its efforts weren't doomed to failure from the outset because of the antagonisms with which FBI and police viewed one another, I thought the prospects for success were poor. Law enforcement agencies had been battling La Cosa Nostra since the days of Prohibition and had only produced a sixty-year history of failure.

Not that the good guys hadn't chalked up some wins. Al Capone had eventually gone to prison on income tax evasion charges (although not for murder). Other bosses, here and there, had been sent to prison on long sentences, as was true of Vito Genovese (who, however, would never have been arrested had it not been in Carlo Gambino's interest to finger him). Yet even in jail, Genovese had been able to continue to run his gang, and it wasn't the first or last time that happened, either. True, we occasionally arrested a hired assassin, as we had in the McCullough case. True, too, the FBI had, in recent years, run a number of successful sting operations that netted low- and middle-level LCN members and associates. And every once in a while an informant like Ronald Raiton came along who helped bring about other arrests.

But law enforcement had stopped nothing. The mob seemed, at times, to flourish on such successes as we had. The leaders who replaced Genovese were more clever and more deadly than he was. In the most evil and fatal of LCN's activities, narcotics trafficking, thousands of arrests had been made, millions upon millions of dollars in drugs confiscated, none of which busywork had even a moment's dampening effect on the mob. We had won battles; they, so far, were winning the war.

Investigating organized crime cases was enormously frustrating, too, as I'd learned in my efforts in the Phil Testa murder. I knew, as Salvy Testa had, without the slightest doubt, that Rocco Marinucci had triggered the bomb, but it was Salvy, not us, who had arrested the guilty person, convicted him, sentenced him to death and carried out the execution. Similarly, I had no doubt that Pete Casella had ordered Marinucci to make the hit, and I knew the motive: Casella's intention to succeed Testa as boss. And for all that I knew, I didn't have enough evidence to arrest Casella either (assuming he could ever be found, another frustration), much less bring him to trial.

In my SIU investigations, each crime represented a discrete entity. Catch the killer and we bring a case to an end. But catch Marinucci and we bring only one killer to an end; the Marinuccis of the organized crime world seemed to be infinitely replaceable. Bring down one and up springs another. In this instance, Salvatore Testa, the killer of Marinucci, became the Marinucci replacement.

Ready access to men willing to commit murder is one reason for the success of the Mafia. Salvy had murdered both Narducci and Marinucci (with Scarfo's authorization) as a matter of revenge, and killings of that vendetta variety are not rare. However, the large majority of hitmen employed by the Mafia have no animus toward the victim; on the contrary, the victim very frequently is a friend. Neither do they, ordinarily, murder for cash. They do it, rather, for the sake of their futures. Not only do they know that they might not have any future should they refuse to perform a killing, but also that by carrying it out, long-range economic benefits can come their way. When they are eligible, in terms of bloodline, to become mafiosos, their first killing gives them entree to the Secret Society and puts them well on the way to becoming millionaires. But even if not eligible (as Willard Moran wasn't), by carrying out a hit they prove their reliability and gain the kind of favor that can be translated into a better drug territory, a prime gambling book, and participation in big-dollar extortion schemes rather than the petty shakedowns they may have been accustomed to carrying out. Tommy DelGiorno, for instance, did not come from one of the wealthy crime families. His parents were solid, American backbone, working-class. When he committed his first murder (of a close friend, on Scarfo's order), he was on the way to becoming wealthy beyond his wildest dreams. Within the Mafia, the economic incentive for murder is a powerful one; hence, the supply of killers.

Membership in the Mafia also provides psychological rewards. The ritual mumbo-jumbo, the long history of the Society of the Men of Honor, inculcates the recruit with a sense of being part of an in-group. Even the associates who are excluded because of lack of proper bloodlines can bask in their insider knowledge of the world of La Cosa Nostra. The feeling of belonging is not unlike that which makes benign secret organizations, such as the Masons, attractive to some. It is all part of the psychic reward of entrance to any inner circle, the achievement of the key to the executive washroom, the acceptance by high society of an upward striver from the nouveau riche. Because in-groups are perceived as such desirable places to be, the possibility of exile from them can take on tragic dimensions. The Mafia differs from other inner circles of privilege only in that exile from it can literally mean death.

Like many business and social organizations, the Mafia also provides "sick" benefits: If the member is "sick" in the sense of being in prison, a portion of the profits from the member's criminal enterprises go to support his family until he "recovers."

Regardless of the gains, financial and emotional, that the Mafia offers its members, the continued adherence to the rule of silence (omertà) has been the secret of its success. Because of it, the ranks of the Mafia, unlike those of other gangs, had, by the 1980s, never been decimated by the principal players informing on one another. While an LCN member or associate was always aware he might be killed or robbed by another member or associate, he believed (and usually was right in believing, the Gambino example to the contrary) that not even his enemies would go to the law on him. For someone whose business is crime, that is a great source of confidence to have.

The rule of omertà might not have prevented the destruction of the Mafia if it had only internal applications. From the early days in Sicily onward, however, the Mafia has been largely able to extend omertà outside itself.

From my experience as a patrol officer and a detective, I knew that witnesses to crimes often are fearful—sometimes justifiably so—of the consequences to them if they cooperate with the police. Nevertheless, in the overwhelming majority of instances, the public does cooperate. It wants the criminal caught. The eyewitness will identify the culprit. Others who didn't see the crime committed add bits of information that contribute to making an arrest.

With Mafia crimes, traditionally, that hardly ever happened. Those who lived in Mafia neighborhoods perceived it as a government unto itself, with its own rules, its own police mechanism. That it had always succeeded in enforcing its rules strongly suggested to outsiders that it always would (unlike other gangs, which might be violent and dangerous but which the citizenry perceived as *possible* to eradicate). The Mafia usually did not need to extend the rule of its government beyond its immediate neighborhood either, since almost all of its crimes of violence occur there. With only a handful of exceptions, the murders of the Scarfo era took place in South Philadelphia. As Tommy DelGiorno once explained it, "Down there, if people see us, they wouldn't say nothing because they would know we was with the mob." When DelGiorno led a squad of killers in the murder of his associate John Calabrese as Calabrese was emerging from Cous' Little Italy Restaurant, the murderers didn't even bother to hide their faces despite the presence of pedestrians on the scene.

Just as success begets success, so failure begets failure. Because police didn't expect to solve gang murders—because they knew they would not get cooperation as they did for other crimes—they had a tendency to just go through the motions on them. They'd prepare the requisite binder reports outlining all the supposed diligent activity they'd expended on them, and then—then the binder went on the shelf, and the police went on to crimes they thought they had a reasonable chance of solving.

Thus it was that when Jerry Kane, who was always getting me to do things I didn't want to do, told me he had recommended me as the right person to help head up the Organized Crime Task Force, I responded in terms of that defeatist psychology. I said I thought I was more valuable to the public where I was. If an unsolved murder I was investigating involved organized crime, fine, I'd work it as I had McCullough and Testa, but since there were only so many resources and so much talent, I said, we should put it where it would do the most good. I was, I thought, quite convincing.

Jerry didn't make light of my objections—I think he shared them—but he had an assignment and I was it, so he came up with a compromise. Six weeks, he said. If at the end of that time I was convinced it wouldn't fly, then I could go back to heading the SIU. When he agreed to let me bring my best SIU detectives with me, I had no more excuses.

My men were no more enthusiastic than I, but orders were orders. Within a week they had packed up and we had left the Roundhouse and were off to our new quarters on the FBI's turf—which none of us liked either—in the Federal Building a few blocks away.

Accompanying me were John Main and Jimmy Jackson as well as three other detectives, to make up the team of five that had been agreed upon. One of them, Chester Koscinski, was even bigger than Main. About my age, with prematurely white hair, Chester was one of the most physically intimidating men I've ever seen. However, he was also gentle by nature, thoughtful, and extraordinarily good at talking to people, a useful quality in any cop, vital in a detective. In some ways the opposite of Chester was Frank Diegel; in his midforties, he was tall and slender, hyperactive where Chester was calm. Frank could be opinionated, sometimes too quick to make up his mind about a case—facts had a way of crumpling before his theories—but the flip side of that was his outstanding analytic abilities. He had another virtue, too, a realization of the importance of the scut work. Rounding out the group was Frank Suminski, who was my age, a big earthy man who, like Koscinski, was good with people, and who had a sharp, incisive mind. Always good humored, he was our jokester and relaxer.

After we had settled into our new space, which we shared with FBI agents and which was a great deal less spartan than the one we'd departed (federal tax dollars provide comfort;

city tax dollars provide misery), we met in a conference room with our new counterparts. Dennis O'Callaghan, my opposite number, was a tall and well-built man in his late thirties. He had been an agent for about ten years—had helped put together the Abscam prosecutions. The fact that he was Irish was a good omen. None of my men were, but the Philadelphia Police Department, like those in most other big cities, has a strong Irish influence, so that O'Callaghan's ethnicity made him acceptable in a way that the more typical Waspy agent might not have been. He had an even better credential: His family was New York City police, and as time went on, his stories about Uncle Bob the Cop were ones my team (if not necessarily his) could relate to.

O'Callaghan brought along to the table—in addition to SAC John Hogan and a couple of other local FBI brass—the five agents he'd selected from his squad. Rather like preadolescent boys and girls at their first dancing lesson, cops and agents kept their distance, eyeing one another warily.

Unlike my team, which remained intact for most of the next four years, there was considerable turnover among the agents, in accordance with the FBI's frequent-transfer policy. The five who were present in the conference room made up a cross-section of the agents I would be working with. One was Gary Scalf, who had shown up at the hospital on the night of Testa's death. We called him "The Bear": big, blond, round-faced, built like a University of Southern California linebacker; he was strong on research. Another, Andy Sloan, shorter and slighter than Scalf, a physical fitness fiend, I came to admire for his subtle mind and his ability to develop information. Jimmy Maher, built along Scalf's lines, was the take-charge guy of the five, very bright, very effective. Charley Kluge, a native Philadelphian, we used principally for surveillance. The fifth man, Eddie McLaughlin, short and curly-haired, was a former Philadelphia highway patrolman, with good street smarts—the one who was easiest for my men to relate to—and with an easy, relaxed manner in dealing with people. Coming on board soon after was Bud Warner, a big and seemingly perpetually angry man, tough, confrontational. Some of the others had difficulty getting along with him, but I grew to like him and seemed to have a calming effect on him; we often worked together.

As the meeting progressed, I listened as Hogan and O'Callaghan explained the FBI approach to organized crime cases. Until then, I had not realized how profoundly different their attitude toward law enforcement was from ours. Instead of upsetting me, my recognition of the distinction gave me my first flicker of excitement about the project. If a way could be found to make their way and ours mesh, I thought that a fruitful cooperative structure just might be possible.

I had the typical police philosophy in that I was case-oriented. For that reason, when I investigated McCullough's connections to organized crime, I wasn't interested in learning about La Cosa Nostra as an entity, but only in absorbing enough knowledge to help me find a motive and solve the crime.

The FBI, in contrast, is information-gathering-oriented. It compiles data for its own sake, often long before there is any need for it. In LCN terms, that means agents approached individuals—frequently small-timers swimming around the edge of the organized crime moat—and let them know that if they ever had any intelligence to report, they would be paid for it. We had our junior version in our Organized Crime Intelligence Squad, which took photographs and compiled surveillance reports. It had not been chosen for the Task Force because its members had no experience working homicides. Its activities, in any event, were necessarily limited to the city, whereas the FBI ranged with no boundaries, so that it had a detailed knowledge of mob goals and interrelationships among LCN families that we could not begin to approach.

The FBI also had money. That gave it the ability to conduct long-term and expensive surveillance, wiretaps and infiltrations, and to hand out money for information on a scale we couldn't imagine. At one point during the history of the Task Force, the FBI paid $25,000 for information on the hiding place of two murderers from another jurisdiction who had escaped prison. Our Detective Bureau budget for informants was $500—that's not $500 for a single piece of information, but $500 for all informants for a year. As a result, cops were constantly taking money out of their own pockets but, necessarily, in relatively minuscule amounts. Not that, theoretically, we wouldn't get repaid. I could have put in vouchers for the drinks and meals for my various informants, but the five-to-ten-year wait to get reimbursed didn't seem to make it worthwhile. Another kind of out-of-pocket cost was also commonplace: In one case, I recall, I needed $100 to put someone up safely for a single night; I had about $40 on me and got the other $60 by passing the hat around the office. In a later Task Force case, I needed $5,000 to store a witness out of town for several weeks; for the Police Department to get that kind of money, I would have needed an appropriation from City Council; the FBI had the $5,000 in my hands in an hour.

Garnering information for its own sake, however, can have its drawbacks. To begin with, it can mean a pride in quantity and not quality. Probably no law enforcement agency in the world has more worthless junk in its files than the FBI. And it can also lead to inaction—the compulsion to find more and more information can delay arrests when they should be made. As one example, the FBI had a veritable cornucopia of knowledge about McCullough's labor union activities (it put our sparse hoard to shame). Yet we in our straightforward detective work broke the McCullough murder, not the FBI.

Their method, therefore, put into their pipeline all kinds of information we didn't have, but our own plugging, on-the-cheap system turned up facts they didn't have. With that realization in mind, I finally spoke up. I said it struck me that the way to begin was to exchange our complete files on each of the gang murders, see if any of our pieces fit their holes and vice versa. To an outsider, that might seem such an obvious proposal that it went without saying. But it was something that had never been done before. Anywhere. Parts of files, yes, oral exchanges, yes, even occasional by-the-case cooperative investigations, but complete files, no. Why give the other side something that will let them make a collar first?

Based on that history of secrecy, when Scafidi suggested working together on a task force and Hogan agreed, it was far from clear that the degree of cooperation I suggested was wanted, on either side, or would be forthcoming. Dennis O'Callaghan considered my request. It would be done, he said.

My next suggestion was based on what I believed to be true, but also had as its purpose to show we were not going to stand on any false pride. Recognizing the FBI had made the first overture, I wanted to equalize the situation by showing our need for its help. The FBI laboratories, I said, are superior to ours; perhaps if we supply them with every piece of physical evidence we were holding—the plastic bags and carpets in which we'd found bodies wrapped, the rope used to tie them, and so on—its technicians might find something we missed. That idea, as I expected, was well received. It too would be done, and it was. (Unfortunately, no new leads were turned up.) The atmosphere was now less wary than it had been when the meeting began.

The next day, Dennis O'Callaghan and I met to discuss the animosity problem. We were equally aware that back-biting, competitiveness, bickering and (regardless of promises) withholding of information was certain to plague and probably doom the Task Force unless firm steps were taken right from the start.

We agreed that the only approach likely to succeed was to force cooperation. At no time would two cops work together, at no time two FBI agents. Instead, we would have five teams, each consisting of an agent and a detective. We knew nobody was going to like that—cops prefer working with cops, agents with agents—but (one of the benefits of a paramilitary structure) nobody was going to disobey our orders, either. They would have to try to make it work.

Despite some problems at the outset, the plan succeeded better than either of us could have hoped. By sharing cases, the men had no choice but to share information, which was as we had foreseen. The serendipity was that they got to like each other. The detectives began to realize that the agents, on a one-to-one basis, weren't as arrogant as portrayed by cop folklore, and the agents reached the conclusion that cops were not the corrupt Neanderthals that FBI folklore had taught them. Soon enough, all the guys were getting together after hours to trade war stories over a couple of beers. Between Dennis and me, the same relationship grew. We too started out wary of one another, developed respect, then friendship.

We also proved compatible in the division of duties. Dennis enjoyed administrative work and was good at it. That freed me to do what I liked best and was best at—street investigations. By that, I don't mean just hunting for clues or pumping informants, though that's a big part of it. Whenever possible, I also liked to meet suspects—long before I was ready to make an arrest—not in any interrogation room where the suspect is least likely to act naturally, but on his home turf where he feels most comfortable. That's how to get the measure of a person, and I'd found, time and again, it paid off when the time for formal questioning came.

And that's what I now intended to do with the Philadelphia mafiosos. But I knew research was in order, too. From the McCullough investigation, I'd picked up some facts about the structure of the local family, but I now needed more precise and historical information. For that purpose, I had the FBI's voluminous files available, which went back to the earliest days of the mob, when Salvatore Sabella became its first boss prior to World War I. Therefore, during the early weeks, when the day's work was done and everyone else had headed for home, I stayed behind and headed for the archives to do my reading.

Among other things, I was interested in finding out how interrelationships had developed, and why certain gangsters had come to the fore and others hadn't. I wanted to know who had their criminal careers handed to them by birth—as was true of Scarfo—and which ones had to fight their way up, and were likely, therefore, to be the toughest and the cagiest. One example of the self-made leader was the man Scarfo now saw as his rival, the Hunchback, Harry Riccobene. He'd been prominent in mob circles for more than fifty years, a genuine leader; but would that also be true of his two younger half-brothers, Mario and Robert, who had risen in the mob on the basis of Harry's name? While it doesn't always work out that way, those who follow tend to be less strong than leaders, and weakness was what I was looking for.

The information I culled from the FBI files not only helped me get a fix on who the gameplayers were but also gave me something non-threatening to talk to them about when I saw them. And I also wanted them to see me and my men, get used to the idea we were around, and were going to stay around. I might drop by one gangster's house unannounced, run into another on the street, or go to a bar I knew was frequented by Mafia members and associates. Some of them even had legitimate places of business, so I'd seek them there. It was in those passing-the-day kinds of meetings that I made my assessments of who was likely to crack, who wouldn't; and it was for those meetings that I needed a topic of conversation that interested them. Gang history filled the bill, especially for mob veterans like Harry Riccobene. He was particularly receptive. My knowledgeable remarks sparked his reminiscences about the good old days of murder and treachery, and he would regale me with anecdotes about the dead, usually using nicknames (I think he'd forgotten some of the last names or may never have known them). The oral history I obtained this way from him and some others had a vivid quality and frequently much more detail than could be found in the impersonally written FBI files. It helped me enormously. To defeat your enemy, understand him.

Working with the FBI also gave me access to another investigative operation, the Federal Strike Force, an arm of the United States Justice Department that prosecutes organized crime. The Strike Force cooperated with Dennis and me by initiating a grand jury that would continue in existence for the next six years. My principal contact was Al Wicks, a low-key and highly effective attorney. Following a plan we developed, we subpoenaed key Mafia members and associates and forced them before the grand jury. We assumed, correctly, that these gangsters would take the Fifth Amendment, but that didn't concern us. We wanted to ask them questions that indicated our knowledge of their activities. Our hope was they would talk about our questions among themselves and thereby drop new pieces of information when they spoke to each other on phones the FBI had tapped in various mob hangouts. We didn't get much that way—a little piece here, a piece there—but it was enough to make the operation worthwhile.

Having decided on our methods, we tackled the next question: What should be our first investigative target?

That was the subject of our next formal meeting, where the twelve of us sat around a table sifting through the caseload. We agreed that, at least at the beginning, we should focus our effort on one murder. If we could make a breakthrough on that, we would be sending a positive message to the public and a worrisome one to our adversaries. For that same reason, we decided we should concentrate on solving a major killing. The two most important were those of former bosses Angelo Bruno and Phil Testa.

Progress had already been made on the Bruno assassination by both the Philadelphia police and the FBI. Between us we had learned (as I had assumed from my McCullough investigation) that Bruno's death was brought about by the battle for domination in Atlantic City. Shortly before Bruno was hit, an informant told us, Antonio Caponigro, Bruno's consigliere, had approached Frank "Funzy" Tieri, a boss of the Genoveses. Caponigro asked for permission to murder Bruno, pointing out that once the Gambino-allied Gentle Don was removed and Caponigro installed as the new don, the Genoveses could count on his support on everything concerning Atlantic City. Tieri told him, "You do what you have to do." Following Bruno's death, however, Tieri informed the National Commission that he had not authorized the Bruno hit. As a result, Caponigro and his brother-in-law, Alfred Salerno, who, some of our information indicated, was the gunman who murdered Bruno, were themselves tortured and slain. (Tieri's treachery had a purpose. Several years earlier, Caponigro had been awarded a lucrative gambling territory in Jersey City that Tieri had wanted for himself. With Caponigro out of the way, it was Tieri's. He didn't live long to enjoy it; he died of natural causes about a year later.)

Even though the men we believed were the chief conspirators in Bruno's death were now themselves dead, the case still had a number of avenues to explore. For one, we were far from sure that Salerno was the shooter, and our eyewitness to the murder had seen two men running off. That meant that one and possibly two killers were still on the loose. The role of John Stanfa, the Sicilian immigrant who had driven Bruno home that fatal night, also continued to raise questions. Shortly after the murder, under surveillance, he had gone to New York, where he met with members of the National Commission. He denied the meeting, was convicted of perjury but was showing no signs of talking. (He never did talk. He remained in prison until 1988, whereupon he fled back to Sicily after learning a murder contract was out on him, a strong indication that he could have fingered someone.) We also believed there was at least one other conspirator to be caught, someone who had been in Cous' Little Italy Restaurant when Bruno had his last meal and had phoned the killer or killers to say that Bruno was on the way. My guess was that that person had been Raymond Martorano.

As intriguing as these angles were, the Bruno murder was now two years in the past, and we all knew that the older an unsolved crime gets, the harder it is to clear.

The Testa murder was now more than a year old itself, which wasn't good, but otherwise it looked more promising. The apparent revenge murders of Frank Narducci, Sr., and Rocco Marinucci, over just the past few months, could mean that the young man who was in the van with Marinucci when he detonated the bomb was fearful he was next. Locate him and we might be able to convince him he was safer in our hands than the mob's. With him, if we were lucky, we'd get to Marinucci's boss, Pete Casella, now believed to be still alive and who, we were all confident, had ordered the Testa murder. There was always the real possibility, too, that by solving Testa's murder, we'd get new information on Bruno's.

My main lead to the young man in the van remained the eyewitness sketch. Based on the patrol lieutenant's glimpse of him, we had circulated it throughout South Philadelphia without success, probably because those who recognized him feared mob retribution if they identified him. The FBI's investigation of the Testa killing had picked up information about a gang of youths that Marinucci controlled. About them, we had no knowledge, just as the FBI hadn't known about our sketch. Now, through the Task Force, we finally pooled our information. It worked. An FBI agent recognized the youth in the picture. We had a suspect.

10
The Young Murderer with the Good Manners

Teddy Di Pretoro—no stalwart "Ted" for him—sweet of face, peaches and cream complexion, black curly hair, could readily be visualized in the white lace smock of an altar boy, holding the priest's vestments (or perhaps lead soprano in the Philadelphia Boys' Choir; that could be imagined, too). He was 21 when I met him; he looked to be no more than 16.

Teddy's manner matched his appearance. His was an accommodating personality, one that apparently served him well in his job as a waiter at Old Original Bookbinders, Philadelphia's most famous restaurant. In his tux, white towel over one arm, he was popular with the customers, quick to do their bidding; his tips excellent.

Teddy's ambition in life, however, went well beyond becoming the world's best waiter.

His role models, for almost as long as he could remember, were the men on the corner. While the fathers of boys like him worked long and hard for not much money in factories, the corner men idled all day long. By their expensive clothes and by their generosity—"Here, son, go buy me a paper," handing him a five, "and keep the change"—they silently told the tale of their government within our government.

The boys of Teddy's neighborhood did not, for the most part, look on the corner men as he did, but avoided them—just as boys in the black neighborhoods of North Philadelphia I patrolled were not, for the most part, impressed by the drug lords, with their gold chains clanging, lounging on their corners. But a few boys always are impressed. The models know this. They are their own historical documents, ever ready to pass on their traditions to the susceptible ones like Teddy.

Once Teddy emerged as the person who most nearly fit the eyewitness sketch for the Testa murder, I assigned teams to surveil him around the clock. We also checked his background. He lived with his mother, who was employed by the Philadelphia courts, and he had a girlfriend, a hostess at Bookbinders. As a boy, he had one arrest, for possession of firearms and silencers. The charge was "adjudicated," juvenile court jargon which means, in effect, the case was dismissed. He also had attended a gunsmith's school.

And he was also, by the time we started to surveil him about six weeks after Rocco Marinucci's murder, a worried young man. My team noted that whenever he went out to his car, he inspected it before starting it. As he drove about, he constantly checked his rear-view mirror. Before emerging at his destination, he first studied the scene, and the faces and pace of every passerby.

After keeping him under watch for a week—he probably picked us up, adding to his concern since he couldn't be sure who we were—I had one of our two-man teams bring him in. He arrived accompanied by a lawyer for whom his mother had done stenographic work. The lawyer did all the talking for Teddy, which was fine with me. I merely told the lawyer we wanted to question his client about a homicide, but didn't press the issue. My only purpose in seeing Teddy at this point was to get a first measure of him and to let him know we were thinking about him. I noted that he displayed no hint of Rocco's surly defiance nor of Willard Moran's wiseguy shuffle. Rather, he reminded me of myself when, as a little boy, I was sent to the principal's office for some minor infraction—sitting there for the lecture that was about to come, quiet, nervous, oh so respectful—that attitude.

A few nights later, I tightened the screws another notch. When Teddy got off duty at Bookbinders, he found me waiting for him. I asked him if he minded taking a ride with me. I promised him I wouldn't ask him any questions—not without his lawyer present—but said I did have some information that I thought he ought to be aware of. With a deferential smile—I was, after all, old enough to be his father—he agreed and got into the passenger seat beside me. I drove along in silence for a few minutes before saying, "Teddy, we have reason to think there's a murder contract out on you." He didn't answer, but his ruby lips moved inward as if to force words back inside himself. He stared out into the night. He didn't ask who might want to kill him.

Helpfully, I described how Rocco Marinucci's assailants had been careful to keep him conscious at all times, as they beat him, as they choked him, as they stuffed the cherry bombs one by one into his mouth. They wanted him to witness his own death, I explained, "and I have no doubt," I went on, "that before they finally killed him, they tried to force him to name his confederates." I stopped with that, glanced over. He was not taking the news well. I have my boy, I thought, if I can get him before Salvy does.

After about fifteen minutes, I was back at the restaurant and left Teddy off. I wished him a good night. He responded, "Goodnight, Lieutenant Friel. Thank you, sir." As if I'd given him a tip. Which I had, intentionally.

The tip had nothing to do with telling him that Salvy murdered Rocco. I had no doubt he already knew that. It was common street talk, and most likely he'd heard it long before we did. He also had to assume that Salvy knew who Rocco's followers were and might suspect one or more of them as participants in the murder of his father. The various precautions we'd observed Teddy taking while we had him under surveillance obviously had sprung from that knowledge. What hadn't occurred to him, judging from his reaction to my tip, was that Rocco might have named him before he was killed. If Rocco did, Teddy knew, he was a walking dead man.

Compounding his problem—and this may have been a second reason for his precautions—was the possibility that Petey Casella (assuming *he* was still alive) also wanted Teddy dead. With Rocco gone, Teddy might be the only remaining person who could link him to Phil Testa's murder. Casella still had allies in Philadelphia. It would take only one to take care of Teddy.

Teddy's parting good wishes to me indicated, however, that he wasn't ready to talk yet. The screws would have to be tightened still a little further and quickly, before Salvy acted. I arranged, therefore, to have him called before our federal grand jury. After filling prosecutor Al Wicks in on what we knew and guessed about Teddy, I wrote out questions I thought would be helpful for him to ask. We didn't expect Teddy to answer them; we assumed, as with the others we'd called, he'd take the Fifth Amendment. My purpose, rather, was to show him we now considered him not merely involved in the Phil Testa murder but our prime suspect. The question "Did you make the bomb that killed Phil Testa?" was guesswork on my part, based on Teddy's mechanical aptitude and his training at the gunsmith school. Even if I was wrong—and I had a hunch I wasn't—the question would show him what we thought he had done.

We also picked up the name of an associate of Teddy and Rocco who, we believed, had purchased the dynamite. (That person was never arrested.) We brought him in for questioning; before he arrived, I placed on my desk a new sketch of Teddy made from his photograph. Below the picture was the message: "WANTED: For Investigation of the Murder of Phil Testa."

After questioning the young man, I left him alone in my office, going where I could observe him without being seen. As I hoped, he rummaged around the top of my desk, seized the "WANTED" poster, studied it, put it back. I then returned to my office, released him and had him followed. He went directly to Teddy's house where, I assume, he told Teddy that the cops must have a description of him from an eyewitness. How otherwise could they have come up with such a detailed likeness of him?

That gave Teddy something new to brood about, on top of all his other problems. After twenty-four hours, I had him brought in. This time, he didn't ask for his lawyer. I assured him that if he told us the truth, we'd protect him and I'd speak on his behalf at sentencing. He split right open.

Yes, he said, it was true. He had bought a number of the parts for the bomb. Casella, Rocco told him, supplied the dynamite.

Rocco and Teddy did the assembling of the bomb in the basement of Rocco's pizza shop, after which Teddy delivered it to the murder site in his car. (That explained why there were no traces of it in Rocco's van.) Teddy placed the bomb on the porch and ran the antenna wire of the detonating device along the side of the house. Once that task was accomplished, he drove off. We had, therefore, come up with the right suspect but for the wrong reason: Teddy had never been in the van with Rocco; our drawing from the patrol lieutenant's description was of someone else. (Subsequently I established, to my own satisfaction, the identity of the youth in the van with Rocco, but I have never had sufficient evidence to arrest him as an accomplice.)

In order to entice him to participate in the murder, Teddy said, Rocco explained to him that once Testa was out of the way, Casella would be the new don, and Rocco and Teddy would become Casella's right-hand men. They'd have suit-cases of money, Rocco said, all the women they wanted, big cars—why, they'd run Philadelphia for the old man, he and Rocco would, and here Teddy was not even 21 yet!

I asked Teddy why Rocco had chosen him for this fine future. "Because he knew he could trust me, sir," replied Teddy.

"How did he know he could trust you, Teddy?"

"Because he knew I'd already committed a murder," explained the lad with a modest smile.

That was the one answer I'd not been expecting. That Teddy, with dreams of mob glory dancing through his juvenile mind, and heroworshipping the tough-guy Rocco, would help with a murder by building a bomb, maybe even planting it, I could readily believe. But I had bought into Teddy's sweet appearance and gentle manner to the extent that it had never occurred to me he could actually kill someone himself. I asked him who. "Oh, it was a friend of mine, sir, Edward Bianculli," he replied.

"But why would you kill a friend of yours, Teddy?" I inquired.

He nodded as if this were a good question, and said stoutly, "I had good reason, sir." It happened, he continued, two years earlier, before he got his waiter's job at Bookbinders. He was then working as a delivery boy for a pharmacy, and the 21-year-old Edward frequently hung out there with him. One day, Edward stole a box of candy from the druggist and blamed the theft on Teddy. "That's why I had to kill him."

I told him I wasn't quite sure I understood. "Well," Teddy said, "Edward seemed to think it was real funny, me being blamed for taking the candy." He made jokes about it in front of other members of Rocco's gang. "The thing is," Teddy explained in an aggrieved tone, "Edward knew full well I was doing stick-ups of drug dealers while I was making my deliveries." For someone of his advanced criminal credentials to be accused of a childish prank like stealing a box of candy was keenly humiliating, which was why Edward had to die.

To carry out the deed, Teddy enlisted the help of 24-year-old Michael Rinaldi. Like Teddy and Edward, Michael was one of Rocco's "walkies" (a mob term for someone who runs errands for and commits crimes on the order of a more experienced criminal). Michael Rinaldi agreed to help Teddy kill Edward, with whom Michael had had his own problems. Teddy told Edward that Michael and he needed Edward's help to rob a drug dealer who, they'd supposedly learned, was going to pick up a delivery at Philadelphia International Airport. Edward agreed to go with them. When they arrived that evening, Michael remained behind in the car and Teddy and Edward walked to the field behind the airport to lie in wait behind some bushes for the dealer's approach. While Edward acted as lookout, Teddy took his position behind him, rose, cocked his gun at the back of Edward's head and pulled the trigger; it misfired. Hearing the click, Edward looked around at him. Apparently thinking Teddy had taken the gun out in preparation for the ambush, Edward innocently again turned from Teddy. The providence of the misfired chamber had given Teddy the opportunity to change his mind. He didn't. He pulled the trigger a second time. The bullet entered Edward's back. He fell, writhing on the ground. Teddy went over to him and, kneeling by him, fired his remaining bullets into Edward's head. He returned to the car, and he and Michael drove back to Philadelphia, along the way throwing the murder weapon in the river. Edward Bianculli's body was not discovered for months, by which time it was so badly decomposed, it could be identified only by the jewelry he had been wearing. We'd never had a suspect in the killing.

Teddy's confession to the murder now probably had nothing to do with any outburst of conscience. If that had been the case, he would have expressed at least a semblance of regret for the murder, and he didn't. On the contrary, there was an element of pride in his tone, and he may have told me about the murder for much the same reason he had committed it: He was sensitive about his angelic looks that made him the butt of jokes by people like Edward, and he felt a need to prove to me how deceptive his appearance was. I also had the strong sense that his accommodating nature was at work. I had asked him a question and he had answered it because it was the polite thing to do.

I next asked him what he thought Michael Rinaldi would say when I brought him in. My question referred to Michael's version of the Bianculli murder, but again Teddy surprised me. "Oh, he'll probably accuse me of two other murders, sir, but I didn't commit them. Rocco did."

Now realizing I had opened an entire box of evil I hadn't expected, I inquired which murders. "You see," Teddy explained, "there were these two young guys, neighbors of Rocco's, and they had electric guitars that they played late at night, and that annoyed Rocco, you know, so naturally he killed them."

I am still not certain if Teddy was telling me the truth about not being involved in the guitar-player murders, which have never been marked officially solved. After confessing to one homicide we had no idea he'd committed, even he might have decided it wouldn't be to his interest to confess to more. One thing is certain: The guitar players were struck by bullets from three weapons, so that there had to be at least two gunmen, probably three. Teddy could well have been one of them, which would have given Rocco more reason to trust him than his participation in the Bianculli murder, which Rocco knew about only secondhand.

While he was chatting away, Teddy also informed me that the late Rocco had claimed to be the murderer of Angelo Bruno. Rocco, Teddy said, told him he used a gun belonging to Edward Bianculli and had worn a long dark green overcoat, inside which he had hidden the weapon as he approached the car. (On hearing this from Teddy, I had Rocco's pizza shop searched; the overcoat was found in the basement, but no gun, nor were we ever able to trace any weapon to Edward Bianculli's possession.)

I have no doubt Rocco told Teddy he killed Bruno, and the coat does match a description we have of the one the killer wore. That Rocco would have been selected for the job, however, is improbable, unless his mentor Casella was involved, and we have no reason to think he was. My guess is that Rocco had been bragging; he wanted to impress his altar boy. (No one has ever been arrested as the Bruno gunman; our information at the time of the killing, that it was Alfred Salerno, Caponigro's brother-in-law, remains unsubstantiated.)

Several months after making his confession to me, Teddy Di Pretoro entered a plea of guilty to the murders of Phil Testa and Edward Bianculli. Based on his testimony, we also convicted Michael Rinaldi of the Bianculli homicide; he got a life sentence. Teddy got one life sentence for Testa, one for Bianculli, but since they were to be served concurrently, Teddy, in effect, had gotten one free murder. He probably would have received consecutive life sentences or conceivably the death penalty—both crimes were premeditated—had it not been for an eloquent defender on his behalf: me.

I made good on my promise to plead mercy for him at his sentencing if he told us the truth about the Testa murder, and even though the coldblooded (and to me, more horrifying) Bianculli homicide had come up in the course of his Testa confession, I could hardly renege on my promise. Also as part of our deal with him, he was given a new identity, and no doubt he will eventually charm a parole board into releasing him. I hear from Teddy frequently. He calls me for advice or sometimes, it seems, simply to pass the time of day. His are always pleasant calls and respectful ones. He is a polite young man.

Teddy has his guaranteed place in the history of crime, too. He was the first hired killer of a Mafia boss ever arrested and convicted in the United States.

Both the print and electronic media gave our accomplishment headline treatment. (I think they loved who Teddy was, too; nothing like a choirboy killer—and one who was a waiter at the famous Bookbinders to boot—to make good copy.) The FBI brass was pleased. The Philadelphia Police brass was pleased. Their public relations stunt in approving the Task Force, if that's what it was, had suddenly produced gratifying results.

We of the Task Force, were pleased, too, at least within limits. That we had succeeded in our first case was a morale booster. We also recognized that Teddy's confession might be a trailblazer.

It was not that Teddy himself was particularly significant. He was nothing more than a walkie for Rocco Marinucci, who, in the grander scheme of mob activities, was himself a minor figure. But Teddy was different from the two men arrested in the McCullough murder in one important way. Both Howard Dale Young, who'd fingered Willard Moran as McCullough's shooter, and Moran himself, whose trial still wasn't scheduled, were outsiders, punks fit for a job or two and nothing more. There would thus be no great surprise in LCN circles that the likes of a Young would talk, and there must have been doubts about the swaggering Moran, too. (Swaggerers are usually bullies and bullies are cowards and cowards talk.) But Teddy was from South Philadelphia, had imbibed the Mafia culture from childhood on, had the right heritage—as Young and Moran did not—to become a made-member, something he passionately desired. Once arrested, he would be assumed to hold fast to the rule of omertà. He didn't.

Teddy, therefore, could send a message to the mob that Young and Moran (assuming Moran eventually confessed) were incapable of. If one of their own informed, might not someone else the next time the screws were tightened? We needed more talkers than Teddy, but he was a good start.

Otherwise, he led us nowhere. His entire knowledge of Casella's role in the Phil Testa murder plot came from the deceased Rocco; we couldn't get into court with that kind of hearsay. Casella was still safe from us. (It turned out he was alive. He turned up in Florida, living with his daughter. He died there in 1984 of natural causes.)

Teddy's confession in and of itself, aside from the chance it would set off the domino effect we hoped for, also failed to move the Task Force toward its goal of arresting Scarfo and dismantling his mob. But even had Teddy been able to give us evidence against Casella, the future of the mob wouldn't have been affected. In removing Phil Testa, Casella set the stage for the ascension of Nicky Scarfo, but he had no role in the new scene. We would have loved to have gotten him, but for crimes past, not present or future.

However, in the present tense, it now appeared that Scarfo, with one bloody year of rule behind him, had espied a rival on the horizon—not a Gambino either, or a Genovese, or any of those prowling about Atlantic City who could be challengers to his power, but rather the old-time Philadelphia gangster, Harry Riccobene.

11

Scarfo Tries
to Kill Harry;
Harry Shoots Back

Not quite five feet tall, bent perpetually forward by his hump, the Sicilian-born Harry Riccobene was, in 1982, 72 years old and about to grow a long white beard that would give him the look of a depraved Santa Claus.

He was, almost beyond doubt, America's oldest extant drug dealer. His first arrest on that charge came in 1932, just three years after his initiation at the age of 19 into the Society of the Men of Honor. Frequent stays in prison had followed; they had not stopped him from becoming a wealthy man.

By the late 1970s, Harry had become a kingpin in the meth

business in alliance with the Pagans, the most violence-prone of all the motorcycle gangs. Harry supplied the capital, they the meth cookers, his men and theirs combining to form the distribution network. Harry's profits, however, came not only from narcotics and the old staple, gambling, but from legitimate businesses as well. He owned a trash hauling company and a ticket agency, controlled jukeboxes and cigarette machines, and, he once told me, had even turned an honest penny or two in real estate investments.

Almost from the day in the spring of 1981 that Scarfo declared himself boss of the Philadelphia/Atlantic City family, the Hunchback had done nothing to hide his disdain for the new leader. I made it my business to get to know Harry a year later, immediately after the Task Force was formed, calling on him at his home. After we had discussed early mob history, I managed to bring him around to the subject of Scarfo. "He's a brash, violent dope," was Harry's considered opinion. As he saw it, Scarfo lacked the "mental fire" to run any self-respecting crime family. "This new breed," he complained, "they're not like us old guys who knew what we're doin'; we took our lickin's and kept on tickin'." Scarfo, on the contrary, he muttered, went around knifing people—an apparent reference to the 1963 murder of the longshoreman Dugan—"and gettin' into fights." On that last point, he was referring to an episode in which Scarfo and his nephew Phil Leonetti, accompanied by Scarfo's lawyer, Bobby Simone, had engaged in a tussle with guards in one of the Atlantic City casinos. The brawl caused the kind of publicity that Harry deplored. Do as Bruno did, was Harry's motto; keep a low profile and you (and your men) will make your millions.

Harry was much more than talk, too. He had a gang of twenty, not counting the Pagans, at his beck and call, which—even though outnumbered by Scarfo's men by at least three to one—was a formidable force.

When the war between Harry and Scarfo broke out in April

1982—coincidental to the formation of the Task Force—
Harry was out on bail following a conviction on gambling
charges, the result of an FBI sting operation which had made
its arrests the year before. As a result, Harry was facing a 9-
year sentence of which he'd have to serve at least a third
(probably more, considering his record), a prospect which
did not deter him for a moment from his plans to take over
the mob from Scarfo. He'd already spent half his life in
jail—seemed in fine physical fettle from it, had a 22-year-
old mistress—and didn't expect he'd have any difficulty continuing to guide his organization from behind bars if his appeal
failed. Genovese, Angelo Bruno and others had succeeded
in doing that, and if they could, so could he. (Ambition runs
high among the elderly in the Mafia; whatever it can be
accused of, ageism is not one bias it suffers from. Pete Casella
was in his seventies when he tried to become boss by killing
Testa. And then there was, even more remarkably, Dominick
Pollina. According to FBI sources, in 1978, when he was
86, he approached Angelo Bruno—the man he'd tried to kill
nearly twenty years earlier—and asked to be appointed to the
then-vacant post of consigliere. The Gentle Don gently turned
him down and instead named his own murderer-to-be, Antonio Caponigro, who himself was in his early sixties.)

Shortly after our Task Force got going, an FBI informant
advised us that Scarfo had compiled a death list. Harry's
name was at the top, followed by his associates (other than
the Pagans—even Scarfo didn't want to tangle with them),
including Harry's two half-brothers, 50-year-old Mario, and
Robert, who was 42.

Once we learned of Scarfo's list, we spread across South
Philadelphia to warn those whose names were on it. We did
that because as peace officers we had an obligation to warn
any prospective victims of danger to their lives, and also
because of the possibility such news might inspire cooperation

with us. Harry's reaction was typical: "No one is going to kill me, but if you can prove it, maybe I'll consider helping you out, Mr. Friel." Since he already had all the proof we had, that closed the books on help from him.

By warning the Riccobene faction of Scarfo's intentions toward them, we were aware we were also courting the danger that Harry would be inspired to strike first, leading to new bloodshed. Our concern proved needless. By the time we learned of the list, Scarfo was already putting it into action. His first target was the Hunchback.

To set up the killing, Scarfo called in 52-year-old Frank Monte, his consigliere, whom I'd last seen in the company of Salvy Testa at the hospital on the night of Phil Testa's murder. At that point, Monte was in trouble himself. He was suspected by Scarfo (probably rightly so) of skimming profits off the Philadelphia gambling operations, a foible on his part that could lead to his own death warrant. He was, therefore, eager to prove how helpful he could be to Scarfo, even if that meant violating his duty as consigliere to be a neutral arbiter between warring factions within the mob.

According to information I garnered two years later, Monte turned to Raymond "Long John" Martorano for assistance. Both men allegedly agreed that Harry's vulnerable spot was his half-brother, the stocky Mario. His white hair combed straight back mob-style, Mario was a foot taller than Harry, but that had not stopped him from living his life under Harry's shadow. In or out of prison, Harry had retained control of the family businesses. Mario was lacking both in authority and—as he saw it—a fair share of the profits. Mario also resented the fact that Harry had never permitted him to participate in a murder. In taking that position, Harry was not concerned with protecting his baby brother from a life of violence, but rather feared that if Mario gained Mafia membership by making his bones, he'd have the opportunity to become independent of him. Mario's eagerness to join the select circle of the Men of Honor was widely known. Long John apparently figured that Mario would consider his half-brother's life an entrance fee well worth paying.

Sometime in late April 1982, therefore, Long John met with Mario at Cous' Little Italy. As Mario later told the story, Martorano said to him, "Your brother's no good," a code phrase in LCN circles that means the person so described is cooperating with law enforcement and must be assassinated. Terrified at being made privy to this announcement (which he didn't believe), Mario asked, "Longy, what do you mean?"

Martorano replied, "You've got to do your duty."

"What ya talkin' about? Whatta you mean?" demanded the agitated Mario.

"You gotta do your duty, like I have." Martorano then held five fingers out, Mario recalled. "I've done five," Martorano said. "McCullough, Stevie, Angie [Angelo Bruno] was no good, Calabrese—" Mario had no doubt Long John was telling him the truth about all these murders, but he also knew it could be dangerous knowledge for him to have. "No, no!" He held his hands out palms up to stop Martorano. "No names. I don't wanta hear. I don't wanta hear." Then, referring to the plan to kill his brother: "I don't know about this. I wanta hear from the consigliere on this. He should decide about this."

Since the consigliere was in on the scheme, Martorano proved agreeable to Mario's proposal and departed. Mario decided not to inform Harry, at least not yet. The situation, he reflected, had its good side. No more Harry could mean more for Mario. But he also had to consider the possibility that when I dropped by his jewelry store and told him Scarfo had a death list and he was on it, I was telling him the truth, which—since Mario didn't trust cops—he had doubted.

The following Sunday, around noon, Long John arrived at Mario's house with Monte in tow. Mario remembered he began by asking Monte why he had to set his brother up.

Monte replied, "Harry is a rat. He won't support Scarfo. His time has come."

Mario objected, "I don't know about this. It's your job to stop things like this, talk things out."

"No," said Monte. "This thing has to be done. When it is, good things will come your way. You'll take over your brother's business and become a made man."

Martorano, according to Mario, then outlined the murder plan, which was predicated on bachelor Harry's habit of having dinner every Sunday afternoon at Mario's house. Naming the date when the hit was to take place, Martorano said, "When your brother comes, you will say to him, 'Harry, we have to talk,' and you'll take him out of the house, and that deserted stretch by your house? You take him there," where Martorano and his lieutenant, big bull-necked Frank Vadino, would be waiting in the shadows to gun Harry down.

Martorano had no sooner finished his explanation than Harry arrived for dinner. He exchanged pleasantries with Long John and Monte, after which those two worthies left. Mario meanwhile was thinking. He was thinking about becoming rich beyond his wildest dreams—and also dead. With absolute prescience, he saw the guns spitting out their bullets not just at Harry but at him. He'd be lying there right next to Harry. Such reflections caused an unprecedented swelling within his bosom of fraternal feeling, prompting him to relate to Harry what had transpired just before his arrival. Harry coolly replied, "Oh, yeah? We'll whack them."

After giving Mario that pep talk, Harry contacted his two most trusted aides, one valued for his brawn, the other for his brain.

The brawny one was the craggy-faced Victor DeLuca, leg-breaker and extortionist, over six feet tall, weighing around 220 pounds, all of it muscle. The brain belonged to Joseph Pedulla who, at 34, was ten years younger and a good five inches shorter than Victor. A good-looking fellow and a former marine, Joey was a bookmaker for Harry, and a very successful—and honest—one. The muscleman Victor was fond of Joey, and felt protective toward him. Despite their outward differences, the two of them had become nearly inseparable. Unlike Victor, Joey did not have a reputation for violence.

Victor, Joey and the two Riccobene brothers met at Joey's mother's house in suburban Cherry Hill, New Jersey. There, the four men sat in the living room making up their own death list. As Harry saw it, Frank Monte, the consigliere, should be their first target. Scarfo and Martorano, after all, were only enemies, but Monte was a traitor to the standards of the Men of Honor by having violated his oath of neutrality.

To carry out the deed, Joey, Victor and other members of the Riccobene gang, including the squat and fortyish Joseph Casdia, whose body and arms were covered with tattoos, set up a surveillance on Monte. On the evening of May 13, a camper belonging to Casdia and Pedulla was parked in a lot behind a gas station to which Monte, earlier that day, had brought his car to be cleaned. When Monte arrived to pick it up, Joey Pedulla, proving himself capable of violence after all, placed his rifle through the gun port in the back of the camper, peered through its site to his target thirty feet away and squeezed the trigger. Monte fell. Pedulla pumped seven more bullets into him. He then sat back, watching as people began to run toward—and from—the scene, shouts, screams, calls for the police. Five minutes later, Casdia strolled up to the camper, got inside and drove off with Pedulla. Victor DeLuca was in a separate car to block traffic if necessary, along with Harry, who had given the signal for the hit when he saw Monte leaving his house to walk the few blocks to the garage.

No one in the Task Force was surprised to hear of Monte's death. Rumors were all over the street that he was cheating Scarfo, and he apparently had paid the price for that. Arguing against that assumption were conversations we had taped on a bug we'd placed in a mob hangout in South Philadelphia.

Those present, all Scarfo men, seemed genuinely surprised by Monte's death.*

It was, however, possible that these men might not have been informed in advance of the assassination. They were older gang members, and we had been picking up information that all or most of the killings over the past six months had been carried out by the group I was now thinking of as the Young Executioners.

None of the Young Executioners was older than thirty, and most were still in their early to mid-twenties. Salvy Testa was their capo, and while I didn't know all of their names then, their number included two sons of the old-time mobster Blond Babe Pungitore, two Grande brothers, two Milano brothers, and the two Narducci brothers, Frank Jr. and Philip, who, at 21, was the youngest of the Young Executioners. (Several years later, when I was questioning Frank Jr., I asked him if he knew that Salvy Testa and Joseph Pungitore had murdered his father. Replied Frank, "Tell me something that'll bring him back and then I'll help you. Otherwise, I don't wanta hear.")

Unlike us, Scarfo knew who was responsible for Monte's death, and so he stepped up his efforts to murder the Hunchback. This time, Harry's killer was to be Jimmy DeGregorio, a leader of the Pagan motorcycle gang.

According to statements made to me by DeGregorio following his confession to a series of crimes, he was approached by Raymond Martorano a few days after Monte's murder. (Martorano was never charged for this or for the previous attempt on Riccobene's life.) Assuming DeGregorio's story is true, Long John probably selected DeGregorio because he knew Harry trusted the Pagan from their meth business dealings together. According to DeGregorio, Long John guar-

---

*According to our information, Monte's successor as consigliere was Scarfo's uncle, Nicholas "Nicky Buck" Piccolo, who was then 78 years old.

anteed him $20,000 if he'd rub Harry out. That's almost certainly a gross exaggeration on DeGregorio's part; $5,000 for outside killers is the usual ceiling.

After accepting Martorano's offer—whatever the real figure was—the brawny DeGregorio, who still looked like the football player he'd been, trotted off to see the aged elf. When he had him alone, he informed him, "Longy gives me twenty if'n I off you, Harry." The Hunchback waved him off. "Ah, go an' kill Longy instead," he suggested.

DeGregorio had expected that, but he'd also expected that Harry would mention a counter dollar figure. Harry hadn't, which was typical; his thriftiness was legendary in crime circles. "I don't think you understand, old man," opined DeGregorio as he picked Harry up by the lapels and held him suspended in mid-air, their eyes, in that fashion, meeting. "I can kill you right now, you little assbag," DeGregorio advised him. "I can kill you this very minute and get me $20,000."

Even in the face of death, Harry was not about to commit himself to that kind of cash outlay. "Nah, nah," he riposted. "You don't kill me. You go kill Longy and then you come back. We'll talk about it then."

DeGregorio was so dumbfounded, he told me, by the Hunchback's fearlessness (and his cheapness) that he couldn't think what to do. With a shake of his head, he set Harry back down on the floor and departed. (He didn't try to kill Martorano either; he figured he'd never get a dime out of Harry for doing that.)

It was during the course of debriefing DeGregorio following his confession to other crimes that I got my first indication that the Monte killing hadn't been the work of Scarfo but of the Riccobene gang. DeGregorio's story was confused—he admitted he had been doing drugs—and some of it turned out not to be accurate, but he did recount a credible conversation with Casdia in which Casdia complained that "Victor bailed out" in the Monte killing, an apparent reference to

Victor DeLuca's failure to block traffic with his car after the shooting.

Victor failed in another murder assignment that summer, as I subsequently learned. The Hunchback, who was becoming annoyed at Martorano's apparent persistence in trying to kill him, asked Victor if he'd mind ridding the world of his once-good friend. Victor said he'd be glad to, and proceeded to John's Vending Company, which Martorano owned. There Victor spotted Martorano standing in front of the premises, but just as he was preparing to shoot him, a bus stopped at the corner and disgorged passengers. Not wanting to risk killing innocent people, Victor held fire, and by the time the crowd dispersed, so had Martorano.

By now, Scarfo had developed his third plan to kill Harry the Hunchback. It was known that Harry rarely made calls from his home phone—he feared it might be tapped—and instead used a booth a short distance away. On the evening of June 8, 1982, Harry was seated inside it talking to his girlfriend when a young man in his late twenties came up to the booth, took out a revolver, and began shooting at Harry, hitting him four times. After the sixth shot, the little old man charged out of the booth, wrestled the would-be assassin to the ground and disarmed him. Covered with Harry's blood, the shooter broke free and ran for his life.

Police were on the scene within minutes, and Harry was rushed to the hospital. I was notified and ran a check to see if we had any information about the period immediately prior to the incident. A police patrol wagon, I was told, had observed a suspicious car in the vicinity of Harry's house and (as was routine) took down the license plate number. I traced the car to an auto leasing firm, which had rented it to the wife of Wayne Grande, one of the Young Executioners. I obtained a mugshot of Grande and took it with me to Harry's hospital room. He was asleep. I laid the picture on his chest. When he awakened—and despite his wounds he seemed in good spirits—he studied the picture and gave me an appreciative grin, but claimed he simply had no idea who shot him or why. I remarked, with absolute sincerity, that he had shown great courage, wounded as he was, going after this kid who still had a gun trained on him. Harry winked and replied in a self-deprecating tone, "Nah, to tell you the trut', Mr. Friel, he was done with that. Y'see, while he was shootin' me, I was keepin' count of the number of bullets he was firing. So I didn't go after him 'til I knew he didn't have any left."

"You *counted* the bullets while you were being shot, Harry?" I asked.

He nodded, as if that was what anyone in his position would have done.

Seven weeks later, on July 31, Victor DeLuca and Joey Pedulla were cruising through South Philadelphia, Victor doing the driving, Joey literally riding shotgun. They were on the lookout for Martorano, with Joey prepared to kill him if the chance presented itself. Their journey took them through South Philadelphia's bustling Italian Market, one of the city's prime attractions for tourists—part of *Rocky* was filmed there—and for presidential candidates, who love to get themselves photographed in the market mingling with the common folk. It is also where native Philadelphians know they can get splendid buys on the fresh produce, fish, meats, cheeses, sold from the many outdoor stalls.

As Victor threaded through the heavy traffic and the throngs of pedestrians on the street, there, directly ahead of them, seated on a rickety red stool which he had propped against a wall, was Scarfo's lord high executioner, Salvy Testa, eating clams from a plastic cup with a plastic fork. Salvy saw Victor and Joey, laughed at them. "Think I should shoot him?" inquired Joey of his good friend. Before Victor had the opportunity to render a judgment, Joey brought up his shotgun. He pulled the trigger, expelling nine .32 double-O buckshot pellets, one of which missed, the other eight lodging in Salvy's left arm which he had raised in reflex to protect himself.

As horrified and screaming spectators tried to scatter, a police officer arrived on the scene in his patrol car. He started after Victor and Joey. Victor wheeled around and raced the car through the crowded street, the officer hot on their tail. Victor headed in the direction of the airport in southwest Philadelphia, as the first patrol car was now joined by several more. Eventually, the officers forced Victor off the road. The car smashed into a bridge abutment, and both he and Joey were arrested.

They didn't stay in custody long. While being processed at the Roundhouse, one of them offered a bribe to an officer with the understanding that a portion of it was to go to the arraignment judge's clerk. The judge later denied any knowledge of the deal, but Victor and Joey were released on low bail and immediately left the city. DA Ed Rendell denounced the judge, ordered an investigation, and demanded that the two men be rearrested. Ten days later, they were back in jail.

On the evening of August 21, Harry Riccobene, completely recovered from the wounds he'd received in the telephone booth, was seated in his car on a South Philadelphia street waiting for his girlfriend to arrive. A man in a jogger's suit, Joseph Grande, the brother of the man who had shot Harry in the phone booth, trotted up to the car, took out his gun and began to shoot at Harry. Glass went splattering, bullets entered the body of the car, but Harry, his tiny size coming to his rescue, was able to duck out of sight. His only wound this time was a crease where a bullet grazed his scalp. The assassination attempt ceased and the jogger ran off when a police officer, hearing the gunfire, arrived. Unperturbed,

Harry shook the glass off himself, waved off assistance, and drove on home.

Just as on the occasion of the telephone booth shooting, I was immediately notified of this attempt on Harry's life. I drove to see him at his house. He opened the door himself, welcomed me in. Harry always seemed glad to see me. However, when I asked him what had happened, he blithely denied he had been shot at. Referring to the damage to his car, he suggested, "Probably neighborhood vandals."

"Vandals?" said I. "Harry, your car is full of bullet holes."

"Well, we got tough vandals around here, Mr. Friel," he noted.

"And what about your head, Harry?" I asked, pointing to the bullet crease.

"Oh, that," said he; "I bumped my head going through a door."

"Harry," I replied, "they don't make doorways low enough that you could bump your head going through them."

He grinned at that, and allowed as to how maybe somebody had shot him, couldn't imagine why. "And you still don't know about the last time either?" I asked without any expectation. In response, Harry shook his head, as if marveling at the mysteries of the human experience.

I then urged Harry to think about his future. He was facing 9 years in prison on the gambling charge, would at least be in his late seventies when he got out. If, however, he cooperated with us, I told him, we'd put him in the Federal Witness Protection Program. "With all your money," I said, "you can go anywhere you want in the entire world, do whatever you want."

He replied, "I can't help you, Mr. Friel. Where would I go if I left South Philadelphia?"

I understood what he meant. Even with his wealth, in the Witness Program he'd be just a little old man out where no one knew him, while in South Philadelphia he was a man of respect. He was a mob guy. He had a need for it, and it was worth any risk to continue to have it. Counting his gold in a retirement community might have been the only thing that ever could have killed Harry the Hunchback.

12
The Riccobene Murders

From the first time I met him, I had little hope that Harry
Riccobene, steeped as he was in Mafia tradition, would
ever cooperate, and his response to the attempts on his
life convinced me I was right. His younger half-brother,
the stout and fiftyish Mario, who'd spent his life in the
shadow of Harry's criminal substance, struck me as more
promising.

I first met Mario in the spring of 1982 when I warned him
he was on Scarfo's death list. After that, I visited him on a

fairly regular basis at the store his son Enrico operated on Sansom Street's Jewelers Row, just a few blocks from Independence Hall. Like Harry, Mario always seemed pleased to see me. Neither of them were, of course, but Mario's nature was essentially a gregarious one; he lacked, I thought, his brother's craftiness, and he was also more emotional, both positive signs from my point of view. I didn't try to push him into any admissions. It was much too early for that to work. My goal, rather, was to establish myself through my visits as a sympathetic, nonjudgmental person in whom (should he eventually find it to his interest) he could confide.

Each time I dropped in on him, he seemed more nervous than the time before. Brother Harry might regard the Scarfo vendetta against the Riccobenes with marked aplomb, but Mario apparently did not. Also facing prison on the same gambling charges for which Harry had been convicted (Mario's sentence the shorter of the two), he didn't attempt to hide his concern that Scarfo would try to get him before he went away, and if that attempt failed, that Scarfo would be waiting for him when he got out. It was not a pleasant prospect.

Adding to his worry, he told me several times, was his fear for the safety of his son. Enrico, he assured me, had no knowledge of the "family business," by which he meant crime, not jewelry, but even so he believed Enrico was also marked for death. (Mario wasn't quite telling me the truth about Enrico; he had been present, I later learned, at several of the Riccobene planning sessions against Scarfo, although he probably never took an active role.)

Just before going to prison, Mario subsequently told me, he attempted to negotiate peace between the two sides. To do so, he approached Joseph "Chickie" Ciancaglini, whom Mario had known for most of his life and trusted as a friend.* Chickie, a capo who was two years younger than Mario, assured him he would intercede on his behalf with Scarfo.

Chickie was lying. Even as he was proffering help, he was planning to murder Mario on Scarfo's orders. He gave the hit contract not to Salvy Testa and the Young Executioners, but rather to three mobsters who were more nearly his own age, Charles "Charley White" Iannece, Nick "Nicky Crow" Caramandi, and Pasquale "Pat the Cat" Spirito, who was designated by Chickie as the shooter.

When the conspirators heard that Mario was to attend a viewing at a funeral home, Ciancaglini directed that the killing take place there, a thoughtful gesture that would save the undertaker the trouble of going out to pick up the body. Pat the Cat, however, never showed. He was a career criminal but he didn't want to be a murderer. (His failure to carry out the order cost him his life soon afterward.)

When the attempt to murder Mario was aborted, all became quiet on the Riccobene-Scarfo battlefront and remained that way for more than a year, in large part because neither Harry nor Mario were around to be shot at anymore; their appeals having failed, they were in prison on the gambling convictions. Neither was there any opportunity to shoot Joey Pedulla

---

*The big and burly Chickie, like his bosom pal Mario, was an affable sort. One of our conversations went like this:

Chickie: "Lieutenant, I just want to tell ya how tough I think your job is. You know, I'm a great supporter of the police myself."

Me: "I'm certainly glad to hear that, Chickie. You could make our job less tough if you could help us."

Chickie (exuding sincerity): "Hey, I'd be glad to. Just tell me how I can help."

Me: "You could tell us who's killing all these people."

Chickie (puzzled frown): "What people, Lieutenant Friel?"

Me: "All your friends."

Chickie (shocked expression): "Hey, you don't think *we* kill people, do you?"

and Victor DeLuca; they were jailed, too, for the Salvy Testa shooting.

For Scarfo, the situation was aggravating. He wanted to get rid of the Riccobenes himself; instead, it was the police who were doing it. Worse yet, he was zero-for-five in his attempts to murder the Riccobenes, while they had one scalp on their belt (Monte) and one palpable hit (Salvy).

Not that Scarfo was about to give up. He still had his list and he still had his pride. He, also, however, had a legal problem of his own (described in Chapter 13) to occupy him. In large part because of this problem, it was not until more than a year later, in the fall of 1983, that he was able to get back to dealing with the Riccobene gang.

Scarfo's first attempt on the new round seemed to indicate that Harry's men were going to continue to live the same charmed existence Harry did. On October 14, 1983, a Riccobene associate, Frank Martines, Jr., was shot in the chest by (according to informants) Eugene Milano and Charley White Iannece. Lying on the street, bleeding heavily, he peered up at the police officer who came to his aid, saying, "I know you from the neighborhood, but I can't give you any information. I have nothing to say to you." He survived.

Less fortunate was Sammy Tamburrino, a partner in a Riccobene video cassette business and Mario's closet friend. On November 3, Sammy was shot and killed by two of the Young Executioners, Nicky Whip Milano and Phil Narducci, inside a variety store he operated on the ground floor of his house, as his horrified mother watched.

Robert Riccobene, Harry's other younger half-brother and Mario's full brother, was the next target. Robert's duties for the "family business" included collecting money from a string of jukeboxes and cigarette machines that Harry owned. One cigarette machine was located in Conti's Variety Store at the corner of Hutchinson and Catherine streets in South Philadelphia, right in the heart of Scarfo territory. We learned from an informant that the next time Robert went there, he was to be blown away. We warned Robert but he scoffed at us. We set up a surveillance for the Saturday on which the attempt was to be made. Our men must have been spotted, because Robert made his collection call and left with no problem.

However, Robert took our warning more seriously than he had indicated. He now went about armed. He also began taking his mother with him on his rounds, in the belief—imparted to him by Harry—that the Men of Honor never kill anyone who is in the company of dear old mom, a theory that had already been disproved in the Tamburrino murder but in which Robert still had a touching faith.

On December 6, Robert and his mother went to visit Harry in the slammer. For this outing, Robert was not carrying a weapon. (Prison officials tend to look askance on armed visitors.) He and his mother arrived back home around ten o'clock in the evening. Robert got out of the driver's seat and walked over to the passenger side to open the door for his mother. As he did, two men, tall, athletically built, 36-year-old Francis "Faffy" Iannarella and squat fiftyish Charley White Iannece, came advancing out of the shadows toward him. Faffy was carrying a sawed-off shotgun. The defenseless Robert lit off for the house; not daring to take the time to fumble around for his keys, he dashed around the side and into the backyard, which had a chain-link fence that he tried to climb over. He was at the top and about to jump into the alley behind when Faffy arrived. Unlike the Salvy Testa shooting in which eight of nine pellets hit their target but none fatally, here Faffy missed with eight of his, but the ninth entered through the back of Robert's head. He tumbled down from the fence, dead.

Robert's mother had chased after Faffy—Charley White had gone back to the car—screaming at him, and she arrived in the yard just in time to see her son's murder. Faffy, who can be quite a charming fellow when he's not killing people, turned and whacked her across the side of the face with the shotgun, using such force that the barrel broke off from the stock. (Faffy apparently had not heard of any Mafia bylaws concerning mothers.) Leaving her to lie next to her dead son—she survived—he ran back to the front of the house, got into the car with Charley White, and drove off.

A week or so later, on a weekday morning, I was on my way to South Philadelphia and was passing the corner of Eighth and Sansom when I saw police sergeant Walter Coughlin and several of his men confronting three pedestrians. I got out of the car to help Coughlin. Being frisked were Salvy Testa, Crazy Phil Leonetti and Larry "Yogi" Merlino, the younger brother of Scarfo's underboss, Chuckie Merlino.

Finding no weapons on them and having no charge at the moment to hold them on, we let them go. I drove off; Coughlin and his men left the scene. According to a witness, the threesome then proceeded along Jewelers Row until they reached the store owned by Enrico, Mario Riccobene's son, who always gave discounts on merchandise to mob members and associates.

Like that of most of the Sansom Street stores, the front door to Enrico's was kept locked. A guard, who was a Riccobene associate, answered their buzz, recognized them, asked them their business. "We want to see Enrico," explained Salvy with a pleasant smile and a wave of his good hand; he was still having trouble with the one that had taken the eight pellets from Joey Pedulla. The guard relocked the door and turned to ask Enrico if he should admit the Scarfo-ites. Enrico said no and walked to the back of the store. The guard relayed the message to Salvy, who didn't seem upset by the rejection; he and his pals left.

Enrico had, by now, gone into the store's vault. He was holding a gun. He must have listened to see if the men had gained access. When he heard nothing, he must have guessed they weren't going to get him. Not this time. He lifted the gun. They had murdered his father's friend, Sammy. They had tried to kill his father. They had tried to kill his uncle Harry. They had just murdered his uncle Robert. They had nearly murdered his grandmother. He placed the gun against his temple. He pulled the trigger. He was 27 years old.

13
Nicky Pockets a Mayor and the Wiseguy Sings

By the time of Enrico Riccobene's suicide in December 1983, a number of changes had taken place in the Scarfo crime organization that were unrelated to the war with the Riccobene faction. One of these was that Scarfo bought himself a mayor, a second was the rise in the ranks of two hoodlums who had hitherto been nonentities, and a third was the fall from power of a talented mob figure, Raymond Martorano. The buying of the mayor had the greatest immediate impact, but the other two events were eventually to play greater roles in determining the fate of Scarfo and his gang.

* * *

Scarfo, even as he was terrorizing the Philadelphia mobsters into obedience, had not been ignoring the profit potential of his home base, Atlantic City.

A Scarfo enterprise that federal and New Jersey agencies had long been keeping under scrutiny was Scarf, Inc., the cement firm. Scarfo's nephew Phil Leonetti served as its president, and presumably its principal purpose was to provide a legitimate source of income for himself and his uncle. How legitimate that income was remains uncertain. The company picked up contracts for five of the first nine casinos constructed as well as for a state-subsidized housing project in Atlantic City, but no indictments alleging extortionate influence were forthcoming.

Much more substantive information about wrongdoing was raised regarding two businesses that shared quarters with Scarf, Inc.: Bayshore Rebar and its parent, Nat Nat, Inc. Both of these companies were owned by Scarfo underboss Chuckie Merlino and his brother Larry, and they dominated the steel reinforcement business in Atlantic City. Between 1979 and 1986, they picked up millions of dollars in casino and publicly funded contracts obtained from the Atlantic City government. When the New Jersey Gaming Commission lifted Bayshore's and Nat Nat's permits to continue seeking casino work, charging undue influence, G&H Steel allegedly became a front through which the Merlinos continued to make bids. According to the New Jersey Commission on Investigation, G&H Steel was also involved in a scheme with Nat Nat to defraud ironworkers of their health and welfare pension benefits.

Scarfo and his cohorts, however, never appear to have made an effort to take over the construction business. Scarfo's diffidence on that score can probably be attributed to his willingness to defer to the New York mobs, which had staked out most of the construction turf for themselves. But Scarfo was hardly diffident elsewhere. By 1982, he held the major casino union, the Hotel Workers, in the palm of one hand and the government of Atlantic City in the other.

His access to the municipal government stemmed from an event that occurred at Giovanni's Restaurant in Folsom, New Jersey, in December 1981. There, a number of Scarfo associates, including Al Daidone and Teamster boss Frank Lentino, met with the brother of former New Jersey state legislator Michael Matthews. An envelope containing $125,000 in cash was handed to the brother (who apparently was unaware of the content, and was never charged for any crime) for forwarding to Michael Matthews. The payment's purpose was to buy the future mayor of Atlantic City. When Matthews took over that office early in 1982, he proceeded to supply to Scarfo and his associates advance information on the sites of proposed new casinos. This insider knowledge permitted Scarfo to buy highly valuable land in and around the sites cheaply from unsuspecting owners. Not all the owners, however, were eager to sell, especially at the prices Scarfo was offering. When that happened, the mob's good friend in the mayor's seat had the recalcitrant owner's property upwardly reassessed to levels that made the taxes virtually confiscatory; that usually worked.

Owning the mayor could have benefits other than those derived from land speculation. Legislation could be influenced, particularly the passage of favorable zoning variances. Licensing and inspection regulations could be altered to fit the mob's needs, and selective enforcement of liquor laws could also come in handy. Bars that the mob openly owned or in which it had a secret financial interest would be free from regulation even when they were—as often was the case—bust-out joints featuring prostitutes and watered drinks.

A bar that the Mafia was interested in buying but that the owner didn't want to sell, on the other hand, would be repeatedly cited for violations, with threats of closing it down. When the mobsters next came to see the owner, who recognized why he was being harassed, he would be likely to prove amenable to whatever deal the goons offered him.

A key player in this and other Scarfo schemes was the 70-year-old Lentino. A long-time ally of Bruno and Harry Riccobene, allegedly involved in Bruno's construction business extortions in Philadelphia, Lentino had retired in 1979 from Teamsters Local 158. He then moved to Atlantic City, where he became employed as a "consultant" to Al Daidone's Bartenders Union, which was expanded into the Hotel Workers Union, among its members the security guards who had been the subject of Bruno's and McCullough's earlier organizing efforts. Because of its capacity to call members out on strike, costing casinos millions upon millions of dollars in profits, the union was able to extort contracts for mob-related concessionaires such as the Poultry King (whose exploits have been described in a previous chapter).

Quite apart from its value in shaking down the casinos, the Hotel Workers Union was a growth enterprise for the mob. In the days before the casinos, Atlantic City hotels had about 4,000 unionized employees; by 1990, that figure had risen to approximately 30,000, each of whose employers paid into the Health and Welfare benefits fund, always a fecund source for money to be skimmed by criminal hands.

Business might have been thriving for Scarfo, but for most of 1983 he wasn't on hand to watch it grow. His enforced hiatus came about as a consequence of the Falcone murder in 1979.

The mob hanger-on Joseph Salerno (who had witnessed Scarfo's salivating "I love this; I love it" as he peered down at Falcone's body), afraid he'd be next, had run to the Atlantic City police with the story of the murder. Scarfo, Leonetti and Larry Merlino were arrested on homicide charges. Soon afterward, when Salerno disappeared into the Witness Protection Program, Scarfo attempted to extract revenge on him by proxy. One evening, the Narducci brothers, dressed in jogging clothes, appeared at the office of a motel in Wildwood Crest, New Jersey, managed by Salerno's father. When the elder Salerno, who had no crime connections, answered the door, they shot him in the throat, leaving him for dead. (He survived.)

At the Falcone murder trial, the ever-helpful Lentino supplied Scarfo with an alibi, and the jury apparently chose not to believe Salerno's testimony. All three defendants were found not guilty.

Despite getting away with murder in the Falcone case (temporarily—that crime would come back to haunt Scarfo years later), his luck did not always hold out. During the course of the investigation of Falcone's death, Scarfo, who at that time hadn't yet bought the mayor, was subjected to the embarrassment of a search of his home at 26 Georgia Avenue. While police did not turn up the murder weapon, they did find a .22 Derringer. Since Scarfo was a convicted felon—a result of the murder of the longshoreman Dugan in 1963—he was not permitted to own a gun. He was charged and convicted on the weapon possession charge. After a lengthy appeals process ended, early in 1983 he was shipped to La Tuna Prison in Texas to spend the next eleven months. Despite the distance from his home base, Scarfo continued to give out orders, through visitors. By then he had in place a cadre of men who had good reason to be loyal to him while he was away.

Among them were the Young Executioners. Even though almost all of them had been born with Mafia silver spoons in their mouths, under Scarfo they had advanced more rapidly than they would have in the conservative days of Angelo Bruno. In large part because of the killings in which they participated, their gambling books were enhanced and bulged with profits; their drug territories were expanded. They hero-worshipped the Little Guy.

Within the Scarfo orbit, however, could also be found a sizable number of middle-aged Philadelphia gangsters, like

Chickie Ciancaglini and Charley White Iannece, who had long careers in crime prior to Scarfo's ascendancy and had never been part of Scarfo's Atlantic City inner circle (as were nephew Phil Leonetti, the Merlino brothers, Nick the Blade Virgilio and Saul Kane). The middle-aged Philadelphians knew Scarfo from back in the days when he was just a street punk. They didn't like him, but as long as they paid him proper financial respect, they thrived financially, too. It was two thugs from this group, Thomas DelGiorno and Nicholas Caramandi, who were to take center stage in the years immediately ahead. As I recall, they first began to show up in our surveillance reports with increasing frequency by no later than 1983, which was about when I got to know both of them. Neither impressed me then, save in the sense that taken together, they made up a kind of composite mobster, exemplars, as it were, of the Mafia working class.

By 1983, the swarthy "Nicky Crow" Caramandi was 48 years old. Below average height, he was a Damon Runyon character, slouching along in showy threads, talking gravelly throated mobster lingo out of the side of his mouth. In the pre-Scarfo days, the caricature Caramandi had been a low-level hood but an active one. Based on his own bragging—and he may not have exaggerated by much—he had participated in 300 burglaries, two robberies and twenty credit card scams, and on one occasion had attempted to shake down a clergyman. His pals in crime were contemporaries like Charley White Iannece and Junior Staino, the latter a member of the old Lilian Reis burglary gang (Junior and Lil lived together). Like Caramandi, Iannece and Staino improved their fortunes when Scarfo became boss, in part because Scarfo murdered so many people who were ahead of them on the ladder of success—and ability.

The fate of "Pat the Cat" Spirito was a case in point. The clever Cat had been Caramandi's patron. When Caramandi and Charley White killed The Cat on Scarfo's orders, they were permitted to take over part of his extensive gambling operation. The Cat killing was Caramandi's first; with it he made his bones.

Soon afterward, he was initiated into the Society of the Men of Honor, which, he complained, carried with it "responsibilities." He had to carry out orders, and all his activities were closely monitored as they hadn't been in the past, making it difficult for him to cheat on the amount of tribute he paid. (Victor DeLuca later told me he didn't want to become a member for that same reason.) As The Crow once summarized it to me, being a member "took a lot of the fun out of being a gangster," and he looked back nostalgically to the carefree days when he and Charley White and Junior were "doing scams."

Becoming a made-member also brought about a closer association with Scarfo, which caused The Crow no end of worry. "You never knew how to act around him," he was once heard to say. "If you said hello to him before he greeted you, he might think you was bein' rude, but if you didn't speak, he might get mad at that, too."

Caramandi's basic problem was that while he was making more money than ever before, he was also much more insecure than ever before.

Following Pat the Cat's murder, the Organized Crime Task Force received intelligence that Caramandi was the person who had lured Pat to his death, having been chosen for that role because Pat trusted him. Consequently, we obtained a search warrant for Caramandi's South Philadelphia apartment, where he was living with a girlfriend. When I arrived there with several of our men, I found the woman had left little notes for The Crow. The one in the living room read, "Nick, turn out the lights when you leave." The one in the bedroom read, "Nick, pick up your clothes." The one in the kitchen: "Nick, put the milk away, please." The one in the bathroom: "Nick, *please* flush the toilet when you're done." When I got to know Caramandi better, I could understand why she found it advisable to leave little reminders about.

More competent than The Crow, if meaner, was little Tommy DelGiorno. Born in 1940, DelGiorno wasn't even Scarfo's height and weighed no more than 130 pounds. He had gotten his start in crime, probably while a teenager, as a numbers runner for Frank Sindone, who, over the years, grew to trust Tommy Del and eventually made him a partner in his gambling business. The garrulous Sindone frequently entertained Tommy Del with accounts of the history of the Philadelphia mob, stories which Del, years later, in an expansive mood, related to me.

When Sindone was murdered in the fall of 1980, DelGiorno continued to attend to the numbers business, in which he had the reputation of running a "clean" book. (This meant he cheated neither his mob superiors nor his customers.) He was, however, ambitious for better things, and when Scarfo came along, he found favor with the Little Guy by dancing constant attendance on him. His chances for advancement were stymied by the fact that he had not yet committed a murder. Scarfo provided the opportunity, in the fall of 1981, when he decided to eliminate tough Johnny Calabrese, who had refused to pay tribute to "that dwarf in Atlantic City." DelGiorno and Faffy Iannarella (the goon who later killed Robert Riccobene and smashed in the side of Robert's mother's face with the murder weapon), shot Calabrese in the back five times as Calabrese was leaving Cous' Little Italy (which, by now, DelGiorno owned).

With the murder impediment to his progress removed, Tommy Del was initiated into the Mafia some months later and quickly was named capo. Under Scarfo's favor, his gambling empire grew rapidly, so that Del was soon paying Scarfo some $300,000 a year in tribute, suggesting his own profits were in the multimillions. While the other five Philadelphia capos may not have been turning over that amount, the likelihood is that Scarfo's income from the six of them would have exceeded a million dollars a year on gambling rake-offs alone by 1983.

Despite or perhaps because of his diminutive build, Tommy Del, once he had the power of the mob behind him, developed an aggressive, bullying personality. His character, I thought, was well caught in an episode that occurred in a tavern frequented by gangsters. Law enforcement people, including me, showed up there, too, as part of my plan that we always be visible to the gangsters we were pursuing.

One evening, one of the Task Force members, a man 6' 1", weighing 210 pounds, was seated at the bar nursing a beer when Tommy Del came swaggering up to him. Said Tommy, "If you didn't have that fuckin' badge and gun, I'd knock the shit out of you." To Tommy's alarm, my colleague reached inside his coat pocket, took out his badge and gun and laid them on the bar. Giving Tommy a big welcoming grin, he said, "Take your best shot." Without another word, Tommy Del slunk off.

Organized crime families are filled with men like the dullish Caramandi and the obsequious bully DelGiorno. Initially motivated by greed, and later by a loyalty to their rulers that is based, in large part, upon their fear of what would befall them if they were thought disloyal, they follow the same advice that Sam Rayburn gave to politicians: They get along by going along.

Raymond "Long John" Martorano (my number-one suspect as the man who hired Willard Moran to kill John McCullough) was a different kind of mob politician and, in his capacity for initiating evil, a much more dangerous one. Nearly six feet tall, his most notable features were his glittery eyes and a spade beard that gave him a Mephistophelian appearance. Martorano did not become a made-member until late in his career. He neither sought nor held any formal office—not underboss, not consigliere, not even capo—but as the mob's minister without portfolio, he wielded more power, for many years, than did those who held such titles. He was the confidant, the courtier who advised the mighty.

For him, as I read him, murder was a matter of statecraft, its beneficiary not the mob but himself.

He began the practice of his art with Angelo Bruno. By providing Bruno with a legal income as a cigarette salesman for his John's Vending Company, he bound himself to Bruno and Bruno to him. In serving Bruno, no task seemed too inconsiderable for him, as exemplified by his picking up Bruno and Kossman on the night of Bruno's death rather than having his driver perform that chauffeuring task. Because Bruno rarely hobnobbed with the troops, Martorano's access to the Don—which he made sure everyone knew about—gave him credibility when he declared himself to be Bruno's spokesman. The Don wants this done or that, he'd say. Some of the orders he gave may have come from Bruno, others not, but since no one could be sure when he was talking for Bruno and when for himself, he tended to be obeyed in all matters. He was much disliked and few would have been unhappy to see him dead.

Martorano was, however, also the consummate survivor. Among the alleged conspirators who plotted Bruno's death, he alone escaped with his life, and was one of the few Bruno lieutenants to emerge stronger than before, becoming whisperer-in-the-ear to the new don, Phil Testa. It was he, according to my information, who advised Testa that McCullough would have to be eliminated, thereby positioning himself, through his alliance with Daidone, to strengthen his own hand in Atlantic City casino unionizing activities.

It was Martorano, too, who, immediately after Testa's death, swore his fealty to Scarfo and informed him of who his enemies were. Evidence suggests he was the one who provoked Scarfo's wrath against Calabrese by telling him of the "dwarf" insult, which Calabrese may never have uttered. Calabrese's body was barely cold before there was a new boss of his meth operation: Raymond Martorano. Martorano's eagerness to help Scarfo rid himself of Harry Riccobene had, at least in part, the same self-service in mind. We now know that Martorano's long-standing plan was to gain control of the entire supply of P2P, the chemical necessary for the making of meth. Riccobene, who had his own sources for meth, stood in his way.

Martorano's years in crime had made him rich; one law enforcement estimate put his fortune at around $10 million. Yet, like Harry Riccobene, he had no interest in retiring and spending it. My impression of Martorano, rather, is that to him, unlike the frugal Harry, money was not important in itself but rather served as the symbol of how successfully he had played the game. I doubt he could have let go of the game no matter how wealthy he became.

Despite his associations with the mob going back to at least the early 1950s, Martorano did not become a made-member until shortly after December 1980.

For how that happened, our storyteller becomes the swaggering gunsel, Willard Moran, Jr., the murderer of John McCullough.

Moran went to trial for the McCullough homicide in July of 1982. Primarily because of the testimony by Howard Dale Young and the ballistics evidence that showed the shell casing in Moran's basement had come from the murder weapon, he was found guilty by a jury and sentenced to death.

His conviction had the effect on Moran that I had hoped it would. Within a month, he phoned FBI agent John Louden, who had interviewed him following his arrest. After talking to Moran, Louden called me and told me Moran wanted to make a deal, his life in return for naming who had hired him. I got in touch with Deputy District Attorney Joe Murray, who had prosecuted Moran. He agreed that if Moran gave us information leading to the arrest of his confederate or confederates, he would recommend to the court that Moran's sentence be commuted to life imprisonment. No guarantee, just a recommendation.

With only that promise in hand, I had Willard brought down from prison to meet with me. He appeared palpably terrified, much as he had during my interrogation of him on the day I arrested him. The last bubble of wiseguy arrogance was gone. Life, which he had so casually taken away from John McCullough, was now exceedingly precious to him.

He gave me what I wanted, too. He gave me Al Daidone. He gave me Raymond Martorano.

As Moran told the story, the opportunity to participate in a mob hit had been broached to him, probably sometime in October 1980, at a Philadelphia bar called Impressions, which was owned by Daidone, Martorano and Martorano's hulking lackey, Frank Vadino.

At the meeting, to which Moran had been brought by Daidone, Martorano licked Moran all over with flattery. He'd long had his eye on him, he lied; he thought Moran was promising; he had an opening on his team for a driver-body-guard and Moran might just be the fellow for the job. That is, he would if he could prove himself. There was, it seemed, a murder that had to be done. Puffing himself up like Mr. Toad, Moran vowed he would prove his ability as a killer. Meanwhile, Daidone fumed. Moran was his discovery, his private thug, and he didn't appreciate Martorano's co-opting his protege. Shortly after the meeting, Daidone sharply reminded Moran, "Willard, don't forget me. I introduced you."

A week or so later, at lunchtime, Daidone took Moran to the Rickshaw Inn in Camden. Standing inside the entrance, Daidone nodded to a table where two men were eating. "Remember the brush haircut guy," Daidone murmured to Moran, who nodded and studied the man he now knew was to be his victim. (The other person at the table with McCullough, I subsequently learned, was his good friend Frank Sheeran, a Teamsters Union official, who not long afterward was convicted on labor racketeering charges and sentenced to 18 years in prison.)

It was another several weeks before Moran learned McCullough's name and that he had to be eliminated because his union activities in Atlantic City were threatening Phil Testa's own unionizing plans there. On hand for one of the meetings at which the murder was plotted, according to Moran, was then-capo of Atlantic City and Phil Testa's right-hand man, Nick Scarfo.

Moran apparently had no idea of McCullough's prominence in Philadelphia; the publicity the killing received, he told me, amazed him. To him, McCullough only meant benefits. Martorano had promised him a new and exclusive drug territory in South Jersey as payment for his services, and that was something to think about. But much more important to Moran, as he made clear to me, was the honor of it. He wanted to be known as Martorano's trusted aide. He wanted to be known as a contract killer.

Daidone also saw cash and honor coming his way with the carrying out of Testa's order. His participation in McCullough's death would make his bones (the honor) and let him take over McCullough's unionizing efforts in Atlantic City (the cash). Martorano would also find the mob-authorized murder to be his own entrance ticket to Mafia membership, but he may not have included in his plans any long-term enjoyment by Daidone of the fruits of his labors.

At about five o'clock on the evening of December 16, 1980 (Moran told me), he pulled into the parking lot of the Pub Restaurant at the Airport Circle outside Camden. He was dressed in a three-quarter windbreaker jacket and a visored cap and had dyed his brown hair red for the occasion. He had with him the .22 caliber Ruger with the silencer and his .38 automatic. He walked over to a Lincoln parked nearby in which were seated Martorano and Daidone, and got into the back. The three men then drove to Philadelphia over the Benjamin Franklin Bridge, which spanned the Delaware River. Once in the city, they turned north until they reached a secluded side street where Daidone had earlier parked the van. Moran transferred from the Lincoln to the van and followed the Lincoln into Northeast Philadelphia. There they made their second stop at Stein's Florists, where Martorano purchased the two poinsettia plants. He delivered them to Moran, and their little caravan started off again.

When the two vehicles arrived at Foster Street, Mc-Cullough's car was nowhere in sight, but they were confident their target would show up. (They apparently had learned—I have never found out how—that McCullough's scheduled meeting for that evening would be canceled.) They turned off Foster, circled around and returned to it, and this time were rewarded by seeing McCullough as he got out of his car. The Lincoln continued on; Moran parked the van and, pulling his cap down over his forehead, walked up to the McCullough house with the first of the two poinsettias. That delivery, he explained, was for reconnaissance purposes. "I wanted to see who was in the house," he told me. "I was prepared to kill everyone there to get McCullough."

When he saw during the delivery that only McCullough and his wife Audrey were home, he returned to the van, secreted the Ruger in the top of the second box, and went back to the house. I asked him why, after he murdered McCullough, he hadn't also killed Audrey. "I would have," he said, "but she was so hysterical, I knew she'd never identify me."

After committing the murder, he drove the van to the parking lot. Leaving it there, he got into the Lincoln. Nobody spoke. Martorano had been firm in his instructions on that; he always believed it safest to assume that any car he was driving was bugged by law enforcement. When they were halfway across the Franklin Bridge on their way back to New Jersey, they stopped. Moran got out, threw the Ruger over the side of the bridge into the river, returned to the car, and they continued in silence until they arrived back at the Pub parking lot, where all three got out. Daidone asked: "Is he dead?"

Moran told me that question annoyed him. It was as if

Daidone doubted his professionalism. "I know," he answered. "I put six in his head."

Moran then strolled back to his car and drove to the Admiral Bar, where Young saw him; and just as Young said, he ordered the three drinks, throwing the third against the wall in honor of the guy with the brush haircut. With his parting comment about watching the eleven o'clock news, he left. He felt great.

Following the murder, Moran told me, he had several meetings with Daidone and Martorano. At one point, fearing arrest, arrangements were made, he said, for payments to come to him for his defense. Daidone's Uncle Bennie was to act as middleman, sending the money through Moran's wife, Debbie, who cooperated with law authorities.

Martorano apparently had been pleased with his McCullough performance, Moran said, because Martorano assigned him to commit another murder. The victim this time was to be the Greek mobster, Steve Booras. Moran agreed to do the job, and on the appointed evening in early May of 1981, he arrived at the Meletis Restaurant, where Booras was having dinner as a guest of Martorano's. Moran, however, had to scrub the mission, he said, when he spotted a police patrol wagon parked nearby. When he read in the newspapers several weeks later that Booras had been killed at the Meletis, he was furious and called Diadone to find out why the hit had been given to someone else. As he recalled, Daidone replied, "That's the way these things work out sometimes."

Moran's information about the Booras murder surprised me. As far as I knew, Martorano had never been suspected of being involved, perhaps because it seemed inconceivable that even someone like him would bring his wife and her three girlfriends to a site where he knew a murder was to take place. However, I could not imagine any reason that Moran would make up the story which, as with everything else he told us, tested as true when we polygraphed him.

The murders at the Meletis had not been my case originally, nor had the case since come under the auspices of the Task Force—no reason it should; it was not supposed to be an organized crime hit, and besides, it was marked closed with the arrest and conviction of Ferber. I thus had no authority to do anything with Moran's statement other than bring it to the attention of Sergeant Danny Rosenstein, the detective who had collared Ferber. He thanked me, and I gave the matter no further thought. Once Ferber confessed, as everyone was still sure he would, if he named Martorano, we could deal with *his* involvement in those murders. Meanwhile, I had Martorano on the McCullough assassination. That was the bird in hand, and I decided to take a look at the bird myself.

In my travels around South Philadelphia for the Task Force, I had picked up a good deal of information about Martorano but had not yet met him. He was serving a sentence of ten years—he would be eligible for parole in three—on the P2P conviction that had resulted from his meeting with the informant Ronald Raiton in Rittenhouse Square in 1981. After dispatching two members of our team to arrest Daidone, I drove with one of my detectives to the federal prison in Lewisburg, Pennsylvania, where Martorano was incarcerated. During the course of the 150-mile trip back to Philadelphia, where he was to be arraigned on the McCullough charge, I hoped to take my own measure of Long John.

I got little from him verbally. He had been dealing with cops all his adult life, was well versed in the way of the Mafia and its rule of silence. Thus, to the extent he talked at all, it was on safe subjects. I learned from him, rather to my surprise, that he loved to read, preferring books of nonfiction. He also struck me as a vain man—I noted the little notches from his hair transplant—and a self-centered one. I had no feeling that he disliked me—apparently I was right about that; he later sent me a gift of a book he'd particularly enjoyed, *Cry of the Kalahari*. His attitude toward police was typical of the older mafiosos; he saw cops as doing their job, just as he was doing his. (The young mobsters tended to be more surly.) My conclusion was that Long John was unlikely to become an informant. None of the telltale signs were there —no wiseguy, no bravado, no little cracks of fear. I would have been happy to make a deal with him, too, but only if he gave me Scarfo.

But movement like that from Martorano, I judged, was still a long way off and probably depended entirely on his not only being convicted of McCullough's murder but sentenced to death for it. Daidone, I suspected, was the weaker of the two (between them I would have preferred to make a deal with Daidone—he had less blood on him), but I was convinced that he also didn't have the amount of knowledge that Martorano did. Long John could break the Scarfo mob wide open, and while he was at it, clear up murders and other crimes that had occurred long before Scarfo's rise to power, probably including Bruno's murder.

But even if Martorano and Daidone never talked, convicting them for the McCullough killing would be a major step forward for the Organized Crime Task Force in its efforts to dismantle the Scarfo organization. Not only would we be removing permanently two of Scarfo's most trusted aides, but we would simultaneously make the remaining members feel vulnerable, as they had not felt before. The more exposed they sensed themselves, the more likely it was that we'd gain defectors.

On the Riccobene side of the ledger, convicting Harry the Hunchback for the murder of Scarfo's consigliere, Frank Monte, could provide the same good dividends. Mobsters were accustomed to doing stretches in prison for relatively minor felonies—it went with the territory—but not murder, and it was the wages of murder that I was anxious to teach them.

14
The Riccobenes
Roll Over

I may have been anxious to make an object lesson out of Martorano and Daidone, but I also had to be patient. The usual delays set in; 1983 passed without their going to trial, and by the beginning of 1984 a date still hadn't been set. As for the murder by the Riccobenes of consigliere Monte, my only source continued to be the Pagan motorcycle gang leader Jimmy DeGregorio. But he, with his second-hand and drug-hazy recollections, couldn't possibly be used as a stand-alone witness. To get our indictment, we needed one—preferably several—of the conspirators in the Monte hit on our side.

My only prospects on that score were Harry's team of Joseph Pedulla and Victor DeLuca. They had been convicted for the Italian Market shooting of Salvy Testa, but 1983 was drawing to an end and they still hadn't been sentenced, as posttrial motions continued to be heard. Both were facing the probability of substantial prison terms. The seriousness of the crime had nothing to do with its consequences—we had plenty of assaults worse in degree of victim injury every day—but with the brazen circumstances. Pedulla had blasted away with a shotgun in broad daylight in a crowded area where innocent people could have been killed. The shooting itself had then been followed by the high-speed escape attempt, which jeopardized the safety of still more citizens. Besides, the shooting had made headlines, as had the subsequent bribery scandal. High profile time. The right judge would throw the book at them.

Prior to their trials, by way of a fishing expedition, I had Pedulla and DeLuca brought down separately to my office in the Federal Building. Like Martorano, the hulking DeLuca had no tough-guy swagger, which suggested he really was tough. Neither did he give me much to probe with. He had a son and a daughter, he told me, but they didn't live with him; he was separated from his wife. My sense of him was that of a self-contained person. Until he had teamed up with Pedulla, he'd usually worked alone, and considering his bulk and menacing appearance, he probably didn't need any help. He had one hero, Angelo Bruno, "who did things right." But that was about all I got. It would be a long hard road toward any zone of trust with Victor DeLuca.

Joey Pedulla surprised me. For someone who had, I believed, committed one coldblooded murder (Monte's) and attempted an equally atrocious one (Salvy Testa's), he struck me as having a sensitive, introspective character, a man who was deeply troubled, perhaps even shocked at himself. As our conversation went on for three hours, never touching on his crimes, I became aware that his center of concern was his family. He had a wife with whom he was happy (somewhat unusual in mob sociology, where the men "respect" their wives, but if they have close emotional relationships with any females at all, it is with their mistresses). Joey also had two children whom—not so much from what he said but the way he said it—he obviously adored. He also seemed to be a responsible man in broader family terms; he was the principal provider for his mother and sister as well as his wife and children. He did not hide his worry about what would happen to the adults of his family if he went to prison, but I sensed it was the children that counted most. "I don't want to miss them growing up, Lieutenant Friel," he said. I decided he was promising.

That Joey was likely to miss the growing up became clear to him following Victor's sentencing in the Testa shooting, which finally took place on January 5, 1984. Victor was sent away for 17½ to 25 years, of which he'd have to serve at least the minimum. And Victor hadn't even shot Testa. Joey had. He had to wonder what sentence he'd get.

He didn't find out. Not right away. I went to see the trial judge, Lynne Abraham, a former deputy DA. I told her I thought it was possible Pedulla could become a cooperative witness; as long as he wasn't sentenced I had room to maneuver in making him a deal. She agreed to the delay I requested.

I immediately brought Joey down to see me again. With Victor's sentence before him, I sprang the Monte killing on him. I told him we knew he was the shooter and were making a case against him. "If we convict you on that," I advised him, "you'll never again see a day when bars aren't between you and the sunlight, Joey."

He professed not to be worried about that possibility, and I hoped he didn't realize how right he was. Nevertheless, I didn't think it would do any harm to let him know I knew he had killed Monte. He couldn't be positive I didn't have evidence. He couldn't be positive someone wasn't talking.

During this meeting with Pedulla, more so than in the first family-oriented one, I became impressed by the quality of his intellect. I'd heard he was something of a mathematical genius. My own impression was of a man with the capacity to quickly grasp abstract concepts, a hallmark of intelligence which—except in the brilliant Ronald Raiton—I'd not found in the criminal world.

Wrapped around that mind was the emotional persona— he wept when talking about his children—that I had observed at our first meeting. His volatility, however, apparently had never displayed a violent bent until he fell under the sway of the massive, less articulate Victor, after which he became more violent than Victor.

Whatever Freudian conjectures that chronology might suggest, Joey's escalating violence, I gathered (from that and later interrogations of him), proceeded solely from what he saw as a simple and dangerous situation. Scarfo's forces were out to kill him and his boss, Harry Riccobene, who had always been good to him and to whom he owed loyalty. He saw himself as Harry's soldier, and in war (just as he'd been taught when in the Marines), you don't try to reason with the enemy, you kill him. His various acts were merely the happenstances of battle. He did not view them as criminal. His regret and shock, therefore, had nothing to do with the acts themselves but with the enormous effects they could have for his family. He hadn't thought of those before he acted, and they were what perturbed him now.

Focusing on his regret, I told him he could get out of the worst of his troubles by telling us the complete truth of the Monte murder. He'd have to do time—I wasn't going to mislead him about that, I said—but I indicated it wouldn't be so much time that he'd miss all the growing years of his children; and he would again, relatively soon, be in a position to support his family. I didn't suggest how much time he'd do; I had nothing specific in mind at that point, and he didn't ask me.

By now I was fairly convinced of what his decision would be, but I'd also reached with him the delicate stage in which the desired resolution could be jeopardized by trying to force it. The time had come to leave him alone to ponder and determine his own fate.

Less than four weeks after Victor's sentencing, on February 1, 1984, he called me: "Frank," he said, "I want to talk to you." He hadn't ever called me by my first name before. From that, I knew what his decision was.

Since we hadn't the faintest hope of making arrests, much less getting convictions on the Monte murder, without Joey, the fact that he was the shooter became irrelevant. The only issue was how good a deal it was necessary to offer him. Because of his children, it would have to be short, nothing like ten or twenty years; he'd never dump on Harry or Victor for terms like these. Increasingly, as I thought about our total situation—not just the Monte case—Pedulla struck me as offering an opportunity we'd not had before. The previous deals we'd arranged—the life sentence for Teddy Di Pretoro, the promise the DA would move to vacate Moran's death penalty—had been favorable for them, considering the magnitude of their crimes. But they had not exactly been enticements for others to come forward. Joey could be the belled sheep I was looking for. He could tinkle out our message to other organized crime soldiers that they could do well, too, if they gave us their bosses before somebody else did. First in, first out.

I discussed sentencing ideas with Dennis O'Callaghan, but ultimately the responsibility for a recommendation was mine. I hit on four years. That seemed to have the right bell ring to it, four years total for the shooting of Monte and Salvy Testa. Could anything ring more enticingly than that?

Joey and his lawyer, Lou Ruch, a former assistant U.S. attorney, agreed to my proposal. Guarantee us that, said Ruch, and you have yourself a cooperative witness.

That was the easy part. When I informed DA Rendell that we could reach an agreement with Pedulla, he objected to the shortness of the sentence—he was worried about public relations repercussions—and insisted we tie Joey in with a full signed confession before we negotiated any deal.

I went back to Joey, described to him Rendell's position. As I expected, he refused to sign. Shrugging his shoulders, he said, "I guess I'll have to take my chances," referring to his sentencing in the Testa shooting.

Almost immediately a new complication entered, one which caused me to reflect (not for the first time) that I had more problems with the good guys than the bad. When Police Commissioner Solomon learned of Rendell's veto of the Pedulla deal, he was furious at what he saw as Rendell's interference with police work. That was a sore subject with Solomon. Recently, Rendell had stripped the police of their authority to place charges against people they arrested, transferring that function to his office, as he had a right to do, and may have been right in doing; but Solomon considered it an insult. This move of Rendell's on the Pedulla deal was more of the same. He called me, John Hogan and Dennis O'Callaghan in to see him. "There will be no negotiations with the DA," he declared. "Don't let him dictate the course of this investigation." As diplomatically as I could, I pointed out that we had no right to finalize any sentencing arrangement; only Rendell could do that. Solomon, who can glare with a glacial authority I've never before or since encountered, repeated: "No negotiations with the DA."

That didn't mean Joey's lawyer couldn't try, but he got no farther than I had. I was now faced with the likelihood that Joey would get at least the same sentence Victor had in the Testa shooting, the Monte murder would remain unsolved, and the only bell anybody would be wearing would be all of us in the Task Force to remind us of how we had failed on the brink of success.

Despite Solomon's orders—I figured he wouldn't mind if

I negotiated and *won*—I went back to see Rendell. At that meeting also present was the head of the Homicide Unit, Arnold Gordon, a very bright, go-by-the-book, law-and-order type. Rendell wouldn't deviate from his stand that Pedulla had to give us a statement before we made any agreement with him, but did compromise by saying I could tell him that the confession wouldn't be used against him in any subsequent trial as long as it was truthful and he testified to its content. On the sentencing issue, Gordon dismissed my four years out of hand. Ten years was the least he'd recommend. I continued to negotiate, and eventually we reached a second compromise. When we got before Judge Abraham, Gordon would argue for his sentence, I for mine.

Gordon had reason to think he'd win on the sentencing. Abraham, who had been one of the toughest prosecutors in the history of the office, was now famed as a judge for her stern sentencing, a reputation she'd hardly tarnished with Victor. But I had hope, too. In my conversation with her when I asked her to hold off sentencing Pedulla, she had indicated she trusted my judgment.

Knowing I had won all the concessions I was going to get from Rendell and Gordon, I got back to Joey with the bad news that law enforcement couldn't guarantee him four years, and that he was still going to have to give us a statement before we would agree to anything. He seemed distraught. He buried his head in his hands. "Joey," I said, "I think this is the right thing for you to do. I'd like you to trust me and trust the compassion of a fair-minded, community-spirited judge, but you've got to know you could get as much as ten years."

His ever-expressive face showed the web of tensions he was feeling, his desperate desire for his family, his guilt at the price of that reunion—informing on Harry and his dear friend Victor. He shook his head back and forth. I waited. He said, "All right, Frank. I trust you."

I stood before Judge Abraham. I made my recommendation; Arnie Gordon made his. Judge Abraham had Joey rise. She sentenced him to 4 years in prison and 16 years of probation. I had my bell and Joey had his deal.

The final step took place a few days later when we trundled him off to federal court to plead him guilty to conspiring to murder Monte under the Racketeer Influenced Corrupt Organization (RICO) statute. (Murder is not a federal crime but can be listed as one of the offenses that goes to make up a RICO conspiracy.) Joey, as had been prearranged through the FBI, received 4 years on that charge, to be served concurrently with his 4-year sentence on the Salvy Testa shooting. (It was through the federal conviction that he and his family became eligible for the Witness Protection Program.) In the end, therefore, Joseph Pedulla got a maximum sentence for shooting Testa that was less than a quarter of Victor DeLuca's minimum for being the driver, and a freebie for killing Monte.

Our bell would ring uselessly, however, if Pedulla's testimony didn't lead to the conviction of Harry Riccobene and the other conspirators in the Monte murder. In that event, those who might think of cooperating when they were arrested would draw back. Testifying against a powerful mob figure like Harry is a risky proposition at best; should that leader go free, he becomes more powerful than before, and woe betide the informant then.

And it was far from certain we would win. Pedulla's testimony got us into court. But, like Moran when he agreed to testify against Martorano and Daidone in the McCullough murder trial, Pedulla was a "polluted" witness, someone who could be viewed by a jury as implicating others in order to get a reduced sentence for himself. That, of course, was exactly what was happening, not just a matter of jury impression. (In the instructions on the law the jurors receive, the judge tells them they should be careful about giving credence to a witness who stands to gain personally by giving testimony.)

That was why our chances would be much better if we could add to the number of conspirators ready to testify. I brought the problem up to Joey. He replied, "Let me talk to Victor alone. I think I can convince him to testify."

I rejected that idea, and so did Dennis when I discussed it with him. It was simply too dangerous. Once Victor learned from Joey—assuming he hadn't heard already; that kind of news gets around fast—that Joey had flipped, the huge and powerful Victor might strangle him before we could separate them.

Neither did we have anything attractive to offer Victor in return for his testimony. Except by a pardon from the governor, which was exceedingly unlikely, his present sentence could not be reduced. He'd be in his sixties, possibly seventies, when he got out. Thus, even the dropping of all charges against him on the Monte case would not likely be seen by him as any monumental benefit.

Even so, with nothing to be lost, I brought Victor back to the Federal Building for a talk. The best tactic, I decided, was to be completely open with him. I told him he was about to be arrested in connection with the Monte murder and the conspiracy to kill other Riccobene enemies. His chances of ever getting out of prison again were remote, and in any event, I could do nothing about the term he was already serving. Nevertheless, I went on, and hoped he'd think about cooperating with us as his friend Joey was. "Joey loves you, Victor, like an older brother, but he decided he had to concentrate on saving his family," I explained, "that they came first, and he couldn't do that if he was going to stay in prison for the rest of his life."

Victor mumbled, "I understand."

"You don't hate him for testifying against you?" I asked.

"Nah," said Victor. "I'm not mad at him. A man's got to do what he's got to do."

That was the last reaction I'd expected from the violent hard case I assumed Victor DeLuca to be. I probed a little further. Victor did feel "hurt," he told me, but not by Joey.

His distress, rather, derived from the way "guys I've hung around with all my life turned on me and Harry." It had been an enjoyable life, as Victor perceived enjoyment, and while he had no close friends among them—"we was all in it to make a buck, that's all"—he couldn't understand, he said, how guys like that would now try to kill him and Harry, who was a man of respect. "You don't try to kill guys you've hung with, just because some little jerk in Atlantic City tells ya to," said Victor.

But it wasn't even himself so much, he went on. What got him mad, he said, was when he learned Joey was on Scarfo's death list. "He didn' do nothin' to deserve that." Scarfo, as Victor figured it, must have decided Joey had to be hit because he knew how bright and capable Joey was. (Victor described Joey's intelligence like a proud father bragging about the A's his son got on his report card.) "That was wrong," Victor said. "He shouldn'a held Joey responsible."

I told him I wasn't quite sure what he meant by that. "What's right," Victor said, "is if you have a problem, you oughta take it up with the big guy," meaning himself, "what brought the guy in, not with the guy that got brought in. Like Joey, he's just a numbers guy," Victor explained, "until he meets up with me and becomes my pal and I make him into a murderer."

And that was it, I realized, startled. To Victor, the guilt was his, and Joey, it followed, could not be held accountable for ratting on him, because if it hadn't been for him, Joey never would have been in the position where he was likely to spend the rest of his life away from his family if he didn't talk.

In his way, the leg-breaker Victor DeLuca was one of the most moral men I have ever met.

As he spoke, I felt Victor's sadness, too. He didn't want his fate. "Nobody wants to be in fuckin' jail; I'd do almost any fuckin' thing to get out of it," he said; but he was also resigned. In his heart of hearts, he never believed anyone would do anything for him, and in a way he was pleased that "things could go good for Joey. We been t'rough a lotta things together," he said fondly. I asked him, "Victor, what would you do if I put you and Joey alone together in this room?"

Victor said, "I'd give him a kiss an' wish him well."

At the conclusion of the interview, I went to Dennis. I told him I believed Victor was sincere, but I couldn't be positive. We agreed that we should bring him down from prison one more time before deciding on any meeting with Joey, so that Dennis could join in questioning him and make his evaluation. When Victor arrived, he said, "I don't like you guys doin' this, bringin' me down like this." I assumed that was because he didn't want to talk to us anymore, but I asked him why anyway. (I'd learned by now to always ask questions; sometimes you don't get the obvious answer, and that's what happened now.) He'd just managed, Victor explained, to get himself a cell at the end of the block, and that was important to him: "Those fuckin' assholes play their fuckin' boom boxes all day long," and the noise, he said, isn't as bad in an end cell as it is in the middle of the row. Now that he was called down again, he would probably lose his end cell. I remembered how when I was in the Homicide Unit, I'd sneak out for coffee to avoid its noise for a half hour; the noise in prison was ten times louder, with no way ever to end it, even for a minute.

Dennis asked Victor his feelings about Joey. With a glance at me—hadn't I told Dennis?—Victor said, "Always liked him."

Dennis: "What if we put the two of you together to talk?" (That was the second time that had been brought up, too, and Victor was more cautious this time, asked us why.)

Dennis: "Joe needs to know he's doing the right thing."

Victor: "I wouldn't hurt him, but I doubt very much *I'd* ever testify."

We got no further with him than that. While Victor was being shipped back to prison, I made a phone call there and arranged for him to keep his end cell.

We brought Victor down one more time. We placed him in the only room in our offices that had a window through which we could monitor everything going on. It had another window, too, a big plate glass one. I could visualize Victor picking Joey up and throwing him through it, eight floors down to the ground. That would make for an interesting headline.

But when I brought Joey to the room, he showed no fear. "Victor'd never hurt me," he said.

I opened the door. Joey entered. Victor turned to face him. They stared at one another. Victor came over to Joey, his powerful arms extended. Joey waited for him. Victor put those arms around him. They embraced. He kissed Joey on the cheek.

Then the two men sat and talked. They paid no attention to us. Victor assured Joey that he understood what he was doing and why. After bidding him farewell, Victor left the room. Joey turned to us. He wanted to know what we could do for Victor. I told him, not much, except a concurrent sentence on the Monte charge and—maybe most important —the guarantee of a permanent cell at the end of the row. "Ahh," said Victor, when I told him this, "that's OK." He shrugged his shoulders. "Helps Joey, I'll testify to the truth."

Now I had Victor and Joey. A third member of the Riccobene gang turned informant was to prove more valuable than either of them.

Since July of 1983, Mario Riccobene had been serving his

gambling conviction in the Lewisburg Prison. He was about to get bad news from me. With Joey's and Victor's statements in hand, I had obtained arrest warrants against Mario and Harry Riccobene, Joseph Casdia and Vincent Isabella (who, according to Joey, had supplied the gun he used to shoot Monte), charging them with murder. As I had with Martorano, I drove to Lewisburg to pick up Mario for his Philadelphia arraignment. In so doing, I had nothing particular in mind, but I figured, considering Mario's talkativeness, that during the long trip back, to fill in time as much as anything, he just might drop a few pearls I could use later.

But when we met, I found that Mario's gregariousness was gone. The tragedies, one after the other, that had occurred since he entered prison had exacted their toll. He was distraught and depressed. His dearest friend, Sammy Tamburrino, had been murdered. His brother Robert had been murdered. His mother had been brutally assaulted. And the suicide of his son Enrico was the worst blow. "They killed him," he insisted to me. "I know they killed him." "They" must have come into the vault where Enrico was hiding, he explained, his gaze fixed on me like that of the Ancient Mariner, and shot him. That must have been what happened. Enrico wouldn't kill himself. I tried to convince him that there was no doubt that Enrico had, but he refused to accept it, holding out his hands at me, to push not me but the truth away. It seemed to me that he could deal better with believing his son had been murdered by his family's enemies than with the fact that he had killed himself because of the enemies his family, including his own father, had made.

I felt sorry for Mario, but I also added to his worries. I advised him we had enough evidence to convict him of helping plan the Monte murder, and that we now knew he had been present and even presided over subsequent meetings to plot the murders of Martorano, Salvy Testa and other members of the Scarfo gang. A conviction in the Monte case, I warned him, could lead to the death sentence, and the very best he could hope for was life without parole.

I don't recall any direct response he made to that description of his potential future. He did, however, tell me another of his worries. He was terrified, he said, that Scarfo, unable to get to him in prison, would go after his wife, his daughter and her little boy. His concern wasn't groundless. Scarfo had already done that once, when he had Joe Salerno's father shot after Salerno himself had disappeared into the Witness Protection Program. That was something, Mario said, neither he nor Harry would ever do. They might try to kill an informant, he admitted, "but would never take it out on the family."

I didn't doubt that. While the Riccobenes and their followers were public menaces, I had found that most of them, like Harry himself, were personally likable rogues; they had none of the mean, ugly edge that marked the Scarfo-ites. Thus, when Mario described Scarfo, Salvy Testa and Long John Martorano as "evil" men, I understood what he meant and agreed with the distinction he was making.

By the time we got back to Philadelphia, I had reason to continue my conversation with Mario in my office. As we were approaching the city, in his desperate effort to get out from under the Monte case, he asked me, "What can I do? What can I do? Will you help me?"

I might, I said to him as he sat across from me. But he had to understand we wanted help, too, and we weren't interested in bits and pieces. For openers, he would have to testify against his brother in the Monte trial, and also in any other case in which he might be useful. That meant, I explained, he was going to have to give us a complete and truthful statement about every crime in which he had been involved. If he met those standards, we would advise the judge at sentencing about his cooperation, and place him in the Witness Protection Program while he was in prison and afterward; we would also immediately extend the same protection to his family.

However, I also pointed out to him (and this was part of Joey Pedulla's deal, too) that if, at any time, he refused to testify against anyone, or if we learned he was lying, not only would the deal be off, but we would have the right to use against him in court the confessions he'd made to us about his own illegal activities. If that stage were ever reached, I said, he had to be further aware that protection for his family could be revoked.

In fact, if that situation ever arose, I would have strongly opposed taking away the family's protection, and I'm sure Dennis O'Callaghan would have, too. However, ours were only two votes, and we might not be able to prevail against the Federal Marshal's Office, which runs the Witness Program, and whose personnel, with a few notable exceptions, are so notorious for their self-righteous arrogance—the average gangster is more pleasant company—that even the FBI didn't like to deal with them.

I told Mario to think about all I'd said, and if he concluded he wanted to talk further, to give me a call.

If he did decide to talk, I had a place ready for him, a safe house which the Task Force had rented in a rural, forested area outside Philadelphia. Joey Pedulla was its first guest. With Task Force members on hand at all times to act as guards, I visited Joey there almost daily over, as I recall, about a four-week period. Bit by bit—truth as always came out on the installment plan—I drew him out, adding to my knowledge not only of the Monte hit but of the workings of the gambling business in which Joey was an expert. He was much as I'd found him in my early interrogations, a highly emotional and introspective man who was careful with the facts now that he had decided to reveal them. He'd make an excellent witness.

When it was Victor DeLuca's turn, he took over the house.

By that I mean, during his eight weeks' residence, he became, quite voluntarily, our housekeeper. He made quite a
picture, this hulking man with his prizefighter's punched-in
face, wearing an apron as he did his dusting and vacuuming.
He also cooked our meals, Italian dishes, frequently ringing
up his daughter to get advice on recipes.

Victor's meals were excellent, too, but eating them could
be a problem. Although a city boy, he had developed a pas-
sionate fondness for the animals of the woods, particularly
the possums and raccoons. He had a way with them, too.
They came at his call; he could tell them apart, even gave
them names. While we were at table, he'd hover over us,
warning us "to leave some for the critters." If we didn't
keep digging in, he'd grab our plates from under our raised
forks and rush with them out of doors to summon and feed
his little friends. (This was the same person who told me he
once slit open the belly of a man who'd been murdered near
Scarfo's Hallandale, Florida, mansion and tossed the body
into the Bay of Biscayne in the hope the bloody entrails he'd
exposed would attract sharks so they'd eat the corpse, a novel
way of destroying evidence.)

Often he would call me at my office.

Victor: "What time you gettin' done, Frank?"

Me: "Why?"

Victor: "I'm cookin' somethin' special t'night and it can't
be eaten cold. So I want to know what time you'll be here,
and I don't want any bullshit, and don't invite any of your
drones here unless you tell me, 'cause I'll only have enough
for us."

Or: "Frank, things have to be cooked to the minute. If
you want it al dente, too much cookin' makes it squooshy
and it's not good, so I need to know when you'll be here, or
don't bother comin'."

As a result, I'd feel absolutely terrible if something turned
up at the job and I'd have to call him because I knew how
upset he'd be.

Behind his back, we complained about how he made us feel like ungrateful slobs when we messed up his clean house—we who were his jailers and interrogators, and had him under our control. Occasionally, to make him feel appreciated, we'd take him out to dinner at a nice restaurant, for which the FBI paid.

And all the while, he talked.

In the early afternoon of a sunshine-laden day in April 1984, I arrived at a motel in St. David's, a Philadelphia suburb. When I entered the building, I spotted the plainclothes officers I'd assigned to guard the room in which Mario Riccobene was sitting waiting. He was by now on the verge of consummating a witness agreement with us.

His value for me took a quantum leap forward when, in one of our preliminary conversations, he told me of the dinner meeting with Long John Martorano at Cous' Little Italy Restaurant in which Longy—"I did five"—named McCullough as one of his victims. The trial of Martorano and Daidone for that murder was finally scheduled to begin in June, and Mario's testimony as to Martorano's statement—it's called an "admission against interest"—would strengthen our case significantly.*

Mario also told me that the "Stevie" listed by Longy as one of his victims was Steve Booras. I wasn't surprised to hear this, since, by now, I also had Willard Moran's statement that Martorano had hired him to kill Booras, although he had failed to do so because of the coincidental presence of a police car when he arrived to do the deed. (Throughout my relationship with Moran, this was the one episode in his criminal

---

*As irritating as the delays in bringing criminals to trial can be in Philadelphia, in this instance they worked very much to our advantage. Had Martorano and Daidone been tried in a timely fashion, we wouldn't have had Mario as a witness against them.

career that he always got angry about. He didn't think it was right that Martorano had gone ahead and hired somebody else to murder Booras. It wasn't that he'd lost money by not being allowed to carry out the crime—he wouldn't have gotten paid for it anyway—but he liked to kill people, and it was upsetting to him to have missed an opportunity.)

Mario, however, still had his compunctions about becoming an informant. Before agreeing to do so, he said, he needed the approval of his wife and daughter. "I want them to see," he explained, "that it's so overwhelming for me that I have no other choice." I didn't think he was being entirely truthful in saying that, maybe not even to himself. Organized crime figures almost never consult with their female relatives about their activities, and Mario was no exception. I assumed that his need for their agreement arose from the guilt (and possibly the guilty desire) he felt about testifying against his brother Harry the Hunchback in the Monte trial. If they said he should, he could rationalize that he had done so only for their sakes.

The meeting couldn't take place in prison because of the danger of its being overheard—hence, the secluded motel. I was to be present, to act as the voice of doom. Mario told me he didn't think he could explain how desperate his situation was as well as I could.

When Mrs. Riccobene and their daughter Karen arrived, they had with them Karen's 5-year-old boy. Giving the adults a chance to talk for a few minutes, I turned to the child. Searching around for something to say to him, I finally came up with: "Do you watch Sesame Street? Do you like Big Bird?"

The child considered this for a moment, viewing me solemnly before replying, "I hate cops; don't you?"

I responded, sounding like Big Bird myself, "Why, no, sonny. I think the police can be our friends."

The adults did not seem to have heard this little interchange, which may have been just as well. Almost immediately afterward, Mario turned the floor over to me, saying, "OK, Frank, will you tell them what I'm up against?"

Putting on my most funereal expression, and in a tone of matching sadness, I addressed the women at some length as I outlined the case against their husband and father, concluding with its most likely consequence (which really was highly unlikely), his death in the electric chair.

I let that sink in a moment; then, no less serious of mien but with an upbeat tempo, I gave them hope. Mario had an alternative, I said: cooperation. If he chose that path, he'd not have to face a first-degree murder charge, would be incarcerated not in a state but a federal prison (which, as every crook and his family knows, is the slammer of choice), and would have the Witness Protection Program available to him and—entering now on my peroration—to them, too, immediately, since it was solely Mario's deep concern for their safety that was causing him to even consider taking such a step.

I finished by appealing to wife and daughter to rush to Mario, embrace him, and tell him he had their blessing.

It was, I had no doubt, one of my finer performances. I could see Mario was pleased with it, too; my heart-tugging speech had not only reduced his wife and daughter to tears, but him as well. (The little boy remained silent, engaging, I suspected, in a cops-and-robbers fantasy of his own.) While Mrs. Riccobene did, indeed, give her husband a hug, daughter Karen bravely wiped away her tears (the cause of which I had mistaken) and addressed her father briskly thus: "You're a traitor. Why don't you ever think of me? If you do this, I won't ever be able to hold up my head in South Philadelphia again. I won't be able to go to the beauty parlor or the pizza store. None of the women would talk to me."

When I found my voice—Mario couldn't discover his, and his wife was really crying now—I said, "You realize, Karen,

Mafia Don Nicky Scarfo shows off the flamingos in his Hallandale, Florida, vacation home.

Scarfo and friends in Hallandale, Florida, in the
early 1980s. *Front row, from left:* two sons of Charles
Iannece and the murderers Joseph Ligambi and
Faffy Iannarella. *Second row, from left:* murderers
Nicky Crow Caramandi, Charley White Iannece,
Don Nicky Scarfo, Nick Milano (with his hands on

the shoulders of an unidentified boy), Anthony
Pungitore; and (*far right*) Scarfo's son, Mark, who
attempted suicide in 1988 because he was ashamed
of his father. *Back row, from left:* murderer Phil
Leonetti; Gaetano Scafidi; murderer Frank
Narducci, Jr.; and an unidentified man.

Casablanca South, Scarfo's home in
Hallandale, Florida.

What's unusual about this surveillance photo of Scarfo and
guests is the presence of a woman. When Scarfo and his
friends got together socially, women tended to be few and
far between.

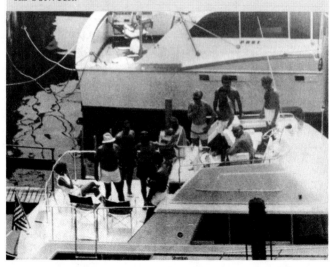

A mob get-together in the late 1970s. *Left to right:* Salvatore Merlino; Frank Narducci, Jr., and Frank Narducci, Sr., standing next to the man who would murder him, Salvatore Testa; Salvy's father, Phil Testa; and Nicky Scarfo.

The Gentle Don, Angelo Bruno (*right*) who reigned from 1959 to 1980. With him is disk jockey Jerry "The Geater with the Heater" Blavat.

Angelo Bruno, moments after his death on March 21, 1980. His murder touched off the mob bloodbaths. Bruno is still holding the newspaper he bought minutes before he was shot.

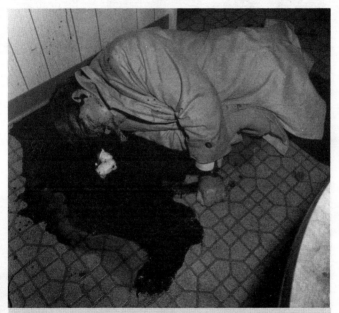

Roofers Union official John McCullough, shot down and killed by a mob assassin in his own kitchen on December 16, 1980. The object lying in the pool of blood is a Christmas ornament.

Phil Testa (*left*) and his son, Salvy, walking the streets of South Philadelphia approximately a year before Phil was murdered.

The interior of Phil Testa's house on March 15, 1981, after the bomb that killed him exploded and hurled him inward. The bomb had been placed outside, on the porch of the house.

One of Scarfo's early murder victims, Vincent Falcone, killed December 16, 1979. Looking at Falcone's battered body, Scarfo had said, "I love this. I love it."

Rocco Marinucci, murdered on March 15, 1982, a year to the day after he murdered Mafia boss Phil Testa. Note the cherry bomb in Marinucci's mouth.

The 4'11" Harry "The Hunchback" Riccobene, whose battles with Nicky Scarfo for control of the Philadelphia/Atlantic City Mafia led to a series of mob shoot-outs.

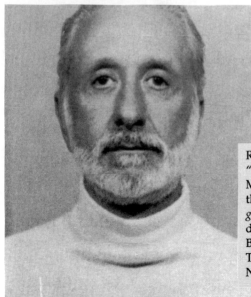

Raymond "Long John" Martorano, the *eminence grise* to Mafia dons Angelo Bruno, Phil Testa, and Nicky Scarfo.

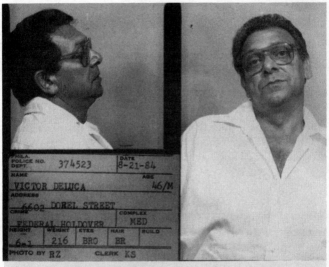

Victor DeLuca , a chief gunman for the Riccobene gang that opposed Scarfo.

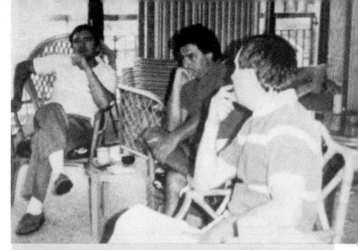

The interior of Tommy DelGiorno's Ocean City, New Jersey, condominium. The condo was bugged for two years by the New Jersey state police. *Left to right:* Nicky ("The Crow") Caramandi, Joseph Ligambi, and Tommy Del.

Mobsters going off to work. *Left to right:* Larry Merlino, Charley White Iannece, and Phil Leonetti, Scarfo's nephew.

Scarfo (*left*) in front of his Atlantic City, New Jersey, house, talking to Phil Leonetti and Torry Scafidi. The house is quite a contrast to his Florida mansion, but many Mafiosi tend to live modestly in the cities where they do business.

Telephoto shot of a Mafia clubhouse interior in South Philadelphia. Joseph Grande is at the table. Above him is a large photo of Scarfo in front of his Florida mansion gates. The other pictures are of mob get-togethers.

Bosom buddies Joey Pungitore (*left*) and Salvatore Testa, on Salvy's boat. The photo was probably taken during the summer of 1984, when Joey was helping to plan Salvy's murder.

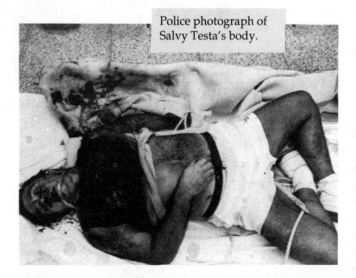

Police photograph of Salvy Testa's body.

Emerging from LaCucina restaurant, where the celebration following the murder of Salvy Testa was held. *Left to right:* Torry Scafidi, Joseph Grande, Frank Narducci, Jr. (*nearly hidden, next to Grande*), Joseph Pungitore, and Tommy DelGiorno. (*Photo by Mark Pinero*)

Frank D'Alfonso, known as Frankie Flowers, who was Scarfo's last murder victim.

Part of the evidence against Neil Ferber in the Meletis Restaurant murders was this artist's eyewitness sketch (*left*). On the right is Ferber's mug shot. On viewing these side by side, eyewitness sketch expert Donald S. Cherry concluded that "The rendering, aside from its limits in technique and anatomical accuracy, illustrates details which could only be obtained from the photo." (*Drawing provided by Dennis Cogan*)

you're sentencing your father to the death penalty? This is a classic lying-in-wait, malice-aforethought capital case.''

''I don't care,'' replied the resolute daughter. ''He's been a member of the organization for a long time, and he's got to do what's right.'' To her father: ''This is your lot in life, and you're going to have to carry through being what you are, no matter the cost.'' And then her coda: ''Where will I go? Who will talk to me?''

My dreams of a best actor award vanquished, I asked Karen if I could talk to her privately. Grudgingly she agreed. We walked around outside while I explained to her that daddy dear was in a lose-lose situation. As matters now stood, he was either going to be killed by us or by Scarfo, and this was his only way out. I pleaded with her to be more understanding. Her response measured my success: ''He's made his bed, let him lie in it,'' she said.

Sweeping back into the room, she gathered up her mother and son and departed. I stayed with the stunned Mario. I reasoned with the stunned Mario. Late into the evening I reasoned with him until I hit upon the right approach, which occurred when I expounded the view that as a husband and father he had to do what was right for his women, even if they—that is, Karen—didn't understand or appreciate his manly self-sacrifice. Adopting that ennobling if chauvinistic posture, Mario agreed to save his own skin and become our witness.

He was good, too. In the McCullough trial, which actually did begin in June 1984, his testimony provided vital collaboration to Moran's, and both Martorano and Daidone were convicted of first-degree murder and sentenced to life imprisonment. (Because the jury did not recommend the death penalty, the life sentences were mandatory.) In the Monte trial, which took place that November, Mario finally had his chance to testify against his half-brother. The evidence he gave helped convict Harry the Hunchback, who got life, as did Joseph Casdia. The supplier of the murder weapon, Vincent Isabella, was convicted of third-degree murder and sentenced to 20 years. Self-sacrificing Mario got four. (He has since been released, as has Joey Pedulla. They are living under new identities. Joey's family is with him; Mario's never did join him. I have no idea how the daughter's social status fared subsequently at either the pizza parlor or the beauty shop.)

While Long John was being tried for the McCullough murder, George "Cowboy" Martorano, his 35-year-old son, had been facing trouble of his own. In a case in which the Task Force played no role, Cowboy had been arrested on charges of helping run a Colombian cocaine network that allegedly netted him and the organization of which he was a part a not inconsiderable $75 million a year. (In addition to cocaine, the American members of the gang were selling marijuana, heroin, meth and Quaaludes via a Philadelphia gang of black criminals who called themselves the Black Mafia.) About a month after his father was convicted and sentenced to life imprisonment, Cowboy was also convicted and sentenced to life imprisonment.

The timing of the George Martorano trial could not have been more fortuitous for us. Coming between the conviction of his father on the McCullough murder and that of Harry Riccobene and his cohorts in the Monte case, it added to the growing public impression that law enforcement was finally making real headway against the Mafia. Much more importantly, from our point of view, the criminals themselves had to be concerned: murder convictions? life sentences? where would the Task Force strike next? against whom?

The Martorano and Daidone trial had also struck an economic blow against Scarfo. Portions of the evidence we compiled had dealt with the role of Daidone's Hotel Workers Union in Atlantic City. That testimony drew the attention of the New Jersey Gaming Commission to the union's activities. As a result, Scarfo's opportunities to extort concessionaire contracts under threat of strikes was virtually removed. It was a major victory, one I could not have foreseen when, more than three years earlier, I had set out on the task of trying to find out who killed John McCullough and why.

Nevertheless, neither trial produced the response I'd most hoped for. No new informant, frightened of the case we might have against him, emerged offering to trade us Scarfo himself for a favorable deal, probably because those who were close enough to Scarfo to give us the quality of evidence we needed were also those who were making the most money from him and who were the most terrified of him, two good reasons for silence that went beyond any Mafia rule of omertà. Neither did we have anyone on hand to help us. Moran came the closest; he, it will be recalled, placed Scarfo at one of the planning sessions for the McCullough murder, but no jury was likely to believe his unsupported word.

Nevertheless, the one-two-three punch of convictions of major mob figures that occurred within one three-month period—Raymond Martorano and Al Daidone in the first, Georgy Martorano in the second, and Harry Riccobene and his confederates in the third—did bring with it media publicity which, in turn, generated phone calls from tipsters. Often, what they had to tell us was useless or false, but we also got some solid leads, including background details about crimes that we had until then lacked.*

Most of our new sources were, predictably, looking to peddle information for cash and had decided that the Task Force, with all that FBI money available, was the place to go. However, we also received a handful of conscience calls from criminals, and they proved to be among the most valuable.

Conscience, I had long since learned to my benefit in solving cases, is by no means the exclusive province of the honest

---

*I can't be specific about the information they gave, because if I did that, I might inadvertently identify them to people who would like to kill them.

and law-abiding. A sense of guilt produces more confessions than any other motive. A criminal's sense of right and wrong, nevertheless, is often quite different from that approved by the straight world. Thus, Victor's conscience was bothered by his "making" Joey Pedulla into a murderer, but not by the murder of Monte itself, which he saw as necessary and even moral, since Monte was a traitor to his duties as consigliere. Along that line, I have known murderers who take pride in killing only those who (as they put it) "need killing," usually drug dealers who cheated them. Such people would consider it morally reprehensible to kill or even harm an innocent person. For that reason, an arresting officer is ordinarily in much less danger from a criminal of that variety than from some scared kid who has just committed his first homicide; the "need" killer recognizes that the cops are just doing their job when they come for him, and that it would be "wrong" to kill them.

It is important for a detective to understand and respect the criminal's sense of right and wrong. In an interrogation, you cannot ask a Victor DeLuca: "How can you talk about morality when you helped set up Frank Monte, when you tried to murder Raymond Martorano, when you sliced a dead man's belly open and threw the body in the ocean for the sharks to get at it, when you go around breaking people's kneecaps and knocking their teeth out?" To ask that—and some detectives do—may give you a momentary sense of self-righteous superiority, but in so doing you deny to the criminal a very precious possession of his, his concept of moral boundaries. It is that concept which, because it is vital to his sense of self-respect, makes him want to talk to you even when he doesn't think he does. Denigrate his sense of right and wrong and you have lost a valuable source of information, and you are also, in my judgment, not acting morally yourself.

Sometimes the sense of boundaries can be helped along. In conducting an interrogation, I may indicate to a suspect who belongs to a gang—any gang, not just the Mafia—that

I believe he wants to get out. In so doing, I'm inferentially telling him he's a fellow for whom I think there's still some hope. With a fair degree of frequency, I hit home with that kind of remark, and I'm especially likely to do so when there's a degree of peer fear involved. (Gang members often are terrified of fellow members.) By suggesting a sense of worthwhileness to the person, I have allowed him to articulate to himself a self-perception that may not have *consciously* occurred to him before.

For the criminal who, consciously or unconsciously, is seeking extrication, the police interrogation provides a prop (in the form of the priestly interrogator who wants to help him) and a concrete benefit (a reduced sentence). Much more difficult is the way of the conscience-stricken gang member who is not under arrest. He doesn't know how to proceed, is often ambivalent about trying. An LCN made-member or associate, for example, is moving within the only world he has ever known, probably from the time he was a teenager. It has not merely provided him income but has fulfilled his human need for fellowship. (Victor's sense of betrayal by the "guys I hung with" and Nick Caramandi's talk of the "fun" of being a gangster both had to do with the fellowship of crime.)

To renounce that world, with its familiar mores and taboos, and try to enter that other world whose people think it is wrong to commit crimes, requires a considerable act of courage of which few are capable. As a result, the criminal who would like to get out but who, lacking a prop, recognizes he can't make the break, may focus instead on a specific crime—almost always a murder—that he defines as "wrong." Because he sees himself capable of making that distinction, he can still consider himself a "good" person. By providing information anonymously over the phone about the "wrong" act, he is hoping to clear his conscience. (It probably won't work out that way, but that's the expectation.)

Such calls are rare even in routine crime investigations,

but they had been unheard of in LCN homicides until the Task Force began getting arrests and convictions, indicating that the gang's power was crumbling. Conscience, I have observed, tends to thrive most when personal risk is reduced.

Our new sources also included people, mostly from South Philadelphia who had always been law-abiding and who, for the first time, had gained hope, because of us, that the mob's hold could be broken. The fear level among them, nevertheless, remained very high, more so than among the criminals who had a more realistic knowledge of the strengths and weaknesses of the world in which they moved. I remember, in particular, one man to whom I must have spoken by phone a half-dozen times between 1983 and 1985. He might have identified to us the man who shot Angelo Bruno. He had witnessed the murder, had gotten a good look at the killer, and thought he'd recognize him if he saw him again. In each call, he seemed to come closer to making a decision to help us, but eventually I stopped hearing from him. Fear won out.

One new informant from the criminal side helped us break a double homicide that had occurred before the Task Force was formed. The bodies had been discovered in the parking lot of the Hilton Hotel near the International Airport. One victim was P2P dealer Mario Pappini, the other a young woman, Kathleen Logan, who had apparently been shot only because she was unfortunate enough to be with Pappini when he was ambushed. Our caller, who seemed disturbed by Logan's death, not Pappini's, but had kept quiet about it for years, gave us sufficient information that we were able to arrest and convict the killers, business rivals of Pappini's.

When an informant appeared to have something substantive to offer, we would arrange debriefing meetings, but never anywhere near Philadelphia or Atlantic City. One site we used was a motel in New Brunswick in northern New Jersey. And many a cold winter night, I'd take the long drive to a safe house we'd established on a desolate and deserted beach area not far from New York City.

We succeeded in keeping our informants safe, too. Despite their fears, none was ever identified by the Scarfo mob, and none was harmed. One of our best informants was among the mob's victims, but he was killed, we now know, for reasons that had nothing to do with his cooperation.

As helpful as our new informants would prove to be, we hoped that their value would be limited to solving past murders, that we would have no need of them for the prevention of future ones. Our expectation was tied into the result of the Monte trial. It meant the end of the Riccobene gang. Its leaders (with the sole exception of the nonviolent Frank "Frankie Flowers" D'Alfonso) were removed from the scene, some through murder, some through imprisonment, some through becoming government witnesses. That meant that with his only effective opposition vanquished, Scarfo might have no one left to kill. If so, the bloodletting that had marked the past four years, with its constant danger of causing the death of innocent people, was at an end.

We were wrong. It wasn't.

15
Scarfo Sends Salvy a Kiss

When Scarfo arrived back in Atlantic City in January of 1984 following his release from the Texas prison, he soon found himself facing two new problems, one concerning his pet mayor, Michael Matthews, and the other his chief assassin, Salvy Testa.

Matthews was in trouble. During Scarfo's absence, his organization had been infiltrated by an FBI agent who wiretapped conversations that produced incriminating information against Matthews and Scarfo's henchman, Frank Lentino. When news of the FBI sting hit the papers, Matthews was subjected to a recall election. Funded by Scarfo, he fought the challenge but lost. Following his indictment, Matthews gave statements against Scarfo and a number of his lieutenants, but—in apparent terror for his life—almost immediately recanted them. He was convicted on corruption charges and sentenced to prison for fifteen years. Lentino, who had been so valuable to Scarfo in the unionization of the hotel workers, was also convicted and went off to prison for ten years.

The convictions of Martorano and Daidone in August of 1984 provided another setback for Scarfo. He seemed to be having a bad year. But not entirely: it turned out that he was beginning to receive income from a new and highly profitable criminal enterprise.

The man in charge of this scheme was the fiftyish Saul Kane. Bespectacled, mild-mannered in appearance, Kane had long been involved in various loan-sharking and extortion schemes, but had never been considered a major player until he joined up with Scarfo. Sometime in 1984, not long after Scarfo's release from prison, Kane was approached by 33-year-old Gary Levitz, who, like Kane, lived in Margate just outside Atlantic City. Levitz was looking to follow the lucrative P2P trail blazed by the criminal genius Ronald Raiton six years earlier. Kane thought Levitz's idea was a sound one and provided the financing in return for a share of the profits. Like Raiton, Levitz developed a contact with a German manufacturer of P2P, which still could not be sold legally in the United States save to pharmaceutical houses. Like Raiton, too, Levitz and Kane shipped the P2P to the United States in a circuitous fashion—they used the Dominican Republic; Raiton had preferred the Bahamas—with the chemical eventually sold in the usual gallon lots to meth cookers. Over the next two years, they would complete at least fifteen shipments with Mark Levitz, Gary's brother, also participating. He would earn $180,000 for his efforts. The dollars were much bigger for Kane and Gary Levitz. Their gross profit was $24 million. Scarfo, who had approved the scheme, received tribute from Kane and Levitz. The amount he received has not been revealed, but it would have been unusual if his share was less than 10 percent.

Business was also booming elsewhere for the ever-greedy Scarfo. A particular beehive of activity was Scarfo's Philadelphia headquarters, a small, shabby, deserted warehouse on South Bancroft Street. To it, in shifts, were summoned low-level drug and numbers dealers for meetings with Scarfo's own brand of IRS agents, led by Chickie Ciancaglini, Tommy DelGiorno and Nick Caramandi. Each visiting crook was advised that his street tax rate had been increased (by whatever amount the collectors thought they could get out of him). Anyone who protested the new assessment was beaten. Anyone who agreed to pay and then didn't was beaten. The assaults might take place behind closed doors, but also in broad daylight on busy streets as horrified spectators watched.

The victim of one such bludgeoning was Louis Turra, who had refused to pay the demanded "shakes" (mob shorthand for shakedowns). Turra, accompanied by his girlfriend, was attacked in fashionable Society Hill. He had his jaw and three ribs broken. His attackers: Tommy Del, Faffy Iannarella, Charley White Iannece, Phil Narducci, Wayne Grande and young Salvatore Scafidi, a distant relative of Philadelphia Police Chief Inspector Frank Scafidi, the originator of the Task Force.

Afterward, several of the thugs responsible discussed the incident in Tommy Del's luxury condominium in Ocean City, New Jersey, which the New Jersey State Police had bugged. The apartment house was something of a mob hangout. Living there during summer months, in addition to Tommy Del, were Wayne Grande, Faffy and a gambler named Joseph Ligambi (of whom more later). During the course of the taped conversation about the Turra beating, Wayne Grande boasted, "All South Philadelphia is shaking." Tommy Del was pleased, too: "That's the way you do it," he boasted. "Right in the fucking street. No hiding. No secrets. Let them know who it was and why.''

There were some second thoughts, however, about administering the beating in front of Turra's girlfriend. ''You gotta understand. A girl's a girl. It ain't a guy,'' explained Faffy, who had slugged Mrs. Riccobene with the sawed-off shotgun he'd used to kill her son. ''Tell that to Nicky,'' commented Wayne wisely. But Faffy continued to have his compunctions. ''I didn't wanna do it in front of her,'' he said. ''We shoulda waited,'' and Tommy Del agreed.

Wayne, however, had the final word: ''I mean, it's the law. You have to pay, right? Hey, you gotta pay.''

(The way of independent drug dealers and numbers bankers was not easy. They not only had money extorted from them by members of the mob, but by freelance muscle as well. Probably the most successful of that breed was Scarfo's old nemesis, who used to punch him around when they were young hoods: Anthony ''Mad Dog'' DiPasquale.

(On one occasion, DiPasquale and a confederate tied a numbers banker in chains and hung him upside down in a garage, every now and again sizzling him with an acetylene torch. At regular intervals, they let the man down to make phone calls to raise money, after which they hoisted him up again. When they released him the following morning, DiPasquale put his arm around the victim's shoulders and congratulated him ''for taking it like a man.'' DiPasquale was convicted for that and related pranks and sentenced to eighty years in prison. It was Mad Dog whom police detectives continued to believe would eventually be named by Neil Ferber as his confederate in the murders of Steve Booras and Janette Curro.)

The South Bancroft Street beatings succeeded for the most part in terrorizing additional ''shakes'' for Scarfo-ites out of the street criminals who were their targets. One potential source of tribute money for Scarfo, however, remained untapped—the Pagan motorcycle gang, which controlled a significant share of the meth business. They simply refused to pay Scarfo a dime, and Tommy Del and pals weren't about to invite them into their headquarters to teach them a lesson, either. They were more likely to get a lesson from the chain-wielding Pagans than to give one to them, as they well knew.

Then, in the spring of 1984, relations between the two gangs took an ugly turn. One evening, Scarfo's underboss, Chuckie Merlino, as he approached Cous' Little Italy Restaurant, deliberately rammed his car into a motorcycle ridden by a Pagan known as The Egyptian. As The Egyptian, cut and bruised, lay on the sidewalk, Merlino swung his car around and made a second charge, running right over his precious bike, which may have upset him more than his injuries did. A few nights later, in retaliation, a band of Pagans roared up on their cycles to Merlino's Philadelphia home and shot it full of holes. (Merlino wasn't hit.)

This brazen insult to the majesty of the Men of Honor was never punished. The Mafia bullies had been bullied by the bike-riding bullies and backed down. As the public perceived it, however, the shoot-out at the Merlino house was but one more proof that organized crime violence continued unchallenged. The cops and the FBI might finally be making some headway in arresting people after crimes occurred—usually long after—but they obviously weren't making the streets safe from the vendettas and bloodshed beforehand.

All this while, Salvy Testa and his Young Executioners were riding high. He was the Jesse James of South Philadelphia. In the saddle alongside him was his version of the Dalton and Younger gangs: the Narducci brothers, the Pungitore brothers, the Grande brothers, the Milano brothers. By early 1984, the Young Executioners had committed twelve murders (that I can trace to them), either directly on Scarfo's orders or with his approval.

At the age of 28, Salvy Testa was rich, too. Money was pouring into his coffers every day. His crew members shoveled wads of cash at him, as capo, in tribute from their gambling and drug operations. His legitimate businesses—Virgilio's Restaurant, inherited from his father, and a restaurant-bar in Atlantic City that he owned with Frank Narducci, Jr.—were both profitable, and he was negotiating to sell the Atlantic City bar at top dollar, which he subsequently did.

Some mob observers were seeing him as Scarfo's heir apparent. The alcoholic underboss Chuckie Merlino certainly wouldn't be it, so it was probably between Salvy—whose father and Scarfo had been close friends—and Scarfo's nephew, the handsome and erratic Phil Leonetti. Salvy had much to recommend him. He possessed more leadership qualities than Leonetti, and was more ruthless. He was a stone-cold assassin, exactly the kind of person Scarfo needed and admired. Some of the older murderers like Tommy Del and Faffy and Ciancaglini were good, but talent like Salvy's didn't come along often. Besides, he was engaged to marry the underboss's daughter, Maria, and that helped his mob positioning, too.

Salvy made his first mistake in January 1984 when he called the Little Guy (on a phone we had tapped) and coolly advised him that Chuckie Merlino was "an asshole who's not taking care of business." Chuckie, he went on, was drinking too much, and he reminded Scarfo how it was all Chuckie's fault that they'd had that embarrassing flare-up with the Pagans.

It was not exactly the kind of call any young man, even one in the crime business, seemed likely to make about his future father-in-law. Why Salvy did it is uncertain. He may have been solely concerned about business, as he said, may have just had one of his fights with Maria—reportedly he punched her around on such occasions—or conceivably he simply thought that Scarfo, just returned from his enforced sojourn in Texas, might not know about Chuckie's unreliability and should be informed.

Whatever Salvy's motives, Scarfo was not pleased. The call carried the implication that Salvy didn't think Scarfo was on top of his own business, and had made the wrong choice in naming Chuckie as his underboss (thoughts Scarfo himself was having but didn't want to hear from anyone else). By complaining about Chuckie, was Salvy suggesting that Chuckie be killed and he himself be named as the new underboss? That meaning could be read into the call, too. "This kid," Scarfo said to one of his men, "thinks he's running Philadelphia."

That was not a good idea for Salvy to have put in Scarfo's mind. Once it had been raised, Scarfo could see reasons for worry. Salvy's crew was getting to be a sizable one. In addition to the various brother combinations, he had by now recruited a half-dozen lesser (but no less ambitious) satellites. If the choice came, Scarfo had to wonder, would the young punks be loyal to him or to Salvy? (He shouldn't have worried. At that point—no way of knowing what might have happened later—Salvy, according to all the information I have been able to put together, never thought of challenging Scarfo. The Little Guy was his hero and he basked in the glory of being his executioner. But Scarfo didn't know that.)

Salvy's wedding to Maria was scheduled for April. It's possible that by then Scarfo had made up his mind to kill him, but the likelihood is that he hadn't. Not only was Salvy valuable, but there could be dangers in having the underboss's son-in-law murdered. Chuckie might not like Salvy any more than Salvy liked him, but if Scarfo had Salvy killed, Chuckie might feel honor-bound to extract revenge for his daughter's husband's death.

Whatever doubts Scarfo had, Salvy accommodatingly removed them when he broke off the engagement to Maria on the eve of the wedding. For reasons that are unclear—but arrogance and stupidity no doubt played a role—Salvy had jilted the underboss's daughter.

The word came down from the Little Guy to the underboss and from him to Tommy DelGiorno. "Get yourself a crew," Chuckie told DelGiorno. "Salvy's got to go."

In June, the sister of Blond Babe Pungitore died. The Blond Babe was the father of the Pungitore brothers in Salvy's crew, and Salvy came to the viewing (which we had under surveillance) to pay his respects. On his arrival there, a smiling Chuckie Merlino came up to Salvy and kissed him on the lips.

From that, Salvy should have known.

We do know that prior to the viewing of the Blond Babe's sister, Salvy was giving every indication of being worried. Because of his careening murderous career, we kept a close watch on him, and I began to get reports that he was not showing up at crime meetings. He seemed particularly careful to avoid the company of Nicky Crow, Faffy, and Tommy Del himself, who he had heard was enjoying the kind of favor from the Little Guy that until lately had been his. He didn't even seem certain of the members of his own crew. When he had business with them, he'd warmly throw his arms around them and hug them, in order to ascertain if they were carrying weapons.

The only member of his coterie of killers that he continued to travel around with was his best friend—they'd known each other since they were little boys—the handsome, clean-cut Joseph "Joey Punge" Pungitore, who had made his bones when Salvy let him help out in the murder of Frank Narducci, Sr. (That could have been another source of worry for Salvy; the two Narducci boys seemed to have forgiven and forgotten their capo's murder of their father, but if they now perceived him as weak and out of favor, would they still forgive and still forget?)

Salvy seemed to think he'd earned Scarfo's displeasure solely because of the jilting of Maria. He wouldn't have been able to think of anything else he'd done wrong, since, in fact, he hadn't. Because he apparently found it hard to believe that Scarfo would kill him over something like leaving Maria at the altar, he could have interpreted Chuckie's kiss as an indication that he, not Scarfo, was out to kill him to avenge

Maria's honor. If so, Scarfo could put a stop to it. Probably almost immediately after receiving the kiss from Chuckie, Salvy decided to try to clear the air with the Little Guy. "We kissed and made up," he told Joey Punge happily. But he couldn't be sure. The talkative Tommy Del once summarized what must have been going through Salvy's mind: "You're never really one hundred percent certain. . . . Scarfo's very good at making you believe you're not gonna get killed." Salvy, in any event, continued his precautions, continued to pal around only with Joey Punge.

What he did not do was try to get away.

He could have. Following the sale of his Atlantic City bar, he had a million dollars or more he could put his hands on immediately. He could go a long way and live a long time on that, virtually free from fear. Tales of mobsters hiring contract killers to track someone to the ends of the earth are the stuff of fiction. As for the Philadelphia/Atlantic City mobsters, they would have had trouble tailing a victim to Newark, much less Los Angeles or Europe. (It took them, after all, more than a year to locate Frankie Stillitano, and he was right there in Philadelphia, hanging out in the singles bars where other gangsters congregated.)

I believe there are several reasons why Salvy didn't flee. The nature of his situation, to begin with, was sufficiently ambiguous to him that he may have, at least at times, managed to convince himself he was safe. It is also likely, I think, that he couldn't encompass the thought of his own death. He was Salvy Testa. He was full of the life of his youth. He was powerful. He was feared. He was adored by his acolytes. He had fancy women. He had fancy cars. He had fancy money. Life was too good for him. It couldn't end for him. Not for Salvy. He was immortal.

But even if Salvy had wanted to flee, he would have, I believe, found it psychologically impossible to do so. The image of Salvy sitting on a stool in the Italian Market eating clams when Victor DeLuca and Joey Pedulla spotted him is an image of the boy at home (and at home nowhere else). It was his market, these were his streets, his people, his world; it was where he was known and what he knew. As with Harry Riccobene, he couldn't conceive of himself as a millionaire nobody someplace else.

So he stayed, and the contract remained in force, and he kept on living.

In the Task Force, we had a betting pool going on for who would be killed next. The fellow who, that summer, drew Salvy's name from the hat was envied. We figured he had the sure winner.

PART III

Solving the Murders at the Meletis

16
Victor Hands Me a "Not for Nothin' "

One day in the late spring of 1984, probably a few weeks prior to the beginning of the Martorano and Daidone trial, Victor DeLuca called me from Philadelphia's Holmesburg Prison, to which he had been returned following his sojourn as cook and housekeeper at our safe house. "Frank? Frank," he said, "I got a not for nothin' for ya."

I recognized the phrase. It was street talk to describe a piece of information for which the snitch didn't expect to get paid or—in the case of Victor—news that didn't concern him but which he thought he'd pass along anyway. "I'm talkin' to this guy in prison," he went on, "and he's up here on a bum rap."

"Who's that, Victor?" I asked.

"Y'know Neil Ferber?"

"The one convicted of killing Steve Booras and the woman at the restaurant, yes."

"Same guy," said Victor, " 'cept he didn't do it. I don't know if you care or not, Frank, like I know it ain't your case."

I paused. "Look, Victor," I answered, "I don't know much about the Booras thing, but I do know there's a lot of speculation now that you may be cooperating, and a lot of guys could be trying to use you to proclaim their innocence, so you'll pass it on to us."

Victor laughed. "Uh-uh. Like I say, Frank, you can do what ya want, but I know this guy didn't shoot Booras."

I thought a moment. "All right, Victor," I said. "I'll have to get you out of there and brought down here. You better not say anything more on the phone, but what you do, have Ferber call me," and I gave him a time and date.

I felt a tinge of irritation as I hung up. Victor's call could not have come at a worse time. I was busy preparing our witnesses for the impending trial of Martorano and Daidone for the McCullough murder, and also for the Monte murder trial (which hadn't yet been postponed to November). But that wasn't all. In addition to my Task Force duties, Jerry Kane had asked me to take on the investigation of the long-unsolved murder of a former Cuisinart executive named Jack Reese who, in December 1980, had been blown away by a hitman disguised as a letter carrier. The case had a TV movie of the week plot—mystery, sex, money, revenge, crooked private eye, political corruption—and even turned out to have an organized crime link, but with the New York City mob, not Philadelphia's. By now, I believed I knew the name of the person who had hired the killer—the trail had taken me to Oklahoma—but I was still pursuing the New York mob angle, which necessitated frequent trips there.

Busy I might be, but I couldn't ignore Victor's not for nothin'. Despite what I'd said to him, I didn't think he'd be taken in by a sob story—he was too street-smart for that—and I was also intrigued by the way he'd chosen his words. He didn't say he *thought* Ferber wasn't involved; he said he *knew* he wasn't. That suggested he had information that was independent of anything Ferber said to him, yet during our weeks of debriefing him, he'd never so much as alluded to the Meletis murders. The more I thought about our conversation, the more curious I became about what he had to say.

My knowledge of the current status of the case was sketchy. I'd heard somewhere that Ferber's posttrial hearing, two years after he was convicted, was still lumbering along (the reason he was still in the general prison population rather than on death row). In the Police Department, I assumed, the protracted hearings for Ferber were a source of aggravation. He would not be likely to talk as long as he thought he had a chance of getting a new trial.

I had no idea which issues Ferber's lawyer was arguing or even who the lawyer was, but the case itself, I reflected, had a way of bumping itself into my attention.

First, it had been Willard Moran telling me that Martorano had engaged him to kill Booras; then it was Mario Riccobene with his story that Martorano had named Booras as one of the five men he had killed. From that, I suspected that the police hypothesis that Ferber and Mad Dog DiPasquale had shot Booras as part of a plan to rob him was wrong. A more likely scenario to me was that Martorano, after Moran's first attempt failed, had hired The Dog, who brought his friend Ferber along with him to act as backup man.

Or was Ferber involved at all? Two other sources had said he wasn't before I heard from Victor. One was Booras's bodyguard, the ex-cop Joseph Inadi, whom I had developed as an informant for a number of crimes. He had told me that the masked gunman he'd seen shoot his boss was much too big to be Ferber and also was taller than the 5'8" DiPasquale. Inadi, however, had only a few seconds to see the shooters, and I had largely discounted his description.

More intriguing was a comment made by John Berkery, Martorano's lieutenant, who had fled to Ireland (from where he couldn't be extradited) on the eve of his arrest on the P2P charges that had resulted in the 10-year sentence Martorano was serving when he was convicted of the McCullough killing. The homesick Berkery had indicated, through his Philadelphia lawyer, that he was interested in striking an arrangement by which he'd give information—but not testify—against other organized crime figures in return for a lenient sentence. Dennis O'Callaghan, in the summer of 1983, had gone to Dublin to meet with Berkery. The proposed deal fell apart, but in the course of their conversation, Berkery had volunteered, "You guys got the wrong guy on the Booras hit. Ferber didn't do it."

By saying we had the "wrong guy," Berkery was implying he knew who the shooters were, and his close association with Martorano certainly put him in a position to have that knowledge. But did he? As I'd long since learned, criminals who are eager to make a deal often state as a fact, for negotiation purposes, information they have only as rumor, if that. The more they claim they can tell, the more valuable they figure they'll be to law enforcement people.

Ferber called me from prison on the day and time I had suggested. I listened as he went through his litany of innocence, much of it devoted to the alleged falsity of a jailhouse informant's testimony against him. I told him I knew nothing about that, but there was information he might not be guilty. I'd be willing to talk to him in person, I said, but I couldn't do that without clearing it with his lawyer, whose name, Ferber told me, was Dennis Cogan. I said I'd get in touch with Cogan and left it at that. In the call, Ferber did nothing to convince me. I'd heard protestations like his from countless defendants who had turned out to be guilty.

My meeting with Victor at my office took place almost immediately afterward. He talked first about his own case, and then turning to Ferber, he said, "You guys think it was Mad Dog."

I said, "Yes, that's the word, Victor. They say he and Ferber were ripping off Booras."

"So what would you say," Victor said, "if I could prove to you The Dog wasn't even in the city at the time of the shootin'?"

I asked him to explain. It all went back, he said, to the days when the squat but powerfully built Dog used to beat up Scarfo. As a result of those encounters, DiPasquale had nothing but contempt for Scarfo, an attitude he saw no reason to change just because Scarfo was now the don. The Dog didn't keep his views to himself. Word got to Scarfo that DiPasquale had called him a "runt" and his mother "a whore."

Either in late April or early May of 1981, a year before the outbreak of violence between Scarfo and Victor's chief Harry Riccobene, Scarfo called in Victor. "He said he wanted me to 'whack the SOB,' " Victor told me, "but I kind of liked The Dog, we went way back, so I said to Scarfo, 'Let me straighten him out,' so Scarfo says, 'OK, but I hear of that asshole again, I'll kill him.' "

Accompanied by his faithful shadow, Joey Pedulla, Victor paid a visit to The Dog and warned him that Nicky wasn't taking kindly to the descriptions The Dog was giving out about him and his mother and he ought to cool it. I asked Victor how The Dog took his advice. "He said to me, 'Fuck him and the horse he rode in on. I'll strangle the little motherfucker myself.' "

Victor said he tried to appeal to The Dog's common sense, which did not seem to be in abundant supply. Almost immediately afterward, The Dog called Scarfo, and not to apologize, either. On the contrary, he repeated the insult about Nicky's mother and added that, in his opinion, Nicky himself performed sex acts with men, and that if Nicky dared come to Philadelphia, "I'll kick you in the balls."

Scarfo again called in Victor. As Victor recalled it, "He says to me, 'This guy's your friend. He's bothering me. You kill 'im,' " an order which Victor took seriously. "If I didn't kill The Dog, Nick'd have me killed."

Thereupon, Victor went Dog hunting. But DiPasquale, who turned out to have some sense after all, had disappeared. "I looked all over," Victor recalled, "and one day" in late May "I went to his girlfriend's house and there was the phone ringin' an' someone says, 'It's from the Poconos,' an' I figured who that must be, and I take the phone from her, and it was The Dog and that's how I knew where he was and he figured I was after him. So it couldn't have been The Dog what killed Booras 'cause when that happened he was hidin' out of town, scared to come back, because he knew I would've wasted him."

I asked, "But couldn't he have come back in town without you knowing it and done the hit for Martorano and Scarfo and that would get him even with Scarfo and Scarfo off his back?"

Victor: "Yeah, he woulda done that in a minute. But he wouldn't come to no closed room, Frank, like that restaurant. I mean, he'd stalk Booras on the street and kill 'im out in the open. But he wouldn't walk into no place he don't know, because he'd figure that was a trick to kill him, that I'd step out from the back and blow him away."

(The contract never was carried out on DiPasquale. He left his hiding place in the Poconos to stand trial in federal court on extortion charges, including hanging his one victim upside down in a garage and burning him with an acetylene torch) that sent him safely to prison for 80 years.

Victor's story by no means convinced me of Ferber's innocence, but it did raise a disturbing question. Ferber, I knew, was originally brought into the Meletis murder investigation because of his association with Barry Saltzburg, the alleged killer of the other Greek Mob leader, Peetros. When it became clear that Saltzburg (who was eventually found guilty of robbing Peetros's body but not killing him) had nothing to do with the Booras hit, Ferber remained in the case because of the supposed involvement of DiPasquale. Now, if DiPasquale also had to be eliminated as a suspect—and I did find Victor persuasive on that point—how did Ferber still fit in?

Prior to Victor's arrival, I had taken a look at Ferber's rap sheet. Aside from the robbery arrest with Saltzburg, which turned out to be an attempted robbery, his record consisted of insignificant fraud charges or "scams," as people in his circle call them. Nothing violent. If Martorano had ordered the hit, why on earth, I wondered, would he choose somebody like Ferber as a participant? Why not his trusted strong-arm man, big bull-necked Frank Vadino (who, for that matter, fit Inadi's description)?

It was possible, of course, that Ferber had associations with violent types other than Saltzburg and DiPasquale, and one of them could have brought him along on the murder, perhaps without Martorano's approval. Possible, possible, I thought with growing unease. I much preferred probable.

I'd never met Ferber's lawyer, Dennis Cogan, but I had seen him and heard a great deal about him. With his unruly mop of dark brown hair and his boyish clean-cut features, Cogan looked to be no more than in his late twenties, ten years younger than his real age. He had, I'd heard, a charming courtroom manner which, along with his looks, made juries like and root for him, which meant they voted against the forces of good, namely us in the police and the DA's office.

But it wasn't only at trial that Cogan showed his wares. He apparently had an extraordinary knowledge of the law that let him come up with technicalities that other attorneys would never think of. According to some grousing in the Department, he put more people back on the streets than all the other criminal defense lawyers in the city combined. That was hyperbole, but it indicated the fear and loathing with which he was regarded. The word among detectives was: Don't let him interview you if you can possibly avoid it; your inch will become his yard. (I think it was only after my first contact with him that I learned he'd been a prosecutor himself, attached to the homicide unit of the DA's office, at which time he was admired for the same abilities that now made him the enemy.)

Whatever he was, he wasn't a mob attorney. I'd have known if he was, and had that been the case, upon hearing his name I would have immediately dropped all interest in Ferber, because I would have assumed the Mafia was paying his legal fees, proof of his guilt.

When I called Cogan to tell him I'd like to interview his client, I didn't have much expectation of a favorable response. Even if he wasn't one of those hotshot defense counsel types—you can see them every day in City Hall in their three-piece suits, shooting their cuffs—he had to be aware of the police antagonism toward him, and the chances were he reciprocated it.

But I didn't get that impression. Instead, I was listening to a voice streaked with the kind of concern which is not readily simulated, a thrust in it of real anguish. He had not been Ferber's original lawyer, he told me, but had been hired by his family after Ferber was convicted to see if he could discover technical errors in the proceedings that could become the basis for a new trial. He had found several such issues, and at the beginning these had been his only concern, he said. However, as he began to study the evidence further and did some detective work of his own, he had become convinced that Ferber was innocent. From the moment of that realization onward, the case became a consuming passion for Cogan. (His secretary once counted up the time she knew he had put into defending Ferber and discovered his earnings on the case by then were 63¢ an hour.) Despite the new evidence he had discovered, Cogan went on (and here was the reason for his anguish), he feared he was going to lose the posttrial motions. The judge, who'd also presided at the trial, was balding Robert A. Latrone. He had a reputation as a strong law-and-order type—we in the police loved him—and, Cogan believed, could never be swayed to overturn a guilty verdict.

For that reason, he was ready to reach out to whoever he thought might help. He gave me a virtual free hand. You can bring Ferber down, he said: "I'll either be there or not; it's up to you; you can ask him anything you want." Even under the circumstances, it was a remarkable offer. Defense attorneys, in my experience, rarely if ever turn to the people who have arrested their client, much less agree to be absent when the client is being interrogated by them.

That was the first of several phone calls between Cogan and me, and during one of the early ones, he sprang a surprise on me. There was, he said, a problem with an eyewitness sketch used against Ferber at his trial. The Homicide Bureau, for which I worked, had fabricated it, he charged, in effect railroading Ferber to the electric chair.

His was as serious an accusation against the police as can be made, as he must have been aware. At the moment, I assumed—rightly, I think—that he was telling me this in order to test me. If knowing that he was charging my fellow officers with misconduct was going to make me back off, he wanted to know it; I'd almost certainly find out eventually anyway, as the allegation was part of the posttrial hearing record. But I also now think Cogan was acting in accordance with his character, as I learned it to be. In all my dealings with him, he acted with absolute integrity. With him you need no bond, his word will do; he never lies. He was going to be open with me, and if I was open in return with him, a relationship of trust was possible. So he was testing my openness, too. I said, "Dennis, I'm going to look at the evidence but that's all I'm going to do. I'm not going to investigate the investigators. That would be a certain way to grind everything to a halt right away.''

I think he liked that answer and understood what I meant by it. It was one thing (as he may have known from his long experience in the DA's office) to take a fresh look at a case when new evidence surfaces. That *should* be done; but one didn't *ever* question the motives of one's fellow officers. All detectives at one time or another have misunderstood evidence; that's explicable, and no one is critical of a detective when it happens. But to accuse a detective or any officer of falsifying evidence is not just accusing him but also bringing into question the integrity of the entire department, suggesting it countenanced such procedures. The very hint of such an accusation by a cop against other cops causes the bulwarks to be thrown up, all cooperation to cease, and the accuser to become a pariah, to be transferred out of his unit because none of the others would want him around any longer.

I'm not saying such a response is fair, but it is police mentality, and it is probably not that much different in kind from the reluctance of doctors to question the motives of other doctors, lawyers other lawyers. Overt corruption—soliciting or accepting bribes—is different. Every police department has a unit designed to ferret out such occurrences, so it is recognized as a temptation endemic to police work.

Fabricating evidence, however, is not a recognized possibility, and so the institutional assumption is that it doesn't happen. I knew that the institutional assumption was false in certain regards as, I'm sure, did the institution itself. Particularly in drug cases, cops have been known to plant evidence or to swear they saw a buy take place when they didn't; this kind of misconduct almost always occurs when the arresting officers "know" that the buy must have taken place; they can't prove it honestly, but they want to get the "bad" person and that's how they do it. However, to deliberately and maliciously frame someone for murder with a faked eyewitness sketch, that was something I couldn't conceive of as a possibility. I had no doubt Cogan was sincere in making the charge, but he had to be wrong.

I had Neil Ferber brought down to the Federal Building, where I met with him in one of the FBI offices. He was not an impressive looking person. About 5'8", 140 pounds, somewhere in his late thirties, he had dark curly hair streaked with gray, a quavery voice, undistinguished features—the kind of person who always reminds people of someone else. Before he arrived, I had checked out his background. He was the black sheep of a family of respectable Jewish shopkeepers in Northeast Philadelphia, had been in scrapes with the law going back to the time he was a kid. His younger brother Jay, whom I'd later get to know, was puppy-dog friendly, intensely loyal to Neil. Unlike Neil, he was the self-sacrificing sort who keeps a family together rather than tearing it apart.

Probably because Neil was the firstborn son (although maybe in hope of straightening him out), he had been given the family's furniture business to manage and had succeeded in bankrupting it within a few years. I heard Neil once described as the guy who always has a sure thing in the third and then the nag runs last, and I sensed that pathetic loser's quality in him. I'd seen it before, the small-time grifters who think there's an angle somewhere, a magic knowledge of the fix, and if only they can figure it out, they'll be winners, too. They tend to lie (often to impress women) about scams they haven't carried out and whine when they are caught for the ones they have tried to carry out. They aren't usually dangerous people, aren't evil, just weak, drifters along the fringes of crime. Impervious to the lessons of experience, when they get out of one trouble, they get into another. I suspected Ferber had committed many small-time crimes for which he hadn't been caught, but that didn't mean he wasn't the victim of injustice in this big one.

His eyes interested me most. Unlike many of his type, he looked straight at the person he was talking to, yet there was also a flinching quality, rather like the dog that adores his master but fully expects to be hit by him. I knew that look could be the consequence of his death sentence, but my guess was that life had put it there long before he ever heard of Steve Booras and Janette Curro.

I had informed Dennis Cogan I was bringing Ferber down, and asked him to be there, at least for the early stage of the interview. However, I arranged to have Ferber arrive ahead of the time Cogan was due. It wasn't that I didn't trust Cogan, but rather that I wanted to get my first impression of Ferber free from the influence that lawyers invariably, I've found, have on their clients. Clients feel dependent on them and sometimes fear they'll get their lawyer angry if they say the wrong thing; they do not act naturally.

When Ferber arrived, Jimmy Jackson was in the room with me. I introduced him to Ferber as a polygrapher. I watched Ferber carefully to see how he took in this news as I confined myself to small talk about his family.

A few minutes later, Cogan came in. As he was seating himself, I turned to Ferber and asked him, "Before we go any further with this investigation, would you be willing to take a lie detector test?"

I got two simultaneous answers. From Ferber: "Let's do it." Cogan, exploding: "That's not why he's here. It's unfair to ask him and I won't permit it. I have absolutely no confidence in any police-conducted polygraphy."

"Dennis," I said, "let's go outside a minute." We did. I told him I had no intentions of asking Ferber to go on the box, that my sole purpose had been to test his reaction, and he'd passed. In my experience, I said, an innocent person will do anything to clear himself, including taking a polygraph. "If we do decide to polygraph him eventually, Dennis," I assured him, "it will have to be only if everyone agrees. In that event, I can recommend someone from the FBI who will be completely objective."

Cogan studied me. He nodded. "All right, Frank. You ask him whatever you want. I'm not going to stay."

We went back into the room. Cogan turned to Ferber. "Neil, I'm going," he said. "You're to answer all the questions Lieutenant Friel asks you," and with that he left.

When we were by ourselves, I told Ferber that Jackson was a detective, not a polygrapher. If Ferber resented having been misled by me, he didn't indicate it; if I read him right, he was disappointed.

In the interview that followed, which probably went on for more than two hours, my goal was to get to understand Neil Ferber, not the case on which he had been convicted. He was not by himself either, as I talked to him; sitting with him were all the other suspects I'd interrogated in homicide and other felony cases over the past eight years. From them, I'd learned patterns of behavior—little touchstones that suggested guilt, if not the proof of it—and I wanted to see where, if at all, Ferber's responses would fit into my accumulated knowledge.

For a while I continued, as I had begun before Cogan's arrival, with the usual zone-of-trust questions—parents, family, schooling, what he did for a living. From there, I moved to previous crimes for which he'd been arrested. I first focused on an extortion trial in which he and Mad Dog had been codefendants; Ferber, I knew, would feel safe talking about that one, since he had been found not guilty.

I next asked him about his state of mind when he was arrested as a suspect in the Meletis murders. "I thought the whole thing was a joke," he said.

Surprised, I asked him why he'd reacted that way. "Because," he said, "everybody who knows me knows I'm not a murderer. Danny Rosenstein and me go back a long way. He knows I wouldn't kill nobody." (He and Sergeant Rosenstein had been students together at Northeast High School.)

I said, "Neil, I don't understand why you'd think that. After all, just a year earlier, you and Barry Saltzburg were arrested outside a bar with masks and guns, and then two people are killed at the Meletis by men wearing masks and carrying guns, and one's thought to be Saltzburg. That's a trail any investigator would follow."

"No, I just thought it was a joke," he mumbled. "I hang around with those guys, but everybody knows I wouldn't commit no murder."

It was from these words, not their content but the bewildered and retreating way in which they were uttered, that I got my first indication that the crucial fire, the one that allows us to keep our mental health and fight against fate, had begun (ever so slightly) to dampen within him.

I made no judgment about that insight at the moment—it would only begin to prey on me much later—since a guilty person as well as an innocent one, given his situation, could find himself entering the same emotional house of straw.

I then returned to his associates, interested (as a truth touchstone) to find out how much he would admit and deny. "Did you know Steve Booras?" I asked for openers, having no reason to think he did.

Ferber: "Yeah, I knew him. He was a Northeast guy like me. Barry, me and him, we used to drink at the same place, Pinocchio's," referring to a bar in Northeast Philadelphia. He didn't much like Booras, he indicated. He also readily admitted that he and The Dog hung around together, did their drinking at the Silver Dollar Saloon, which was then known to police as being frequented by wiseguys who congregate in singles bars, where they try to come across as organized crime when they put the make on the women who drink at such places.

And it wasn't, he volunteered, just The Dog and Saltzburg he knew. (He liked The Dog, was scared to death of Saltzburg.) He knew mafiosos, too. He'd met Raymond Martorano once. Phil Testa had been a customer at his store, as was Junior Staino, a made-member. He'd give them good buys on furniture, he pointed out; like Enrico Riccobene, he had a mob discount policy. (According to Ferber's brother, that was one of the reasons the store went bankrupt; the other related one was that with customers like that, law-abiding folks stayed away.)

Those responses of Ferber's were typical of the interview. Ask him a question and straight ahead he'd go. Not only did he always answer the question but, time and again, he volunteered information that tended to arouse suspicion about him rather than alleviate it. Admitting he knew Martorano suggested that Martorano could have hired him. Admitting he knew Booras suggested he knew about Booras's wealth, giving him a motive to rob him, and noting he didn't especially like him suggested that the truth was he hated him, giving him a motive to kill him. Admitting he knew Testa suggested the possibility that Testa had recommended him as a gunman. (Testa was killed two months prior to Booras, but the plot against Booras could have been of long standing.)

Ferber's way of responding, however, was highly untypical of a guilty person. Such individuals ordinarily do their best to distance themselves from knowledge of everyone who could be involved in the offense of which they are suspected. In a crime like the Meletis murders, where motive is an issue and the relationships among the parties probably unclear to the police, the suspect will either deny knowing anyone who might have been involved, or if that's impossible, will downplay any association, as in: "Oh, yeah, now that I think of it, I did meet him one time, when I was sitting in the back of a car; it was just a couple of minutes." That type of response is virtually a reflex action on a guilty suspect's part. I'd heard versions of it time and again.

The innocent person, on the contrary, is more likely to answer as Ferber did. Because he's innocent, he can't imagine how anything he can say about the people involved in the crime can hurt him.

In making any assessment of Ferber, nevertheless, I knew I had to be cautious. Cogan, as his courtroom opponents had learned, and as I now had, can be quite convincing. So, in his way, had been Victor when he asserted Ferber's innocence. Which led me to my concern that I could become the victim of a self-fulfilling prophecy: by reopening the investigation, I was admitting to the possibility of a miscarriage of justice, which meant I might subconsciously be looking for indications that tended to prove the miscarriage and ignore those that pointed to Ferber's guilt.

It was with that danger in mind that I'd had Jimmy Jackson present for the interview and asked John Main to sit in for part of it, too. They were aware I had become interested in the case, but I'd not shared any of my reasons. I had kept from them Cogan's version of the facts, and not filled them in on Victor's story. That way, when they listened to Ferber, they'd have the objectivity I might by now be lacking.

After the interview, I asked Jackson what he thought. He shook his head and laughed. "That guy's not guilty," he said. John Main, I learned when I asked him separately, had reached the same conclusion.

I didn't have to ask them why. We'd been working together for more than three years now, knew how each other's minds worked, and each of us also knew, from our long aggregate experience in investigating homicides, the characteristics of guilty people. It's nothing that could ever be explained in a court of law—it's not evidence—but it is what you *know*, the intuition you develop from years of dealing with crime.

Ferber's not guilty, declared the mutual intuition. Yet all three of us had at one point believed Howard Dale Young was the shooter in the McCullough case, and we had been wrong, which was a cautionary lesson to keep in mind.

After Ferber was returned to prison, I sat for a while trying to decide what to do next. Maybe nothing, it occurred to me. If Cogan won Ferber a new trial, there might be no need for me to go further. I found that a comforting thought. I don't recall if, in thinking that, the phrase ''sticking my neck out'' crossed my mind, but it could have. It did, I know, later.

17
Killing Salvy Becomes a Problem

Even as my concern about the Meletis murders grew—we might have not only convicted the wrong person, but in the process, let the guilty ones go free—events were moving forward on the planned assassination of Salvy Testa.*

When capo Tommy DelGiorno was given that assignment,

---

*The story told in his chapter was put together over a two-year period by the Task Force and other law enforcement agencies, with the use of wiretaps and informants who either had indirect knowledge or were present when various events occurred.

he cast about for a likely site to carry out the hit. His first choice was Pier 30 along Philadelphia's Delaware River waterfront. The name suggests a good place for a murder, late at night, fog horns booming, dark creaking wooden corridors, maybe a stab in the back with a longshoreman's pick. But Pier 30 was nothing like that; it was, rather, an indoor-outdoor sports center where yuppies came to play tennis and racquetball, among them the young urban professional killer, Salvy. Pier 30 did have one dark entrance stairwell, and Tommy Del figured to have Salvy blasted there, in broad daylight, with the killers (Del had no intention of being on the scene himself) then making their getaway up the I-95 expressway. The plan was scrubbed after Del became worried about the shooters getting caught in a traffic jam along that heavily traveled route.

The second plan was initiated about four weeks after Salvy left his bride at the altar. He was told a crime meeting was to be held at a clubhouse in South Philadelphia. (This clubhouse had no more pretensions to elegance than the one on Bancroft Street; it was located in a building that had once housed a plumbing supply store.) Due to be on hand when Salvy arrived were Nicky Crow Caramandi and Charley White Iannece. The suspicious Salvy didn't show.

The third attempt took place in June at the viewing of the Blond Babe's sister. The killers were secreted on the floor above, with Salvy to be shot following his kiss from Chuckie Merlino, but only after—as was proper—he had paid his respects to the deceased. The deliberately visible presence of our men taking photographs of everyone entering and leaving the funeral parlor caused the conspirators to drop that scheme.

Following the near-fatal kiss, Salvy became "increasingly hard to clock," as Tommy Del explained the problem to Scarfo, who was curious to learn why it was now more than two months and the simple murder had not been carried out. "Never can tell where he's going to be," groused Del, laying the blame on Salvy. Scarfo then showed why he was the boss:

He had a solution. Joey Pungitore; he's the one Salvy trusts, said Scarfo.

Del considered that an order, and paid a call on the preppy youth. The middle son of the Blond Babe, trim and athletic, Joey Punge wore button-down shirts and horn-rimmed glasses, and had as his ambition to become a real estate magnate. When Del advised Joey Punge he had to kill Salvy, the startled Joey said there had to be a mistake. "Salvy told me he'd made things up with the Little Guy," he said. "No," Del corrected him, "he's a dead man."

As the scene was later described, Joey's eyes "filled up," and true-blue to his friend, he pleaded, "Please don't ask me to shoot him."

Not that, he quickly assured Del, he wouldn't go along with the murder. He probably figured he'd be a dead man himself if he didn't do that. He'd just rather not pull the trigger. Salvy and he, after all, were best friends.

Tommy Del appeared touched by Joey Punge's loyalty to Salvy, and assured him there'd be no need for him to do the actual killing. Del's concession was, perhaps, not as generous as it sounded. In addition to Nicky Crow and Charley White, he already had Faffy Iannarella lined up to do the deed, and there was always, if worse came to worst, the feckless Junior Staino. (At this point, except for Joey Punge, none of the Young Executioners was involved in the plot, perhaps because Scarfo feared they'd inform Salvy, much as, years before, Ignazio Denaro had warned Angelo Bruno that Dominick Pollina intended to kill him.)

His conscience suitably eased, Joey Punge quickly displayed a measure of enthusiasm for the task at hand. He pointed out to Del that he and Salvy shared a place in Margate where they spent most summer weekends. On the way back one Sunday, he suggested, they could stop off at Del's condo in Ocean City and kill Salvy there. The idea initially seemed a splendid one to Del, but he decided against it because, as he later explained, "it's messy to murder somebody in your house.'' One is likely to get blood all over the furniture, which might get one's wife angry at one.

He conferred about the problem with Nicky Crow, who had an idea. His friendly pharmacist, The Crow explained, had come up with a potion that would knock out somebody if placed in a drink. (They have interesting pharmacies in South Philadelphia.) What we can do, said The Crow, is give Salvy a glass of iced tea loaded with the potion when he arrives with Joey Punge, and after he falls unconscious, haul him out and shoot him someplace else. Del wasn't certain. What if the potion doesn't work? he asked The Crow.

Recognizing the merit of that query, Nicky Crow decided a scientific experiment was called for. He trooped off to see the friendly pharmacist, who made him a batch of the elixir. The Crow took it home and administered it to himself. When he awakened several hours later, he reported to Del, with a measure of pride in his accomplishment, that the drug worked as advertised.

Unfortunately for Crow, his willingness to risk poisoning himself for the cause of killing Salvy came to naught. When, on the appointed day, Joey Punge and Salvy arrived at Del's condo, where Del and The Crow were waiting, iced tea mixed, Salvy refused to go in. "I don't trust Del," Salvy said to his bosom buddy.

After the knockout drop attempt failed, Joey Punge, who was really getting into the swing of things by now, came up with another plan. He suggested that he inform Salvy that he and Wayne Grande were having a dispute over a gambling territory. As their capo, Salvy would have the duty to adjudicate the quarrel, since such matters only go to the consigliere if the capo can't resolve them. Because territorial disputes are common—they can be over which side of a street a numbers writer is allowed to work—Joey Punge figured Salvy wouldn't be suspicious when told of the supposed problem.

After getting permission from Scarfo, Del broached the

idea to the heavyset, bespectacled Wayne Grande, who, while one of the Young Executioners, was also married into the Scarfo family. Next to Joey Punge, Wayne was probably Salvy's best friend. The plan to which Wayne agreed was simple and seemed foolproof. During one of their long and relaxing weekends at the shore, Joey Punge would advise Salvy of the dispute and suggest they stop at Wayne's house on their way home to discuss it. Wayne was given a gun by Del, which he was to secrete in a kitchen drawer when he heard from Joey Punge that they were on their way. (A concerned father, Wayne didn't want the gun in the drawer any sooner than that, lest his children get at it.) When Salvy and Joey arrived, they'd go to the kitchen, Joey would ask for cigarettes, Wayne would go to the drawer presumably to get them, pull out the gun and blow Salvy away. (Apparently, unlike Del, Wayne had no worries about mucking his house up with blood.)

As they were leaving the shore that weekend, Joey Punge forgot to call Wayne to tell him they were on the way—possibly some residual sense of guilt at work. As a result, on their arrival at Wayne's house, not only was no gun in the drawer, but there were no cigarettes either. Salvy, however, didn't seem to take notice of anything untoward, and merely asked for the details of the turf dispute. Neither man expected to have to come up with a story, but they apparently managed to Salvy's satisfaction.

When Scarfo learned of this latest contretemps, he was furious at Del, who was furious at Wayne for not having a gun on hand anyway, with Wayne furious at Joey for not calling him, and Joey, in turn, furious at Wayne for the same reason as Del was.

The next plot, a couple of weeks later on September 7, also failed. On this occasion, Joey told Salvy he was still having problems with Wayne and asked Salvy to come with him to the Something Sweet Shop, a candy store owned by a friend of Wayne's which was closed for the summer. As the three men arrived at the store, where Wayne had the gun secreted, they noticed a cop see them enter. That ended that. The task of killing Salvy was by now taking on epic proportions, and an increasingly agitated Del was fully aware that Scarfo was running out of patience with him. At that point, Scarfo was probably wishing he had Salvy Testa on hand to kill Salvy Testa. At least Salvy was competent.

They tried a sixth time, seven days later, same place. Joey told Salvy the dispute with Wayne was still unresolved, and Salvy wearily agreed to try to settle it one more time. He asked Joey to pick him up at his house. Around noon, the two friends arrived at Something Sweet, Salvy in a Temple University sweatshirt and shorts. This time, no police were in sight.

On entering, Salvy and Joey came upon Wayne sitting on a couch facing them. A voice from above, belonging to Wayne's brother Joseph, yelled down a hello to Salvy. Salvy then made his mistake. He turned his back to call a return greeting to Joseph. As he did, Wayne Grande took the gun out from under the cushion of the couch, advanced a step or two toward Salvy and shot him in the back of the head. Joseph Grande came running down the stairs, bent over the body and said, "I don't think he's dead. I think he moved." Wayne Grande put his gun to the back of his friend's head and shot him a second time, and that was the end of Salvy's career as head of the Young Executioners.

The three killers found a rug in the store, wrapped the body in it and laid it behind the couch. It was still only a few minutes after noon. They'd have to wait there for another eight hours until dark, when it would be safe to carry the remains out.

After helping shove Salvy's body behind the couch, Joey Punge phoned Torry Scafidi and asked him to go to Del's house in Philadelphia and advise him the murder had finally taken place. In so doing, Joey and the Grande brothers probably considered they were doing Torry a favor. He was anxious to join them as made-members of the mob, and by helping them even at this stage of the murder, he would earn the credential to become eligible for induction.

When that youth arrived with the good news, a relieved Del called a meeting at the Oregon Diner to discuss disposal of the corpse. On hand for that discussion, in addition to Del and Torry, were Nicky Crow, Faffy and Charley White. Del sent Charley White and Crow on a reconnaissance mission to New Jersey to choose a spot to dump the body. Philadelphia was, by now, gaining too many convictions of Del's friends, and he figured it would be better if the New Jersey cops, not us, be in charge of solving Salvy's murder. (Del knew his police procedures; in murder cases, when it is not immediately known where the crime took place, jurisdiction is determined by where the body is found. That was probably why, a few weeks later, the body of still another Scarfo victim, Michael Micali, who apparently had annoyed Scarfo over some minor matter, was also discovered in New Jersey.)

At 8:45 that evening, a truck belonging to an alleged organized crime associate arrived at Something Sweet. Salvy's body was placed (with some difficulty—it had become stiff during the intervening hours) on the vehicle, wrapped in a blanket that Crow and Charley White had purchased during their New Jersey trip, and tied with ropes. The truck was driven to the spot selected in Camden County, where the body was dumped on a shoulder of a road. A passing motorist discovered it an hour later.

By then, a party in honor of the murderers was going on at Salvatore "Sam the Barber" LaRussa's LaCucina Restaurant, located just a few blocks from Salvy's place, Virgilio's. A delighted Scarfo had come up from Atlantic City for the occasion. At one point, he hugged the flattered young Scafidi. "You done good," he told him. Torry had made his bones.

The next day, after Salvy's body was identified, we had a happy $100 winner in our office pool.

18
Ferber Goes to Death Row

Around the time of Salvy Testa's murder in September 1984, Judge Latrone finally moved on the Ferber case. As Dennis Cogan had feared he would, he rejected all the posttrial motions. Two weeks later, he formally imposed two death sentences on Ferber, one for the murder of Steve Booras, the other for that of Janette Curro. Ferber was transported to Graterford Prison, where he was placed in a cell on its death row. A date was yet to be set for his execution.

Latrone's decision was greeted with delight in the Homicide Bureau and the DA's office. There was no question, I heard, that Ferber would now make the confessing phone call. He didn't.

By that time, I had interviewed Ferber a second time and also had begun to talk with law enforcement officers who had had contacts with him prior to the Meletis murders. I was especially interested in learning more about the attempted robbery a year before at the Halfway House bar. I had been informed by one of the detectives assigned to the Booras murder that "they [Ferber and Saltzburg] had been caught doing the same thing once before," which I took to mean wearing masks and carrying guns. If so, that indicated a propensity for violence on Ferber's part, regardless of his protestations to the contrary. To make sure my understanding was correct, I contacted the arresting officer in the Halfway House incident. I had been misinformed. He said that when he intercepted Ferber and Saltzburg, neither was armed or wearing a mask. Those items had been found in the back of Saltzburg's car.

I next contacted the FBI agent whose investigation had led to the arrest of Ferber and DiPasquale on charges of shaking down a gambler. (This case was *not* the one in which DiPasquale hung the victim upside down in a garage.) The FBI man said that despite Ferber's acquittal, he thought he was involved in the scheme. His impression of Ferber as a person was, however, that he had no tendency toward violence.

That was also the view of DEA agent Ellis Hershowitz, with whom I had contact on a drug case and who told me he had known Ferber for years. He considered him a petty thief, definitely not violent.

During my second meeting with Ferber, he offered a confession. I don't recall the date of that interrogation, but I believe it was between the day that Judge Latrone rejected his motions for a new trial and the date set for his formal sentencing. Ferber said to me: "Lieutenant, I'll say anything you want. If you want me to say it was Mad Dog DiPasquale,

I'll do it, except you'll probably give me a lie detector test and I can't pass a lie detector test if I tell you that. But you tell me who you want me to say killed the guy and I'll tell you I was there and I'll testify to that.''

He was wandering haplessly now, I realized, in a huge room that he was beginning to fear had no exit. I shook my head and said I wasn't interested in hearing what he thought people wanted him to say. I asked him instead to go back in his memory and try to tell me all he could about his activities on May 27, 1981.

He said he remembered filing job applications in the morning and named some of the places. In the afternoon, he'd had a session with his psychiatrist. The early part of the evening was a blank to him, but he thought he might have gone grocery shopping with his wife and daughter. He still maintained, as he had from the beginning, that he'd arrived at his cousin's birthday party in the Philadelphia suburb of Bensalem about 9:30, the same time that the murders at the Meletis were taking place. That alibi hadn't held up at his trial, as I knew from Dennis Cogan. The distance from the murder site to the birthday party at that time of night was about twenty-five minutes, and the people at the party—apparently a good deal of drinking was going on—either didn't remember when Ferber arrived or stated they first saw him around 10:15 or 10:30.

Following our interview, I set about checking out his story. I was able to confirm the job applications. Next, I called his therapist, who also confirmed Ferber had kept his afternoon appointment. When I asked him what had been discussed, the doctor refused to tell me, citing doctor-patient confidentiality. He did say, however, that the content had been innocuous, relating to a "domestic" problem Ferber was having. I had no reliable way to check out the early part of the evening; presumably his wife and daughter would back him up on the shopping, but that didn't mean anything. I did learn that one person at the party, a 15-year-old son of the cousin, had testified he saw "Uncle" Neil at 9:30, but I gathered the DA had raised substantial questions in the jury's mind about the boy's ability to recollect the exact time.

As I had with Ferber, I always conduct "day of the crime" interviews with suspects, a portion of the investigation that some detectives, erroneously in my judgment, either omit or fail to give sufficient attention. At times, the information I gain this way can have legal significance regarding motive and degree of premeditation, but it also helps me, as it should other detectives, to develop a storehouse of information that can be used as a measuring stick to evaluate the conduct of suspects in new cases as they arrive.

Especially illuminating to me are confessions I have obtained from those who have committed pre-planned murders, such as mob hits. I ask the killer how he prepared himself emotionally, and what he did to occupy his time during the hours before the hit was to take place. From these interviews, I had become aware of a consistent behavior pattern. The killer either drinks beforehand, or takes drugs, or both, to lower his inhibitions. He reports being nervous, having difficulty concentrating on anything other than the event ahead of him. I also regularly seek out statements from individuals who were with the killer in the immediate pre-crime period. Almost invariably, they recall he was distracted "as if thinking of other things," as one put it.

A pattern I have never encountered was the one Ferber described to me and about which I now knew he had been truthful. In no instance had I heard of a killer submitting job applications on the day he knows he's going to commit a murder. In no instance had I encountered a killer having a therapy session on the day of the murder. That struck me as virtually a psychological impossibility.

As I considered the information I now had in hand, I remember it was late in the evening; I was alone in our office in the Federal Building, no phone calls to interrupt me, eight stories up, able to look out the window by my desk at the city lights of night. Analysis time for Ferber.

One step of my analysis was easy. From Ferber's documented activities on May 27, I ruled out the possibility of premeditated murder on his part. That, however, did not by itself let him out of the crime. A word that DEA agent Hershowitz had used to describe Ferber was on point. He had said Ferber was incapable of "knowingly" participating in an act of violence. But "unknowing" accomplices are not all that rare, and Ferber, in my assessment, had a number of the qualities of such a person. His generalized hero-worshipping of criminals, the behavior of a mob groupie, fit that pattern, as did his specific attraction to violent individuals like Mad Dog DiPasquale and Barry Saltzburg. Nonviolent himself, he may have been fascinated by the sense of danger that he perceived in them, conceivably saw them as embodiments of a desirable macho quality that he feared he didn't possess.

Such a person is going to be flattered—and incapable of refusing—when an admired tough guy turns to him and says, "Listen, pal, I want you to help me out. There's this guy that owes me money, and here's a gun. I want you to cover me while I go in here and choke the son of a bitch 'til he pays me." Instead of choking, the tough guy shoots and kills the victim as he all along intended. The unknowing accomplice is horrified by what has transpired, but in the eyes of the law he is every bit as guilty as the one who pulled the trigger.

If Ferber had been a dupe in that fashion, then his innocent actions earlier in the day were meaningless.

Having found a way to put Ferber on the scene of the murder, I next had to ask myself: But would there have been a dupe like Ferber in *this* crime?

Based on my experience in working organized crime homicides, that struck me as extraordinarily unlikely. In mob hits, killers are lined up in advance, as they had been for the Salvy Testa murder. They obtain the implements necessary to carry out the deed—masks, guns, a getaway car. They are informed where the victim will be, or else lure him to a certain place at a certain time. Thus, for the crime to take place, each player must know his role. If, for some reason, one of them has to drop out, either the crime will be postponed or a replacement found who is experienced in contract killing, a job description Neil Ferber clearly didn't fit.

The likelihood of Ferber being an unwitting accomplice, therefore, was exceedingly slight but not nonexistent. Conceivably, an independent criminal (like Saltzburg or DiPasquale) could have learned that Booras was to be at the restaurant, had the guns and masks at hand, and dragged Ferber along at the last minute because no one else was available. (With both Saltzburg and DiPasquale out of the picture, who that person could be was a question unto itself.)

I next turned to consider the birthday party. What interested me was not when Ferber arrived, but that—if he was in on the killing—he had gotten there at all.

In multiple-accomplice homicides I have investigated, and those I have otherwise studied, I have learned that the conspirators almost always remain together for a period following the crime. They do this for a number of reasons. One arises from the follow-up duties they have to perform. Primarily, they must get rid of the murder weapon or weapons (a river is the usual depository) and dump the murder car (the one used in the Meletis murders was never located). They also have a need to confer with one another; they must get their stories straight about where they were when the murder took place, so that one of them, under questioning, doesn't contradict what another is saying. They also want to stay together to observe each other. Murder can produce an emotional high followed by bizarre and suspicious behavior, as it did when Willard Moran ordered the shot of whisky and threw it against the wall in memory of the man he'd just killed. If one of their number seems out of control, they may murder him too, lest he draw attention to himself and them.

For all these reasons, or any single one of them, it is highly unusual for members of a murder party to permit one of their number to leave immediately, and particularly not the one they would consider to be the weak link—in this case, Ferber. I tried to imagine their conversation as they were speeding away from killing two people. Ferber: "Oh, drop me off here at my car." (Ferber arrived at the party in his own car.) Accomplice: "Why?" Ferber: "So's I can drive up to my cousin's birthday party in Bensalem and have an alibi." Birthday parties in the circles in which Ferber and his friends traveled don't mean cakes and candles. Accomplice: "Fine, Neil, we'll drop you off and hope, while we're stopped, nobody picks up our license plate number or is able to identify us later. Oh, and by the way, Neil, while you're up there drinking and doing lines of coke, when you get high, try to remember not to mention what we just did, OK?"

It could have happened that way. Anything's possible.

During neither my first nor my second interview with him did Ferber mention an alibi he'd originally given, no doubt because it had been proved false. (I only heard about it in November 1984, two months after Ferber went to death row, from my collaborator on this book, who at the time was also investigating the Meletis murders.)

On the day of his arrest, Ferber was asked to account for his whereabouts on May 27 at the time of the murder. He gave the birthday party story to cover the latter part of the evening, and went on to say that he and his wife Annette had met earlier with his accountant, Ben Fishbein, at his home in Cheltenham, a suburb north of Philadelphia. He and his wife, Ferber said, got there around 8:00 and stayed for more than an hour, after which he dropped Annette off at home and proceeded to the party by himself. If that story was true, Ferber was out of the case. In no conceivable way could he have left Cheltenham, delivered Annette to their house in the northeast section of the city, and gotten to the murder site by 9:30.

Fishbein was immediately contacted by the detectives. His records showed an evening meeting with Ferber and his wife, but on the following evening, not on the night of the murder. Mrs. Fishbein confirmed her husband's story. She had been in New York on May 27, she said, and when she came home from a synagogue meeting on the evening of May 28, Mr. and Mrs. Ferber were there.

To the detectives, Ferber's alibi was broken. He'd lied about where he'd been, further proof of his guilt.

Over the years, I've heard many lying alibis. A typical one in an accomplice killing: "We was playing cards together." Other times the alibi is deliberately vague, as in: "I just went out for a walk. . . . I went to a movie. . . ." or in one case: "I had a fight with my wife, picked up a six-pack, drove up to Trenton and came back when I cooled off." In other instances, the suspect will claim to have no memory of the evening in question. That's not surprising, and can't be taken as a sign of guilt, since unless we have a specific reason to pinpoint a date—most people can recall exactly what they were doing when they heard President Kennedy was assassinated—our memories tend to smudge. We may think something occurred on a Monday when it was a Tuesday, and it is very possible to put two events together as happening one right after the other, when, in fact, they occurred in close juxtaposition, but not on the same day. In my work, I've observed that this form of telescoping time, which happens with witnesses as well as suspects, is particularly likely when the person is under pressure to remember, just as Ferber was when the detectives questioned him.

His mistake—putting the meeting with Fishbein on the night he wanted it to be, not the night it actually took place—was more consonant with innocence than guilt, but that wasn't what interested me about his failed alibi: It was, rather, how easy it was to break it.

If Ferber had committed the Meletis murders, he had eleven days between the commission of the crime and his arrest to develop a credible story, or at the very least, to decide on the noncommittal "I don't remember." But what had he come up with instead? A tale about meeting with an accountant—exactly the kind of person who keeps records—that required just one phone call to disprove.

Far from suggesting his guilt, his broken alibi about the meeting with Fishbein was one of the strongest indications of his innocence I had yet encountered.

19

The Salvy Testa Investigation Continues and Another Murder Occurs

As much as my concern about the Ferber case was mounting in the fall of 1984, I had only a limited time to spend on it. My major effort, and that of the Task Force, was to try to find out who killed Salvy Testa.

At the outset, we had only one negative fact: We knew from the evidence on the site where Salvy's body was found that he had not been murdered there. We soon discovered a clerk at a Two Guys store in New Jersey who tentatively identified the blanket as one she had sold to two men, but she could not give a description of them. Another possible lead was the ropes with which the corpse had been tied. Between the New Jersey State Police and us, we visited stores that sold the rope in New Jersey, in Philadelphia and throughout southeastern Pennsylvania. No luck. We also searched Salvy's boat in Margate for evidence that it was the murder site, or that the rope had come from there. Both possibilities were eliminated. Trying to locate the manufacturer of the rope proved futile. We interviewed the regulars at Pier 30, where we knew Salvy frequently played tennis. None could recall seeing Salvy on September 14.

I conducted the search of Salvy's house just as I had three-and-a-half years earlier when Phil Testa, his father, had been killed. Going back over my written inventory of that time, I saw that I had noted the presence of rope and a blanket similar to the one in which Salvy was later found wrapped. Neither item was there now. His racquet, I observed, was on his desk, where he must have placed it just before going out to meet his death, waiting there like the Little Tin Soldier in the Field poem for its master to come home and play with it again. All I could conclude from my investigation of the house was that the murder hadn't taken place there, still one more negative fact.

Two seemingly positive ones, however, were forthcoming. A police sergeant attached to the Narcotics Unit reported observing Salvy in the company of Joe Pungitore around 6 p.m. on the 14th. (It must have been the 13th.) Soon after, a caretaker on the Girard Estates came forward. He had also seen Salvy, he said, in the early evening of the 14th talking to a nursemaid and her children who lived nearby. The nanny disputed that; she didn't remember seeing Salvy that evening, and added he never spoke to her or the children.

Because of the erroneous information from the officer and the caretaker, we wasted large amounts of time trying to trace the evening movements of a man who had died at noon. (In fiction or the movies, of course, we wouldn't have had that problem; we would have known from the autopsy report the exact time of his death; in the world of reality, the medical examiners can't be nearly that precise.)

From the outset, our chief suspect was Joey Punge, for the same reason that Scarfo had selected him. We knew Joey and Salvy were close friends and that during the summer, while careful about associating with anyone else, Salvy was constantly in Joey's company, making him the probable Judas. I also considered Tommy DelGiorno a likely prospect. We had observed his rapid rise in the Scarfo organization, which could mean he was being groomed as Salvy's replacement; in that event, Scarfo would almost certainly have given him the honor of carrying out the act of succession himself. I didn't ignore the Young Executioners either. The two Narducci boys, in particular, might have been eager to rid the world of the man who murdered their father, and might have been chosen to participate for that reason.

During the months that followed Salvy's death, other officers and I made it a practice to drop by two bars favored by the Young Executioners, Sharkey's on South Broad Street and Joe Dickie's, a few blocks farther west. "Here's your capo," I might say to one of the punks, showing him Salvy's picture. "He's dead; what makes you think you won't be next? You know what Scarfo's like. You know how these alliances are with Nicky. One day you're in, the next you're out, and then you're like Salvy."

It's a technique that never seems to work while it is going on. No one responds, "Oh, yes, you're right; golly, I better tell you all I know." But it does lay groundwork, puts thoughts in the mind that can bear fruit when other pressures build on an individual to talk. In any event, it was worth a try, since we had not a scintilla of evidence leading us anywhere. (Our luck in the investigation was bad all the way; not only were we inadvertently misled about the time of Salvy's death, but the policeman that Pungitore and Grande thought had seen them entering Something Sweet the week before the murder apparently hadn't, or else hadn't recognized them. If he had, he would have made a report on it as soon as he heard Salvy was dead.)

It wasn't only bars we went into. We made our presence felt constantly on the street, too. See a mobster, pull him over, give him the lecture.

One day, a month or so after the killing, FBI agent Bud Warner and I spotted Tommy Del and Wayne Grande sitting on milk crates in front of the mob clubhouse on Camac Street. The clubhouse had a dingy back room furnished with chairs covered with ripped vinyl, a card table, and on one wall, a photo of Little Nicky standing in front of his Hallandale, Florida, mansion, which he called Casablanca South. (Nicky was a great Humphrey Bogart fan.)

The shabbiness of the clubhouse and the men sitting outside on the milk crates define one of the oddities of mob life that has always fascinated me. Tommy Del was, by then, a millionaire several times over, and if Wayne Grande wasn't, he was well on the way. Men like them love the luxuries wealth brings them, expensive clothes, big cars, fancy women for themselves, furs for their wives, marble staircases and similar self-indulgences for their homes—like the state-of-the-art bidet Salvy had installed in his refurbished house on the Girard Estates. Nevertheless, they remain men of the streets, continually returning to their origins as if they could only find their identities, not in a grand plush sofa or behind a huge desk, but sitting on a milk crate in front of a broken-down building. They were Del and Wayne that day, and Salvy Testa on days past, leaning back on the old kitchen stool to eat his clams while watching the throngs in the Italian Market. Such is the ethos and environment of mob life.

Bud and I went up to them. Squat little Del waved me a greeting, and the grim-looking Wayne was cold but polite. I gave them my canned lecture about how the mob was in turmoil, no one sure any more who was on whose side. I concluded by observing to Wayne, "The likelihood is that if your capo is dead, you're not in favor either, and so you'll be dead soon, too. Here, I want to show how you guys will end up."

With that, I took out the two photographs I always carried with me and handed them first to Del. One was of Salvy's body showing the bullet hole in the back of his brain, the other an autopsy picture. In it, Salvy's skullcap has been removed, empty sockets where his eyes had been, flesh stripped from the face, a hole where once there was a mouth.

Del was confused. He didn't think he was looking at a human being. I helpfully pointed out the highlights. "Jesus Christ," he said, going gray, and turning away in horror. I took the pictures from his trembling hand and gave them over to Wayne. He displayed a clinical interest in the autopsy photo. Explaining he'd once worked in a funeral parlor, with obvious relish he said, "Oh, yeah, here's where they took his skull off, and that's where his eyes were."

I considered him a moment. He was my chief suspect as the person who had shot Harry Riccobene in the phone booth while Harry was talking to his girlfriend two years earlier. Stone-cold killers do that kind of thing. Now, regardless of what he learned in the funeral home, the objectivity with which he discussed the remains of his boss and friend made me move him up several notches on my list of suspects. A coward's bullet in the back of the head, I thought, was exactly Wayne Grande's style.

I took my pictures back; I'd use them again. "So long, fellows," I said, and Warner and I went back to our car and drove off, leaving the man who had planned the killing and the one who had carried it out sitting on their milk crates in the sun, contemplating, I hoped, their grim futures. In retrospect, I think it more likely they were laughing at me.

As 1984 ended, with no end in sight for the Salvy Testa murder investigation, it wasn't just Tommy Del and Wayne Grande who had reason to laugh at us. Scarfo did, too. We were no closer to an indictment of him than we had been when the Task Force was formed in 1982. He had—for what comfort that was—been somewhat hurt financially. Thanks to the success of the FBI investigation of Mayor Matthews, he had lost his control over Atlantic City government and the riches that had brought. Even more harmful to him was the New Jersey Gaming Commission's new attention to the Hotel Workers Union—brought about by the Martorano and Daidone trial—which had hampered his extortionate activities against the casinos, if not necessarily his rake-offs from its Health and Welfare Fund. Law enforcement, however, takes no credit for another declining source of income for Scarfo, that provided by heroin. The recession in its sales had begun before he became don and continued into the 1980s, as cocaine and subsequently its derivative, crack, replaced heroin as the number one narcotics choice. The Mafia has never been able to get a handle on the cocaine business. Colombian merchants have retained principal control of it from the manufacturing through the wholesale distribution stage.

Not that mobsters like Scarfo weren't profiting from cocaine. Like dealers of other contraband, those selling coke pay to do business in an LCN territory. According to our information, a major supplier to the Philadelphia/Atlantic City mob, Billy Motta, was assessed around $500,000 a year in the early 1980s for the privilege of selling to the same people who were extracting the tax from him. (In the straight world, businessmen collect sales taxes from customers; in the Mafia world, the customers collect sales taxes from the businessmen.) Since it was not only Motta who was paying but every other cocaine peddler, large or small, who could be located by Scarfo's vigilant enforcers, his share of the proceeds each year was considerable. But it didn't begin to match the amounts that had flowed in during the good old heroin days.

There had been no similar slackening of profits from the meth business. Income from it derived from two sources: the profit from product sales, and P2P. By early 1985, Saul

Kane's P2P importations alone were producing a million dollars a month.

It was early in 1985 that the next murder of an organized crime figure took place. The victim this time was a powerfully built, intimidating man of middle years named Frank Forline. He was typical of the kind of opposition that Scarfo, with his ever-escalating demands for tribute payments, continued to encounter after the fall of the Riccobenes. It wasn't that Forline refused to pay Scarfo; he just kept delaying. In so doing, he probably felt he had some protection in the form of the equally menacing-looking Scarfo capo, Chickie Ciancaglini. They had known each other since they were boys, had been best men at each other's weddings.

By 1985, however, any protection Ciancaglini might have been providing Forline seemed to have vanished. Ciancaglini, by then, was doing a stretch in prison on federal racketeering charges, which ordinarily wouldn't have affected his power, but his associations with Scarfo's enemies, the Riccobenes, which went back for years, probably did. In any event, one day in the middle of January, Scarfo sent Tommy Del and Nicky Crow to visit Forline at the headquarters of Action Concrete, a Philadelphia company in a Philadelphia suburb that Forline controlled. (He had walked into its offices one day and announced to the owners, "I'm now your partner. I'll get you business, contracts." The owners, apparently scared by his physical presence and recognizing who his associates must be, decided that was an offer they couldn't refuse.) On their arrival, Del and The Crow sagely advised Forline that the time had come to pay Scarfo. Forline, according to the account I received, proceeded to deck Del, after which Del and Crow skulked off.

On February 7, while on his way to work, Forline stopped off at a nearby shopping center. There he was met by a man who got into the truck with him. They proceeded to the deserted rear sector of the mall. Forline parked the truck against a snow bank. It was the last thing he ever did.

His body was discovered the next day. When my team and I arrived on the scene, it seemed to me we finally had on our hands a murder that could be solved quickly. The shooter's bloody fingerprints were all over the truck.

I thought too soon. The prints didn't belong to Del or The Crow, nor anyone else in the Philadelphia/Atlantic City mob, nor anyone in the entire United States to whose prints we had access. Aside from the fact that Forline's killer was male, we had no description of him either. It is conceivable that Forline's death had nothing to do with his mob activities, but we were unable to find anything in his personal life to suggest that; neither had he been robbed. To this day, of the thirty-four murders that took place, his is the only one for which we have no idea who the killer was, nor have we been able to tie the order for the hit back to Scarfo or anyone else. It was a sloppy, brazen daylight homicide and apparently a perfect one.

20
Crooked Cops and a Condemned Man's Fantasies

While I was spending my time—sometimes successfully, sometimes not—trying to combat Don Nicky Scarfo and his organized crime family, another version of organized crime was also on the loose in Philadelphia. It had its own dons: They were Philadelphia police officers.

The first crooked police operation to be uncovered was a typical Mafia-style protection racket. I have no idea when it originated (probably long before I joined the force in 1960) but the first evidence of it (that is, someone who was ready to talk) did not turn up until early 1982—by coincidence almost exactly at the same time my Organized Crime Task Force came into existence. The informant was a brothel-keeper who told the FBI that cops were forcing him to pay them off if he wanted to stay in business. The FBI thereupon began a protracted undercover operation, which developed evidence that the extortions of which the brothel-keeper complained were widespread. For the most part, those involved in the payoffs were district captains and officers assigned by the captains to investigate vice. The units to which the officers belonged were called "five squads" to distinguish them from the other four squads in a district that exclusively carried out patrol work. The implicated five squadders did the collections and divvied up the spoils with the captain. But it wasn't just the district captains and their five squadders who were on the take. Inspectors, who are above captains in the police bureaucracy, have their own vice teams, and several of these inspectors and their underlings were also implicated.

As I recall, it was around the time of the Frank Forline murder in February 1985 that the story of the FBI investigation first hit the Philadelphia newspapers. Coming under the heaviest criticism—how come he didn't know what was going on in his own department?—was Police Commissioner Gregore Sambor. A craggy, heavyset, military type, Sambor had succeeded Morton Solomon as commissioner about a year earlier. By March of 1985, matters got worse for Sambor when the FBI investigation led not to him—there never was a suggestion he was corrupt—but to the office next door to his where presided his most trusted colleague, Deputy Commissioner James Martin. (I was present one day when Sambor told John Hogan, the FBI agent in charge of the Philadelphia office, that anytime he, Sambor, wasn't available, Hogan could confide in Martin. "It will be just like talking to me," Sambor assured Hogan, who by then was well aware of the developing case against Martin as the boss of bosses of the police Mafia. As with Scarfo and Bruno and other dons, the tribute money flowed up to him.)

Looked at one way, Sambor's trouble was not of his own making. The corrupt, high-ranking officers held their positions thanks to civil service promotions. Sambor, therefore, had inherited, not created, a problem. Nevertheless, both Sambor and Solomon (who was also, as far as I know, personally honest) failed to recognize or failed to deal with an inherently corruptive situation.

Vice squad cops, as both men should have known, are under constant temptation to accept or demand payoffs from pimps and illegal gambling operations. Not every vice cop, by any means, is on the take in Philadelphia, anymore than all of them were on the take in New York City at the time of the Knapp Commission, but the corruption is widespread and persistent, in part because it is so easily rationalized by the extortionists. They point out that vice figures hardly ever go to jail and that some judges are paid off, too (which in Philadelphia was no fantasy). There was, therefore, no point in arresting these crooks, and since everybody was getting into the act, they might as well get their share of the loot, too. After all, it wasn't as though they were stealing from honest people.

One little-noted reason for the persistence of vice squad extortions, and not just in Philadelphia and New York but elsewhere across the country, is that most honest cops don't want vice squad assignments. They are afraid of getting dirtied by those on the take or of being tempted themselves. As a result, as a former police commissioner (who also did nothing about the problem) once put it, "A cop who asks for transfer to vice, there's only one reason for it."

What was unusual about the Philadelphia vice scandal, therefore, was not that it occurred, but how widespread it was and how high in the Department it reached. By the time the arrests and trials reached an end in 1987, Deputy Commissioner Martin, two chief inspectors, two inspectors, six captains and lieutenants, and twenty-five nonranking officers were convicted.* Still others were dismissed from the force or permitted to resign under pressure, including several more captains and inspectors.

By 1985, also, although indictments did not come down until three years later, the FBI investigation had branched out in another direction: narcotics. At that time, in addition to all the little five squads, we had an elite Five Squad that ranged citywide, busting drug dealers. According to the FBI information, much of it based on evidence provided by two former Five Squadders who had been convicted of corruption and become government witnesses, many members of the squad, including the commanding officer, Captain John Wilson, had used their knowledge of drug activity not to make arrests and protect the public but frequently to enrich themselves. They allegedly either extorted money from the dealers or confiscated their stock (which they then sold themselves) or a combination of both. In the 1989 trial of Five Squad members, Andrew Mainardi, a convicted yuppie cocaine dealer (who had a seat on the Philadelphia Stock Exchange), stated that when Five Squad officers raided his townhouse, they took him up to his bedroom, where they spread out on his bed the fruits of their search: $13,000 in cash, seven grams of cocaine, several ounces of marijuana, some hashish, and about twenty Quaaludes. The officer in charge, whose name Mainardi couldn't remember, allegedly told him he had two choices: Either they could "go by the book" or else work something out.

The officer then went on to point out that most of the drugs would get "lost" if he let them keep the money, Mainardi testified. When Mainardi agreed to the proposal, the officer, he said, went to the balcony overlooking the living room and shouted down to his fellow Five Squadders that the case was

*Martin died of cancer before he could begin serving his sentence.

just a minor pot bust. The other officers, Mainardi went on, cheered this good news. Mainardi was placed on non-reporting probation on the marijuana charge. In their eagerness to make the deal, Mainardi recalled, the cops missed a set of keys that would have led them to a house containing $2.4 million worth of cocaine.

According to another drug dealer, Walter Roeder, the Five Squad wasn't even honest when it was stealing. He said that when two Five Squadders raided his apartment, they found $40,000 in cash in a plastic bag. They agreed they'd take half of it. When the cops left, Roeder said he discovered they'd taken $30,000.

The accusations, coupled as they were with the admissions from two of the cops about their corruption, coming on the heels of similar cases in which there were already convictions, had a disastrous effect on morale within the Department. There were expressions of anger, too, from the vast majority of officers who find such activities and the people who engage in them loathesome.*

In the spring of 1985, when the first set of corruption charges in the vice cases were being aired, I was meeting on a regular basis with Commissioner Sambor to discuss the Task Force's cases. I found him to be a likable and even rather charming man—certainly, compared to his predecessor, the glacial Solomon. (Sambor's public image was entirely different from his private persona and helped add to his woes. In interviews with the media, it seemed to me that he came across as stiff, arrogant and, worst of all, not very intelligent.) Sambor was a great enthusiast of the Task Force, possibly because our arrests had given the Police Department most of what little good publicity it had gotten in recent years, but principally, I think, because he was a professional police

---

*In November 1989, four of the six indicted Five Squad officers, including Captain Wilson, were found guilty by a federal court jury on charges of racketeering, conspiracy and filing false income tax returns. Appeals in their cases were pending at the deadline date for this book.

officer who sincerely wanted to rid the city of Scarfo and his version of organized crime. As a matter of protocol, I had informed Sambor of my investigation of the Meletis murders, my growing belief that Ferber had been wrongfully convicted of them, and the evidence I was putting together that indicated the hit had been orchestrated by Raymond Martorano. Sambor gave me the authorization to treat the Meletis shootings as an open mob murder hit to be handled by the Task Force. The Ferber angle never seemed to interest Sambor much, but Martorano did. Long John had escaped the electric chair in the McCullough assassination, maybe he wouldn't be so lucky if we could convict him of killing Booras and Curro.

Nevertheless, despite Sambor's backing, the Task Force had been under attack elsewhere in the Police Department, an opposition, I noticed, that arose in the summer of 1984 when I began to pay serious attention to the Meletis murders. Leading the opposition was my immediate superior, Captain Gene Dooley, who had replaced Jerry Kane when Jerry was promoted to inspector about a year earlier.

Dooley, a tall and prematurely balding man with intense eyes, I always thought to be a basically good-hearted person, and he was in my judgment a thoroughly competent police officer, but someone who, it was my impression, had accepted from his training that the only way to be a successful cop was to be an intimidating one. He also had the habit of going off in several directions at once in a conversation or an investigation. This trait had earned him the departmental nickname of ''Rick,'' for ''richochet.''

Dooley wasn't happy with the Task Force in general, and was very unhappy with me in particular. A friend of his was the captain who then headed the police organized crime unit that helped us in an advisory role but had been excluded from the Task Force because its men weren't experienced in homicide investigations. This captain had asked me to report to him about all Task Force activities. I avoided doing that; in my judgment, the fewer the people who knew what we were doing, the safer the operation. Besides, the captain wasn't my superior officer; Jerry Kane then was, and he'd never asked me to report to him. (I discussed the cases with Jerry on a regular basis even so, but that was because I valued his insights.)

A few months after he succeeded Jerry as chief of the Homicide Unit, Dooley told me to pack my bags and report the following night to work the 12-to-8 shift on regular murder cases. It was a waste of time, Dooley explained, for me and my SIU men to concentrate on thirty-some organized crime murders when there were hundreds of others we could be working on.

I had no choice but to obey that order, but I did tell him he should be aware that the Task Force had been approved at the top level of the Department. I called over to the FBI and told my codirector of the Task Force, Dennis O'Callaghan, of my transfer. Dennis went immediately to his boss, John Hogan, who called Chief Inspector Scafidi, whose baby the Task Force was. Scafidi countermanded Dooley. The Task Force was back in operation, and more: My new orders were to report only to the Police Commissioner. Dooley wasn't happy about that anymore than I would have been in his position. For the moment there was nothing he could do about it. But the time was increasingly close at hand when he could.

During the spring and early summer months of 1985, I stepped up my investigation of the Meletis murders. Ferber's lawyer, Dennis Cogan, had continued to keep in touch with me and was particularly interested in obtaining the polygraph test that had been given to Jerry Jordan, a key prosecution witness in Ferber's trial. Jordan had testified that Ferber had confessed to killing Booras and Curro when the two men were in prison together shortly after Ferber's arrest. I was interested in seeing the chart, too, but as I told Dennis, because of complex and illogical police bureaucratic regulations, I could not obtain it on my own. I told him he'd have to go to the top for it, which he did. Toward the end of July

1985, I received a call from Police Commissioner Sambor passing Dennis's request on to me for my decision. That gave me the authorization I needed, and I obtained the chart. Before turning it over to Dennis, (who had lined up a polygrapher, William Anderson, to study it), I decided to get my own expert opinion, and I had no doubt about whom I would choose.

Frank Cryan's abilities as a polygrapher had first come to my attention in the Robert Hornickel murder case. Hornickel had been killed on January 27, 1983, after a dispute with his confederates in which he complained he had been cheated out of his fair share of the proceeds in a drug deal in which Chickie Ciancaglini, the late Frank Forline's pal, was allegedly involved. My investigation indicated that the hit was ordered by Ciancaglini. The alleged shooter (yet to be charged) was supposedly accompanied to the murder by Ronald "Cuddles" DiCaprio, the friendly bartender at Cous' Little Italy. Considering Cuddles to be the weak link, I had subpoenaed him before our federal grand jury, where we gave him a grant of immunity. After he refused to testify, he was held in contempt and imprisoned at the federal government's Metropolitan Correction Center in New York. Soon after, a call came in from Cuddles' cellmate, who said Cuddles had confessed to him. The cellmate had been convicted of passing worthless checks and was hoping his information would give him a ticket out of jail. I conducted an interview with him in which he laid out for me in detail the entire scenario. Since he had never been in Philadelphia and had no associations in the city—I checked that—it seemed inescapable to me that his knowledge had to come from Cuddles.

I was prepared to have Cuddles charged with the murder, the cellmate as our star witness. To be on the safe side, however, I asked Frank Cryan of the FBI to put him through a polygraph test. When Cryan completed the examination, he came back to me: "He's lying," he said.

I was stunned. I told Frank he'd better recheck his dials;

the man couldn't know what he did unless Cuddles told him. Even so, I brought the cellmate in. "You just blew up the box," I said. On hearing that, he rather cheerfully admitted that it figured. Cuddles, he went on, had told him the story of the murder but always with the preface: "This is what they're accusing me of." I felt stupid. The truth was so obvious, now that it was obvious. After that I never doubted Frank Cryan. If he said somebody was lying, he was lying.

"He was lying," Frank said as he handed me back the Jordan chart.

The police polygrapher who gave Jordan the examination had called the results "inconclusive" and recommended Jordan be given a second test before he was permitted to testify against Ferber. That was never done, nor was there any rule requiring it. Under DA Rendell's regulations, a witness who *failed* a polygraph could not be used as a witness, but those testing inconclusive weren't excluded. It had, even so, struck me as appalling that the follow-up test wasn't given to a key witness in a first-degree murder case. Now Frank Cryan was telling me that the results, far from being inconclusive, unmistakably showed deception.

I was aware, of course, that two polygraphers could read the same chart differently, but I was also aware, gloomily, that arresting officers can sometimes put pressure on a police polygrapher ("We *know* this guy did it," they would advise before the test was given), and if the polygrapher was accommodating or didn't want to make enemies, the reading could be slanted without entirely compromising the polygrapher's integrity—from "deception" to "inconclusive."

Backing Cryan's analysis of the Jordan chart was Cogan's polygrapher, Anderson, a retired FBI agent. He found it "inexplicable," he said, that any polygrapher could read the Jordan results as inconclusive.

I was convinced that Jordan had lied, but to what extent and for what reason was not yet clear to me. If I were going to interrogate Jordan intelligently some day, I needed to know more about the entire case.

My first step in that direction was to interview Ronald Raiton, who, I knew, had a long-standing relationship with Raymond Martorano. Raiton was in the Witness Protection Program but reachable through his FBI control, Gary Langan. (Raiton had no choice but to cooperate; as part of the terms of his probation, he was required to be available for questioning in any criminal investigation.)

In a letter to his wife, Raiton had expressed the belief that control of P2P distribution was the motive for Booras's murder. When I asked him why he reached that conclusion, he said it was largely an assumption on his part: Martorano and Booras were both buying P2P from him, and a mobster's usual way of solving a competition problem is to kill the competitor. But he also had an anecdote to tell me. By way of background, he explained, Martorano had been after him for some time to become his exclusive P2P franchisee in Philadelphia; as an enticement, he had offered to help Raiton collect money he was owed. With that offer in mind, at a meeting with Martorano a day or two after Booras's death, Raiton (who by then was acting undercover for the government) said to Long John, "How about Stevie?" referring to a mob associate named Steve Vento who was into Raiton for a considerable sum.

Martorano, Raiton said, immediately became furious. "That's none of your business," he shouted. "Keep your nose out of things that don't concern you." Raiton was surprised both by Martorano's vehemence and his apparent reneging on his promise to help him collect from Vento. Then, Raiton recalled, "it suddenly clicked into place," and he realized that Martorano thought he was talking about Steve Booras. "No, no," he said. "No. Vento. What about Stevie Vento? What about my money?"

It was Martorano's turn to look surprised. He calmed down

and began to discuss the Vento problem with Raiton. (As part of his deal with the government, Raiton promised to—and did—turn over the receipts from any new income he was receiving from his P2P distribution. He had, however, every intention of collecting on old debts, like Vento's. During that summer, despite the fact that Raiton was under virtual round-the-clock surveillance by the FBI, he managed to ship millions of dollars out of the country.)

Either immediately before or after the Vento misunderstanding, the Booras case also came up in a meeting Raiton had with John Berkery, who'd later tell Dennis O'Callaghan that Ferber was innocent. In the Berkery conversation, Berkery, in passing, indicated to Raiton that while he hadn't participated in the Booras murder, he knew all about it.

This conversation was taped by Raiton and handed over to the FBI, which at the time was, along with the police, investigating the Booras murder. The agents working with Raiton, however, apparently never advised the ones on the Booras case about the reference to the murder on Raiton's tape of the Berkery conversation. Had that information been passed on, the investigation almost certainly would have focused on Martorano and the members of his crew, like big Frank Vadino. Ferber probably never would have even been a suspect. (As it was, the tape did not surface until 1987, when Berkery, who had been caught while sneaking into the United States, was on trial for his drug dealings with Raiton and others. Berkery's conviction on that charge was reversed on appeal, but prior to his second trial, he pleaded guilty and got a reduced sentence.)

We were by now in the late summer of 1985 and Neil Ferber had been on death row for almost a year. It was around that time that he explained to his brother Jay how he was trying to keep his mind off the little room with the chair. "I imagine," he said, "that I have a lot of money and so I buy this house in Florida, a really big house, and I go through the house room by room, and I furnish it. I choose chairs, tables, beds, the carpeting, the drapes, figure out how they'll all go together. Then, when I have that house furnished, I sell it and I go out and buy another house, and I start to furnish it, all different. I spend a lot of my time doing that,'' the death house fantasizing of a furniture salesman.

That's what he did, lying on his bunk, staring up at the ceiling, unable to sleep, in the noise. The noise, he told his brother, that was the worst, he had to keep it away somehow, the men of death row shouting and screaming and crying, the rattling of the bars, the constant clanging of the doors. It was a place of horror for a guilty person. How much worse for an innocent one?

And I couldn't help Ferber. All I had was theory. All I had was intuition. All I had was experience. I had nothing to go to court with. Like Ferber, I was having trouble sleeping. I was becoming obsessed by the murders at the Meletis.

21
How Neil Ferber Became a Murder Suspect

So far, I had only one piece of ammunition in the Ferber case, Frank Cryan's verdict on Jerry Jordan's polygraph, and it was of limited value. At most, I could use it to show DA Rendell that reason existed to believe a key witness had lied. (The entire polygraph subject, however, was likely to be a touchy one with Rendell, since Cryan's finding bounced right back to the underlying question: Why hadn't Rendell's office insisted on a second polygraph of Jordan when the first tester urged that be done? One inference that occurred to me was that there was fear of what the second test would show.)

In any event, the Jordan polygraph, no matter how it was interpreted, wasn't admissible in court, so I needed more, a great deal more. To try to find it, I decided I was going to have to do what I'd told Cogan I'd not do, investigate the investigation. On the basis of Commissioner Sambor's explicit approval to treat the Meletis murders as a Task Force matter, I was able to obtain the case file. It was time to do some detective work.

I began at the beginning by reading the statements of the people who had been present in the restaurant when the shooting occurred: those who worked there, those who had been part of the Booras dinner party, and the other diners. The total was twenty-one possible witnesses, of whom nineteen had been interviewed. Missing from the file were statements from Raymond Martorano and his wife Evelyn, who had apparently left the restaurant through the back before the police arrived; Detective Chitwood later said he tried to speak to Martorano the next day at his lawyer's office, but that Martorano refused to talk with him.

Several of those in the restaurant had not observed the crime. That group included the restaurant's owner and chef, who were in the kitchen when the gunmen entered. From among those who saw something, I learned that each killer was between 5'6" and 6'7" in height and weighed anywhere from 130 to 240 pounds. I didn't find the diversity of descriptions surprising. The shooting could not have covered more than a few seconds, with the time between the entrance of the killers and their exit well under a minute. During that interval, incredulity—no one expects to see a murder committed while having dinner in a restaurant—was mixed with sheer terror. People were screaming, some diving under tables (making the killers look tall), others frozen into position, possibly with their hands partly covering their eyes to keep out the horrific vision confronting them.

One aspect of the descriptions, however, struck me as possibly significant. Among the witnesses who saw the bullets being fired at Booras, there was agreement that the shooter wore a ski mask. He was the man that "Joey Eye" Inadi, the ex-cop, had described as weighing nearly his own 240 pounds. Some of the viewers believed that the man who fired the bullets into the ceiling also wore a ski mask, others weren't sure, and still others thought he had the lower part of his face covered with a scarf. I turned next to the statements of Mr. and Mrs. John Egan, who were in their car in front of the restaurant when the two men ran out. The man who stopped momentarily in the glare of their headlights, whom they subsequently identified as Ferber, had ripped off a ski mask as he turned to look back at the murder scene. Therefore, if only the killer wore a ski mask, it was the killer they had seen.

In rereading the interviews, and from the absence of any mention of the subject elsewhere in the file, I realized that the original investigators had never made an effort to learn which gunman was the shooter, apparently because they didn't think they had to. They assumed Ferber had fired the shots into the ceiling and were certain that he would eventually confess, and give them the actual killer, whom they first believed to be Saltzburg, and later DiPasquale. I decided to interview everyone who'd given a statement, and over the next several weeks, with the help of my detectives, that task was accomplished.

As a consequence of those interviews, I was able to determine the truth about the masks, and also turned up information that further implicated Martorano. Concerning Martorano, I learned, from two restaurant employees and one of Janette Curro's sisters, that Booras and Martorano had had dinner together at the Meletis about two weeks before the murder, providing important corroboration for Willard Moran's statement that he had come to the Meletis about that time to kill Booras but had been scared off by the police car he saw parked nearby. "Joey Eye" Inadi also supplied a suggestive detail. It was Martorano, he said, who had arranged the seating at the fatal table.

To solve the mask problem, I recognized I needed to find a witness or witnesses who had seen the killers *before* the shooting began. Such a person would have a pre-memory of the appearance of the killers, unclouded by the fear that ensued or by the gaps in vision caused by trying to duck out of the way of bullets.

In studying the interviews, I found two persons who might meet that criterion. One, a waiter, had to be eliminated because he attested to having bad eyesight. That left Marcella Kohler, the barmaid. She had observed the killers entering the restaurant, had them in her vision for ten to twenty seconds before the shooting began. She also struck me as a woman of considerable presence of mind. When the first shots were fired, she ducked behind the bar, pulled the phone down and dialed 911.

On meeting with her, I found her recollection quite similar to that which detectives had taken down on the night of the shooting four years earlier. Under my questioning, she recalled a few additional details—she may never have been asked about them before—which were consistent with what she could have seen and apparently so trivial they they did not appear to be embellishments.

She told me she had first noticed the two men while they were still outside the door to the restaurant, and had the impression they bumped into each other in their eagerness to get inside. On seeing them in their parkas, her first thought had been, "Why are they wearing winter clothes in May?"

Both men were heavyset, she said. One of them—she couldn't be specific about heights—was wearing a ski mask, while the other had his face covered from the nose down with a scarf (she couldn't be sure of the color) and wore a navy blue watchman's cap. That was a new detail and an impressive one to me. People in moments of stress (and she wasn't stressed at that moment) often remember seeing things they haven't seen, but they don't misremember details such as a watchman's cap, much less its color. That's not the stuff of imagination. Marcie Kohler had removed the possibility that both men wore ski masks.

She went on to say that the man in the scarf pulled out his gun and fired into the ceiling. She recalled thinking, "My God, it's a holdup." She next observed the heavyset man in the ski mask begin firing directly at Booras.

Since there was no reason to doubt the Egans when they said they observed one gunman pull off a ski mask, the conclusion was inescapable that that person was the killer. He couldn't have been, as had been assumed, the one who fired into the ceiling; that man wore a scarf. You can't have it both ways, I thought. Either slender Ferber is the heavyset, coldblooded murderer in the ski mask or he wasn't there at all.

I next turned to Mrs. Egan's identification of Ferber from the mugshot array displayed to her and her husband at their home on the evening of June 1, four days after the killing, and three days after they helped create the eyewitness sketch.

Among the seven photos shown to Mr. and Mrs. Egan by detectives Chitwood and Mitsos were those of Ferber and Barry Saltzburg. (DiPasquale, at that time, had yet to come under suspicion, and his was not included.) John Egan, who is an architect, got the first opportunity to look at the pictures but failed to name anybody.

Linda Egan kept a journal of the events of that period. I only became aware of it several years after I completed my investigation; by then, it had become one of the many documents that were part of the court record in the Meletis murder case. In her diary, Mrs. Egan describes the meeting with Chitwood and Mitsos:

> They showed us each (separately) about seven pictures
> . . . and asked if we could identify any of the men.
> John went first, then me. I said #34. I felt a chill when
> I saw him. He was most like the man I saw.

Chitwood took statement. I said I chose #34 from
that group. He wrote something like: "This is one that
looks most like the man I saw last Wed. night, the night
of the murders, or most like the one who pulled off his
mask. As far as I am concerned, he is the one." But
I said, "As far as I can tell, he is the one."

He called John back. . . . He said they don't think
the killings are mob-related as the media has been saying. They think Peetros was robbed of an expensive
ring.* Then Booras, Peetros' friend, vowed to get his
killers. So killers killed him first. Jeannette [sic] Curro
was in the way of one of the bullets.

Mrs. Egan's recollection of what Chitwood wrote is accurate (based on the police statement I found in the file) and
became the grounds for obtaining an arrest warrant for Ferber.
Clearly, the detectives believed in good faith that they had
sufficient evidence for the warrant, but I was shocked—and
would have been even more so if I'd had Linda Egan's diary
available at the time—since her supposed identification in
my opinion wasn't legally sufficient to arrest anyone. My
own policy would have been to ask the question, "Are you
sure, to the exclusion of every other man, that this is the
man?" Quite apparently, she would have answered no, yet
from her diary and Chitwood's version of her words, that
question was never asked. From her "as far as I can tell,"
Ferber clearly should have been a suspect, and an effort made
to find confirming *or exculpatory* evidence concerning him;
but the arrest warrant, which was approved by the DA's office
and a judge, should not have been issued. Moreover, even
if Chitwood and Mitsos thought her identification was
stronger than it was, I would have been concerned about John

*He had been. The motive for the loanshark Peetros's murder has never
been established. The most likely theory is that the contract was put out on
him by someone who owed him a great deal of money.

Egan. He had every bit as good a look at the person who removed the ski mask as his wife had, but he had failed to identify Ferber. Nevertheless, the warrant was obtained and Ferber taken into custody on June 8.

The case was about to take an unexpected turn. It occurred at a police lineup at the Detention Center, a Philadelphia jail for untried prisoners, on June 24. Chitwood drove the Egans there, where they were introduced to Guy Sciolla, the assistant DA assigned to try the case. Again, from Linda Egan's journal:

> Eventually we each filled out a form describing what we had seen to Det. Chitwood as he wrote it down.
>
> Mine said, basically, saw two men, described one, lighted highway. One white male approx. 5′6″, wearing bulky clothing so unable to see weight or build. Light-colored hair. [Ferber's hair was dark brown, almost black.]
>
> At last, they determined lineup would prob. be fair. We went into building, men were frisked, women opened purses. Went up ramp & into a waiting room/ auditorium. . . .
>
> We sat down in the front row of chairs in front of a white-haired man, a woman & another man. The Dets. & the DA came in & stood to one side.
>
> The man running the lineup laid down ground rules. 7 men would come into lighted box. Each would go through series of moves that the man would order. We must sit in chairs separated from each other, view whole lineup, not talk or shout.
>
> At end he would call us out singly & ask if we wanted to identify any of them. If so we would say yes & give the # of the man. If no, say no.
>
> He turned out light in room, turned on lights in box, which shone out into the room some. I think the men in the box could see us nearly as well as we saw them.

Ferber [she knew him by name now because of the news stories following his arrest which featured a photo of him] was #3. I recognized him from his picture as soon as they led him in. His hair was the same as in the picture, but he was very much thinner than the picture.

None of the others looked anything like the man I saw on 5/27.

But I felt Ferber was wrong, too. He was too old, too thin, had wrong color hair. Had more delicate bone structure than man I saw. Also moved completely differently, seemed almost effeminate here, not so then.

He was obviously very scared, but who could say why?

At the lineup I was farther away and farther to the left than on the night of 5/27. I didn't see Ferber in profile too well as a result.

Still he seemed wrong, the wrong man.

So when I was called out, I said, "No"—I did not want to identify anyone.

When John was called out he said, "Yes—#3."

He believes Ferber is definitely the man because he has the unusual hairline he remembers. Also, John said he's never known anyone who looks like Ferber & so identified him based on that.

We all went back down the ramp together, the defense attorney . . . , Mrs. Ferber . . . & the private investigator . . . in the back.

. . . Mrs. Ferber spoke about getting home to feed a baby. The attorney said she has four children! in an obvious play for sympathy.

The DA—Sciolla—said when we went in we were ahead. Now they & we are even. "But that's all right," he said. (!)

Chitwood stood with his back to us, his arms folded, looking out across the landscape.

The DA wants John to go to the hearing tomorrow. Mrs. Curro's sister will testify about what happened inside, John about what happened outside. I am not to come. I guess because the DA asked, "If they ask you in court if he is the man you saw, what will you say?"

"He's not the man I saw," I answered him & explained how he looked wrong.

Chitwood interjected that there was a lot of anxiety about lineups—the old male chauvinist stuff.

Chitwood drove us back home. I asked if Ferber didn't have a younger brother who had different hair. Chitwood paid no attention.

John said, "Well, I sure hope you have more on him than our identifications."

Chitwood replied . . . he couldn't tell us what they had on him & he wasn't going to.

When Assistant DA Sciolla told Mrs. Egan that, as a result of the lineup, they were now "even," he presumably meant that her husband's identification made up for the loss of hers.

In fact, the prosecution had been dealt a serious blow. Because Mrs. Egan was now saying Ferber wasn't the person she saw, she had become a potential witness for the defense, while Mr. Egan's value was weakened by the fact that he had failed to name Ferber from the photo array. Ferber's lawyer could have a field day with the shifting identifications between husband and wife.

I, however, wasn't reading the Egans' statements from a lawyer's point of view, but rather as a detective. From that perspective, I knew that eyewitness identifications can be fraught with credibility problems. One is raised by the polluting effect of after-events. In this instance, following Ferber's arrest, a police spokesman announced that the Department had definitely arrested the right person, the case was solved, and the newspapers carried that story, along with the same mugshot photo of Ferber that had been shown the

Egans. John Egan clipped the story and picture and carried it in his wallet. Who, therefore, was he identifying at the lineup? Was it the person he saw fleeing the restaurant? Or the person whose picture he saw in the newspaper and whom the police pronounced guilty?

His sincerity wasn't at issue. I have no doubt he was positive the person he named at the lineup was the same as the one he saw remove the ski mask. However, he had been subjected to influences that would not have occurred had the lineup taken place before the "guilty" newspaper story and its reinforcing image of Ferber's photo. That Mrs. Egan hadn't been similarly influenced is irrelevant. Different people respond to stimuli in different ways. Had she identified Ferber at the lineup, the question about the intervening polluting effect would have held true for her just as it did for her husband.

My main concern, however, was not with the shifting Egan identifications but rather how reliable their descriptions were at all. They had the ski mask man in their vision, by their own estimation, for about five seconds, during which he looked to his left back at the restaurant, turned away from them, and then looked briefly to his right. Their view of him consequently was a profile one, quite brief, and observed during the course of a startling scene—sounds of shots being fired, masked men running, masked men carrying guns, a frightening and jarring vision for anyone to encompass. Their recollections could be roughly accurate but hardly more than that.

Regardless of the intrinsic value of the Egan identifications, they stuck to them. Shortly before the trial, at a suppression of evidence hearing (a standard and usually unsuccessful procedure at which the defense tries to argue that certain prosecution evidence was illegally obtained), John Egan firmly pointed out Ferber, seated a few feet from him, as the ski mask man. Linda Egan, on seeing Ferber up close, was even more certain he was not the person she had seen.

Linda Egan, however, never did prove of any help to Ferber. Because she had originally identified Ferber, the lawyer who then represented him, who was not the one at the lineup, did not call her as a witness. As a result, the jury heard only her husband's identification.

The eyewitness composite that the Egans helped construct is reproduced on the last page of the photo section, along with the Ferber mugshot that was shown to the Egans and used in the newspaper story at the time of his arrest.

The detectives involved in the investigation and the police artist have denied that Ferber's mugshot was used in any manner whatsoever in the creation of the composite. Cogan's allegation that the drawing was fabricated is based on the extraordinary similarity between it and the photograph. When, as Cogan has done, a transparency is made of the photograph, it fits exactly over the upper half of the composite; the bottom half of the transparency, when shifted slightly, also fits portions of the lower half of the photo.

Perhaps the best way to approach the problem of the composite is to consider it first independently of the photograph. When I did that, I realized it presented problems in believability on its own. To begin with, the composite is full face; the Egans saw the killer in profile. Next, the sketch shows the killer looking upward; in their view of him, the Egans couldn't possibly have seen that. (The eyes-upward pose can occur in mugshots when, as with Ferber, the subject doesn't look directly at the camera.) The composite also shows the killer with his hair combed. I couldn't imagine the Egans had seen him that way. The person they viewed would have had to have mussed his hair from donning the ski mask and then later snatching it off.

The composite, nevertheless, is signed by John Egan as representing his recollection of the killer. (Linda Egan helped with the drawing, and I am uncertain why she didn't sign it, but the most likely reason is she wasn't present when it was completed. In any event, nothing in her diary or any statements she made indicates she was unhappy with it.)

How then could the Egans, who beyond doubt are honest people, have agreed that a rendering of a killer was accurate when it contained crucial elements they could not have observed?

There is an explanation, and it points up a serious flaw in the composite method of creating eyewitness sketches. Police have two methods of making such drawings. In one, the sketch is made exclusively from the witness's recollection. Because it is difficult to describe features to someone—even an artist—who has not seen the person who is being described, such drawings tend to lack detail, are highly impressionistic. To obtain greater detail, the composite method is frequently selected and—according to testimony at Ferber's suppression of evidence hearing—was the method employed to develop the sketch the Egans signed. To create a composite, the eyewitness is given a box of black-and-white photographs, almost invariably mugshots, of individuals who fit the basic description category, in this instance a white male. The witness is asked to sort through these pictures and pick out those having aspects that most nearly fit the witness's memory of the suspect's physiognomy. Thus, one photo might have a familiar jawline, another a familiar nose, a third the right kind of eyes, and so on. Working from these pictures, the police artist creates a face. If the photos are full-face, as they typically are and apparently were on this occasion, that's what the artist draws. He may never ask the witness if the suspect was seen full-face, and the witness may not object to seeing a full-face drawing of someone seen only in profile.

It is at this point that witness psychology enters the picture, which can have its own adverse effect on credibility. While I have no way of knowing how the Egans responded to the situation in which they found themselves, generally speaking, witnesses who are asked to make an eyewitness sketch do so at a time when they are emotionally upset by the violent event they have just witnessed; they are also eager to help the police with whom, if they are like the middle-class Egans, they have had no previous significant contacts and who, they assume, know what they are doing. Moreover, they find themselves in a place that is strange to them, a police station, and turned over to a person they are told is an expert, the police artist. Under those circumstances, they may marvel at the expert's apparent uncanny ability to translate memory to picture, but they are highly unlikely to question *how* he does it. If they wonder at all, they are likely to conclude that the procedure is a standard one, that, for instance, they are supposed to help the artist turn a profile into a full-face rendering. Under his urging, they may point out details that have to be changed to be in accord with their memory, but they will not be surprised if the artist draws a coiffure for the suspect that is *exactly* like the one in the photo they chose that was most *similar* to the hairline they recall seeing. They therefore have no hesitancy in signing the composite even though it contains elements they couldn't have observed or are contrary to those they did observe.

The result is that instead of getting an original (if unde-tailed) illustration of the witness's best memory, the composite literally produces a composite face made up of elements of various mugshot faces *which are drawn in accordance with the way they appear in the mugshots, not as they appeared to the witness*.

If, by some terrible coincidence (and Ferber was luckless enough for this to have happened to him), the Ferber mugshot was among the photographs the Egans went through, and they picked it out as resembling, full-face, some significant aspect of the person they saw in profile, it becomes conceivable that the artist used that picture for the entire upper half of the composite. However, against that theoretical possibility, we have the unqualified denial by everyone involved that Ferber's photo was among the mugshots shown to the Egans.

Assuming that denial is truthful, what did happen? I don't

know, but the possibilities strike me as quite limited. One is that the person the Egans saw in profile became, by an intervention of miraculous proportions, Ferber when drawn full-face. A second is that Ferber's photograph was given to the artist to use as a basic face (that is, it wasn't simply among the mugshots) and the Egans, for whatever reason, never questioned that. A third is that the drawing was altered after the Egans last saw it.

If the Ferber photograph was used in some manner to make the composite, that means Ferber already was a suspect when the Egans arrived at police headquarters the morning after the murders, or very shortly thereafter. That is conceivable. In a homicide investigation, police work around the clock; in this case the Peetros murder in Delaware County was already known to them, and the theory had been developed that because Peetros and Booras were both leaders of the Greek Mob, the two deaths were related. At some point in the Delaware County investigation, Ferber's name surfaced as a possible confederate of Saltzburg, the tip probably coming from one of Sergeant Danny Rosenstein's informants. It also may have happened that someone involved in the investigation knew that Ferber was an associate of Saltzburg's and had been arrested with him in the attempted robbery of the Halfway House bar. Therefore, if the operating theory was that Ferber was guilty and also a weakling who would crack immediately and finger the shooter as soon as he was charged with the murder, then it was necessary to have a basis for arresting him. A hunch wouldn't do; an identification would.

When the composite was shown around police headquarters, an FBI agent who was on hand and who knew Ferber from another investigation said, "That looks like Neil Ferber." (According to Rosenstein, it was only then that Ferber became a suspect.) When, several nights later, Mrs. Egan was asked to select from the photo array, it is small wonder—assuming the picture wasn't changed after she last saw it—that Ferber looked familiar to her; after all, she had just helped draw him. What is amazing is that Mr. Egan didn't pick out the Ferber photo, too.

Regardless of how it came into existence, the mischief done Ferber by the composite was not limited to the pre-arrest period. It also became a prosecution exhibit in his trial. Assistant DA Sciolla, who, at the time, had no reason to doubt the authenticity of the composite (nor did he have any knowledge of the problems connected with the Jordan poly-graph), walked over to the defense table and held up the composite for the jury to see. Pointing to Ferber, he asked if this man was not that man? As Ferber himself said, "If I'd of been on the jury, I'd think it was me, too."

By the time I received the composite, the questions it raised were hardly any secret in the Department. In his posttrial motions, Cogan had used as a witness a nationally recognized police expert on eyewitness sketches, Donald Cherry, who branded the drawing a fake. Although Judge Latrone, in re-jecting Cogan's motions, apparently discounted Cherry's tes-timony, it remained a major appeals issue for Cogan, and had the potential of blowing up into reams of bad publicity for both the police and the DA.

That had already begun, to some extent. My collaborator on this book had first suggested Ferber might be innocent in a *Philadelphia Magazine* article in 1983, and by 1985 was writing about the composite in newspaper articles. Irv Homer, the city's highest-rated talk-show host, was also by then urg-ing a new trial for Ferber, using the composite as one of his reasons.

Despite the allegations of serious police misconduct raised by the sketch, no one in the Police Department or the DA's office had taken a single step to try to learn about its origins. If they had, I would have been the first one they would have come to, since the case was now a Task Force matter. That nothing had been done meant nothing was going to be done.

I could have forced the issue by going to Internal Affairs. Even had I survived the ensuing firestorm—and wasn't kicked out of Homicide and the Task Force as a traitor to my class by pursuing the allegation—an Internal Affairs investigation (as I knew from previous ones I had witnessed) was not desirable, since it would have called a halt to all activity concerning the case, including my own efforts, until the impropriety issue was resolved.

My decision, a comfortable one personally—no one wants to be a pariah—also seemed to me self-evidently the right one: I'd say nothing about the sketch. At least for the time being. That way I'd keep open the door I'd otherwise close to Rosenstein and the other detectives who'd worked the Meletis murders and who, as matters presently stood, were willing to answer any questions I had. My decision paid off, too. Because Rosenstein remained cooperative, through him I was able to reach, in optimal circumstances, the jailhouse informant Jerry Jordan, whom I now considered to be the key to unlocking Ferber's death row cell.

But I wasn't able to get to Jordan—not yet. I had another mob homicide on my hands.

22

Scarfo's Motives
for Murder

Shortly after 7:30 on the evening of July 27, 1985, Frank "Frankie Flowers" D'Alfonso was taking his little dog for a walk on South Ninth Street near Catherine Street. Not far from his florist shop, he happened on an old friend, the short, fat, 64-year-old Alex Marcella, a convicted gambler and numbers booker for the mob. The two men engaged in a conversation, Frankie facing away from the corner, Alex toward it. Suddenly, as one witness described it, Alex's eyes got as big as saucers as he saw two men emerging from a car on the corner of Percy Street. They were carrying guns and advancing toward him and Frankie. Alex heaved to and ran down the street full-speed "as if he was trying out for the Olympics," according to another witness. As the car from which they'd left continued on, the two men pumped five bullets into Frankie, first into his back, and then, as he turned, into his face. The killers dashed north on Percy, tossing their guns into an empty lot as they approached a late model black car, the back door of which was open. They dove into the vehicle and sped off. A passerby noticed the license plate began with the letters "KD."

As Frankie lay bleeding on the sidewalk, people screaming, his dog yipping, his pregnant daughter with whom he lived came up to him and fell sobbing by his side. "We had just finished coffee and watching *Wheel of Fortune* together," she later said. "We were going to go out and sit on the steps and talk about the baby" after he had finished walking the dog. They took Frankie to the hospital. He was DOA.

I had been notified shortly after the murder was committed, and my men and I quickly arrived at the site in the heart of mob territory. We conducted the scene survey, followed by the usual sweep of the neighborhood, knocking on every door to see if anyone had seen anything that could help us.

In the past that would have been an exercise in futility. By July of 1985, however, my squad and I were familiar figures in the locale, and our reputation for making headway against the Mafia was known. We found people willing to talk to us. One of them even gave us a tentative identification of one of the shooters, a hitherto unheard-of courageous act of cooperation.

If the esteem in which we were now held helped the investigation, so did the deceased. Frankie Flowers had been a well-liked man. Slightly built, a little below average height, in his late fifties, Frankie had been one of the last surviving members of Bruno's inner circle who was not in prison. He was not a made-member—we have no indication he ever committed a murder; that would have been contrary to his personality. But he had been valuable to Bruno, representing the mob in crooked prizefight promotions, running gambling junkets to London; and he was also a major numbers writer.

The people in his neighborhood—not just the crime figures, but the hardworking honest folk—were fond of Frankie for the same reason I was. He was, like a number of Bruno's old cronies (Martorano was an exception), pleasant and out-going; he was also warmhearted. Like John McCullough, he was a soft touch. Anyone who might have money problems knew they could go to Frankie and he'd loan them a ten, a twenty, a fifty, and not at any interest rates either. If the person could pay back the amount, fine; if not, Frankie never asked. It was just wrong, the honest folks thought, to murder Frankie, an outrage, which was why they talked. (Even so, they wouldn't have talked if we hadn't shown signs of effectiveness.)

On the surface, it was easy to understand Frankie's murder. An old pal of Harry the Hunchback, he'd allow his florist shop to be used by the Riccobenes to spy on Scarfo's faction, which had its Philadelphia headquarters nearby. Given Scarfo's standards, that, by itself, was sufficient cause to kill Frankie Flowers.

But something else was involved. In the fall of 1981, six months before the warfare between Scarfo and the Riccobenes broke out, Frankie had been nearly beaten to death by Salvy Testa and Eugene Milano, who used a baseball bat and a crowbar on him. Sometime later I learned from a source that Scarfo ordered the attack out of sheer jealousy; he knew the high regard in which Frankie Flowers was held both within and outside the mob. Scarfo bided his time, but Frankie had to die eventually, not because of the Riccobene connection but because, I believe, he symbolized to Scarfo the one thing he couldn't terrorize out of people: respect.

Despite the unusual amount of help we were getting, none of it, including the tentative identification, was strong enough to make arrests.* If the case were going to be cracked, it would probably be by turning still another mob member into an informant. But then again, we were still waiting for that kind of help on the Salvy Testa murder, too.

If Frankie Flowers' death showed one aspect of Scarfo's personality, then two other hits he ordered around the same time as the Flowers shooting, but which weren't carried out, indicate a man for whom, by 1985, murder had become so habitual that he seemed incapable of thinking of any other solution to a problem he might have.

Due to die (according to an informant) in the hits that never took place were Scarfo's old friend, underboss Chuckie Merlino, and Chuckie's younger brother, Larry.

Chuckie was the prime target. Scarfo had decided that Chuckie's drinking problem, about which Salvy Testa had given him warning more than a year before, had made Chuckie incompetent to carry out his duties. Chuckie, therefore, had to die. Since Larry might resent his brother's death and try to do something about it, Scarfo ordered Larry killed, too.

---

*The D'Alfonso murder had a peculiar and frustrating sidelight. A short time before Frankie's death, Bud Warner of the FBI and I warned him he might be in trouble. Our information came from a tap operated by the FBI's narcotics unit on a place of business from which it was believed drug deals were being made. A number of people had access to the phone, including employees who had no knowledge of any illicit activities. For that type of tap, regulations require that the agent who is doing the listening shut off the device if it is clear from the beginning of the conversation that it is an innocent one. On this particular day, immediately after Frankie's murder, the agent doing the listening, who was newly arrived in Philadelphia, heard two women talking about a "bad . . . horrible" event. The one woman said, "But you don't know who did it?" Replied the other woman, "Yes, I do. It was—"

On hearing that, the agent turned off the tap. When his superior went over the transcriptions, he called the agent in and, dumbfounded, asked him why he had cut off the conversation at that moment. Explained the agent, "I'm only supposed to listen to conversations about narcotics."

Chuckie's life and that of his brother were saved by the very weakness that had put Chuckie in danger of death in the first place: his drinking. One evening shortly after Scarfo's decision to have him murdered was made, Chuckie was picked up on a drunk driving charge in Margate, was brought into the police station, told his rights by a lieutenant and advised that their interview was being videotaped to help establish Chuckie's sobriety or lack of it. Probably because he was drunk, Chuckie forgot about the videotaping, and while the cameras were rolling, he offered the lieutenant his watch and cash—I think it was about $400—if the lieutenant would let him go. The lieutenant forthwith arrested Chuckie for offering a bribe, and when the tape was played at the chagrined Chuckie's trial, it was somewhat difficult for him to come up with a defense; he was convicted and sentenced to prison.

Scarfo, for reasons that aren't clear this side of sheer bloodthirstiness, apparently decided to go ahead with killing Larry anyway. His closest advisers were horrified, not out of any love for Larry, but from fear of the possible consequences to themselves. Taking their own lives in their hands, Tommy Del, the Pungitore brothers and Faffy Iannarella all urged Scarfo to call off the Larry hit. They pointed out that once the jailed Chuckie learned of his brother's death, he'd likely turn government informant. The worried Del even blurted out to Scarfo that he'd be "crazy" to go ahead with Larry's murder. Scarfo listened to this good counseling and satisfied himself with stripping Chuckie of his title as underboss, reducing him to soldier. It was a substantial punishment—it meant no more tribute money would come Chuckie's way—and appears to have been the only time in Scarfo's career as don that he was talked out of killing anyone.

That Scarfo would even consider ordering the death of the Merlino brothers, both of them completely loyal to him, illustrates the compulsiveness of his murderous nature. Even such Mafia mass-murderers as Capone and Anastasia could rationalize their decisions in the sense that they could calculate that a certain person's death would either protect their own skins, gain them profits, or improve their hold on their organizations. Scarfo's killings often fulfilled none of those goals. Murdering Larry Merlino, for example, quite apart from whether or not it would have the ill effects forecast by Del and the others, would serve no purpose whatsoever. Larry produced profits, and even Scarfo would have difficulty coming up with some reason to think Larry, at the point he intended to go ahead with killing him, was any threat. Even more clearly counterproductive had been the assassination of Salvy Testa he had ordered. By killing Salvy, Scarfo lost his most able lieutenant in Philadelphia, solely because of the groundless suspicion that Salvy, sometime in the future, might oppose him; and he was forced to replace him with the incompetent DelGiorno.

The aborted Merlino murders and the circumstances surrounding them were to have consequences that would endanger the future not only of Scarfo but of the New York City Mafia as well.

But that was still four years down the road. Returning to the summer of 1985, I found myself facing a situation in which my own career was threatened, the Task Force was on the verge of collapse, and the likelihood I'd be able to help save Ferber's life thereby diminished.

It all came about over a tragic incident in which I didn't play a role but over which Police Commissioner Sambor, whose support I needed to continue the Meletis murder investigation, lost his job.

23
"Your Job Is Not to Unarrest People"

May 13, 1985, was perhaps the single most infamous day in Philadelphia's history. Early on that morning, Commissioner Sambor, accompanied by a troop of heavily armed officers, arrived at a barricaded house on Osage Avenue in West Philadelphia that was occupied by a handful of members of a tiny, largely black, back-to-nature radical organization. "MOVE! This is America!" cried the Commissioner to them, and when the MOVE members refused to come out, Sambor started serving them their eviction notice—firing broke out. By the time the day was done, a bomb had been dropped on the house, eleven occupants—including five children—were dead, and sixty-one nearby private homes had burned to the ground. Philadelphia, Sambor and Mayor Wilson Goode (who had authorized the bombing and failed to order the resulting conflagration put out until it was too late) made headlines around the world.

Fearing indictment, forced to spend his energies trying to explain the unexplainable to a grand jury, to the press and to a citizens' investigating commission, Sambor paid increasingly less attention to the daily operations of the Department. (In the end, the only person who went to prison was the sole MOVE adult who survived the holocaust, Ramona Africa. The grand jury investigation, several years later, cleared Goode, Sambor and everyone who had been on the scene, of criminal culpability. My own reading of the evidence led me to the opinion that sufficient grounds existed to indict several high government officials on charges of— minimally—risking a catastrophe.)

Sambor managed to survive in office until late in 1985, but from May 13 onward everyone knew his days were numbered. He became a virtual nonperson in the 7,000-member force he still nominally commanded. And with his fate settled in reality long before it was officially, I lost my protector in the Meletis investigation.

The first sign I had of that was in June, when Captain "Rick" Dooley, who had earlier tried to remove me from the Task Force, called me in to see him. Referring to my efforts on behalf of Ferber, which, by now, were well known throughout the Department, he informed me, "Your job, Lieutenant, is to arrest people, not unarrest them. And your job isn't to investigate cops."

I answered, "I'm not investigating cops. I'm investigating an organized crime murder and the very real possibility that Ferber wasn't there, didn't do it."

He paid no attention to that. "And under what authority are you meeting with the DA?" he wanted to know. "Only the Commissioner can do that, and I forbid you to do so. You're not to investigate this case and you are not to meet with Rendell.''

Ed Rendell had been elected district attorney of Philadelphia in 1977. A strong-featured, balding, intense man, relentlessly spouting a simplistic law-and-order philosophy, Rendell quickly became a media darling—he knew how to talk in ten-second sound bites, and the cameras loved him—all of which translated into public popularity as well, and in 1981 he was overwhelmingly re-elected. The next year, at the crest of his popularity, he was asked by the Democratic Party to run for governor against incumbent Republican Dick Thornburgh, who later became attorney general of the United States. Rendell declined. Thornburgh looked unbeatable, but he won, surprisingly, only by a thin margin over a virtually unknown opponent. The popular Rendell would have almost certainly defeated him. By 1985, Rendell had decided not to run for a third term as DA but rather to seek the prize he'd let slip by him three years before.

There had been a time when Rendell and Dennis Cogan, Ferber's lawyer, had been close friends. They had served as prosecutors together when Arlen Specter, now a United States senator and the author of the single bullet theory to explain the assassination of President Kennedy, was DA of Philadelphia. In the 1977 campaign, Cogan had been one of Rendell's most enthusiastic supporters—he made speeches for him—and the support and friendship had continued until it floundered over the Ferber case. Cogan had met several times with Rendell in 1983 and 1984, laying out for him, as he had for me, all the reasons he believed Ferber deserved a new trial. That which seemed impressive to me didn't to Rendell. He began to avoid Cogan. At one point, in the first half of 1985, Dennis told me, he put in thirty-five calls to his good friend without receiving a single reply. One of the few times he did reach him, Cogan said to him, ''There's a homicide lieutenant, Frank Friel. He has been reinvestigating the case. If you won't listen to me, Ed, at least talk to him.''

Rendell, of course, had talked to me many times in the past, most recently on the Joey Pedulla plea bargain, and was aware of the success I had in breaking organized crime cases. He called me several weeks before Dooley told me I dared not speak to him and that I must drop the Ferber case.

I went to see Rendell. Between interruptions for phone calls and assistants going in and out, he spent perhaps a half-hour listening to me. I concluded by saying that in my professional opinion, Ferber was innocent. In that quick, hunched-forward way of his, a familiar bit of spittle at the edge of his mouth, Rendell declared, "None of this is evidence. No confessions. No one's confessing 'I did it.' But it's interesting. Go do your stuff. Keep me informed.''

Ed Rendell's a very likable person—mostly because he's basically a decent person—but I was not favorably impressed by him that day. Fair or not, my opinion was that any action he'd eventually take on the Ferber matter (including the most likely one of doing nothing) would be dictated by his strategy for his forthcoming gubernatorial effort. On that score, the Ferber conviction was campaign fodder of the highest order—gangland rubout, innocent woman killed, DA wins death penalty, cleans up those mobsters, tough prosecutor. That kind of thing would play great in the boondocks. That is, it would unless the Ferber conviction blew up in his face during the middle of the campaign. Or sooner: Because of my role in the Task Force investigations, I had been getting favorable coverage in the media, and he may have realized that reporters were likely to listen to me if I went to them with my concerns about the Ferber conviction. I had no intentions of doing so—it was a last resort I'd not begun to approach yet—but Rendell couldn't be sure of that. He could ignore Cogan, but I might be a problem.

Dooley, inadvertently, was solving that problem for Rendell by ordering me off the Ferber case. I didn't obey Dooley; it didn't occur to me to do so. Rendell had asked me to keep him informed (which gave me grounds to ignore Dooley on that score), and while Commissioner Sambor might not be around much anymore, my orders to report to him directly on organized crime matters had not been countermanded, so I had good protocol reasons for my response to Dooley. But I had only one real reason. We had put an innocent man on death row. I would be, as I saw it, simply derelict in my duty as a cop—and as a human being—if I didn't do everything I could to get him out.

Interviewing the jailhouse snitch, Jerry Jordan, was still very much on my agenda. If I could break Jordan, that would go a long way to saving Ferber. But it wouldn't solve the Meletis murders themselves. I wanted to arrest those who were guilty. If I could do that, not only would Ferber be exonerated, but justice would be served all around.

I had a number of pieces to the puzzle, each of which pointed to Martorano. I knew from the McCullough murderer, Willard Moran, that Martorano had hired him to kill Booras but he hadn't been able to carry out the deed. I knew from Ronald Raiton that Martorano wanted to become Raiton's exclusive P2P distributor in Philadelphia and that Booras was a rival, giving Martorano a motive for murdering Booras. I suspected strongly that Martorano's lieutenant, John Berkery, had knowledge of the murders; but in 1985, he was unreachable, still hiding out in Ireland. That left Mario Riccobene, who had told me in passing when I debriefed him in the spring of 1984 that Martorano had bragged to him that he was responsible for Booras's death. At the time, however, I was interested only in Mario's knowledge of the McCullough murder and the various crimes committed by the Riccobene gang—Victor DeLuca had not yet given me his "not for nothin'" tip that Ferber was innocent—and I had not pursued the Booras angle.

Now the time had come to see what else Mario might have

to say, which led me to my next confrontation with Captain Dooley. Mario, in the summer of 1985, was serving his 4-year sentence, under a new identity, at Lompoc Prison in California. According to police regulations, I had to clear any "off-site" trips, as this one would be, with my immediate superior officer. That was never a problem as long as my mentor, Jerry Kane, was in charge of the Homicide Division; he had faith in me and authorized whatever I requested without question. Dooley was a different matter. Considering how he felt about the Meletis murders—"Your job isn't to unarrest people"—I was sure he wouldn't approve a cross-country jaunt to see Mario, so I only told him I wanted to interview a witness in an organized crime case. I think he suspected who. He said no. Not necessary, he said. The Department can't afford that kind of expense, he said.

I didn't bother to argue with him. Instead, I asked for leave time, of which I had several months available. He couldn't deny me that. I headed for California, paying my own way.

When I arrived in San Diego, I checked with my men back in Philadelphia and was told Dooley was looking for me. That struck me as odd; it was as if he wanted to make doubly sure I'd left the city.

Dismissing Dooley from my mind, I went to see Mario. In our talk, I gradually brought him around to the Meletis murders. He had more information. Martorano, he said, didn't merely list Booras as one of his victims but had gone into the background of the hit. As Mario recalled it, Martorano told him that Booras and he had had a conversation in which Booras called Scarfo a "punk" and said he was damned if he'd pay him a penny in tribute. On hearing this, Martorano said he immediately went to Scarfo, repeated Booras's words and was given Scarfo's approval to kill Booras. Thanks to Mario's new specifics, which were admissible in court as they pertained to Martorano, my case against Martorano was measurably strengthened. I hadn't, however, gotten any further on Scarfo. At the time that my investigation of the Meletis hit had led me to Martorano as the likely perpetrator, it seemed next to impossible to me that he would have dared try to carry it out without Scarfo's OK. Mario's recollection of his conversation with Martorano confirmed my belief, but it wasn't trialworthy evidence against Scarfo—he couldn't be charged on Mario's testimony that Martorano had implicated him. To indict Scarfo, we needed the testimony of Martorano himself, or of someone else who was present when Scarfo authorized or later admitted he had authorized the crime. Nevertheless, I had a great deal more information than I had had before—a chronology and a reason—and the more you know, the better the questions you can ask when the time comes. (Whether Booras actually did insult Scarfo and refuse to pay him remains an open question in my mind. Booras might very well have; he was hotheaded and stupid enough. However, Martorano was also quite capable of making up the story in order to get Scarfo's imprimatur to rid himself of his rival in the P2P business.)

While I was pinning down Mario's recollection, back in Philadelphia Captain Dooley was hard at work. He paid a visit to Commissioner Sambor and the new Deputy Commissioner Bob Armstrong. In that meeting, I was later told, Dooley charged that I was a loose cannon. I didn't report to him, his immediate superior, and was insubordinate, which I took to be a reference to my failure to stop talking to Rendell (even though Rendell had told me to keep him informed about the Meletis case).

In response to Dooley's complaints, Sambor allegedly told Dooley I hadn't reported to him either "in weeks," which was true; the MOVE catastrophe aftermath had made Sambor nearly impossible to reach. Armstrong, according to Dooley, said I hadn't conferred with him, either, which was not true; I had been keeping Armstrong advised of the activities of both myself and my men. We were frequently out of town interviewing witnesses, some of them in prison like Mario, and I had always let Armstrong know why we were going to be absent. He had said, "You do what you have to do."

Dooley next went to see Al Toland, the assistant special agent in charge of the Philadelphia FBI. According to Toland, he told Toland that everybody in command in the Police Department agreed I had been lying about whom I was reporting to, lying about the cases I was working on, and had defied Dooley's direct orders by talking directly to department heads such as Rendell, the Commissioner himself, and even John Hogan, Toland's boss. (I often conversed with Hogan, who was interested in the progress of the Task Force.)

Toland said he replied, "I'm shocked to hear this. We'll address the problem when he gets back."

Dooley, Toland recalled, stated, "No, when he comes back I'm relieving him of his command and sending someone else over to head the Task Force."

Toland's response to this seemingly irrevocable decision was: "That would be a matter of consideration." He didn't want to appear to be interfering in a Philadelphia police problem. However, replacing me affected the FBI's operation, and that did come within his province. As soon as Dooley left, Toland called me in California and asked me, "What the fuck is going on?"

I said, "I think Dooley has concluded correctly that I'm here pursuing my investigation of the Booras case," and told him I'd defend myself when I got back. Toland next conferred with my co-commander of the Task Force, Dennis O'Callaghan, who reminded him that I had had previous problems with Dooley. Dennis said he suspected I was perceived as a threat to Dooley's homicide unit which had gotten a good measure of the credit for solving the Meletis murders. If I succeeded in overturning Ferber's conviction, Dennis speculated, I'd inadvertently be making Chitwood and the other detectives in the investigation look bad.

In my conversation with Toland, while I was still in Cal-

ifornia, I said I believed Danny Rosenstein, who had arrested
Ferber for the Meletis murders and still believed he was
guilty, was to be named as my replacement. I'd picked up
that story from my own detectives who'd heard—rumors get
around fast in a police department—that Rosenstein had ordered his squad to pack up their files because they were going
to the Federal Building.

While I was still in California, the news of the decision to
remove me from the Task Force was brought to the attention
of Al Wicks, the attorney on the staff of the United States
Justice Department's Strike Force against organized crime
with whom I'd worked in helping prepare grand jury presentations since the days of Teddy Di Pretoro in 1982. Wicks
—probably in response to a query from Hogan, Toland's
boss—stated that the position of the Strike Force was: "You
can remove Friel, but if you do you better remove the Task
Force because without Friel, you have no Task Force. He is
the driving force behind it, and all the successes of the Task
Force are a direct result of his initiatives, above those of the
FBI, so without Friel you don't have a Task Force. It will
be nonexistent."

Because the Strike Force was, in effect, the prosecutorial
arm of the FBI in Mafia cases, Wicks's view of my capa-
bilities was taken seriously, providing confirmation of the
FBI's own evaluation of the role I played. Toland phoned
Dooley: "We will not," he assured him, "interfere with the
internal workings of the Philadelphia Police Department, but
if you remove Friel, do not send anyone over to replace him.
If you do send someone over, they will remain in the lobby.
We will not grant them entrance to working space."

By now—all this happened in a two-to-three-day period
—I had wrapped up my business with Mario Riccobene and
was ready to return to Philadelphia. I called my squad and
asked to be picked up at the airport. Dooley somehow learned
of my request, countermanded it, and sent one of his admin-
istrators to fetch me. The administrator seemed embarrassed,

and I felt as if I were virtually being kidnapped. I was taken directly to the Police Administration Building, rather than my Task Force headquarters in the Federal Building, and marched into Dooley's office, where we were left alone with each other. He wasted no time on preliminaries. The Police Commissioner and Deputy Commissioner, he said, agreed that I was a liar, that I was unreliable, and that I was now forbidden to talk to them.* I was also, he said in a satisfied tone, relieved of my Task Force command with Sambor's approval.

As I listened to these accusations, I had no doubt of their implication for me. Unless the damage to my reputation was undone, I no longer had a future in the Police Department. I'd be branded forever, just as Dooley said, as unreliable and a liar. I'd become the pariah I had told Dennis Cogan that I might become if I investigated the investigation into the Meletis murders. I'd broken rank by trying to find out if we had sent an innocent man on his way to the electric chair, and for that I must be punished.

Dooley wasn't quite done with me, however. I had, he said, one final—and humiliating—order to carry out as far as the Task Force was concerned. He directed me to take Sergeant Rosenstein to the FBI headquarters and introduce him to all the authorities there as my replacement. Somehow, Dooley went on, the FBI had gotten the impression that he, Dooley, was forcing me out, and I was to correct that mistaken idea by saying I was voluntarily stepping aside.

Dooley could remove me from the Task Force, but he couldn't force me to lie. I refused to carry out that order. I said, "This whole thing is a sham on your part to replace me with your personal selection, and I'm not going to mislead the FBI about it."

---

*Dooley also touched base with his immediate superior, Chief Inspector of Detectives Frank Scafidi, who later told me he "regretted" he hadn't backed me.

Whenever Dooley got excited, he began to glow, and now, as his anger mounted, the familiar bright red color began at his neck and spread to the top of his head. He told me I was confined to quarters. During my shift, I was not to leave the building and not to use the phone, lest I get word to my colleagues in the FBI and the Strike Force who might want to save my job. "I'll do better than that," I said. "I'll sit right here in your office, Captain, and the only time I'll leave is with Danny Rosenstein."

And that's what happened. I found myself a chair, and for the next two days I sat in Dooley's office. He stared at me. I stared at him. Whenever I left, for coffee, for lunch, to go to the bathroom, I called Danny to act as my guard so that I wouldn't be accused of making the calls I believed weren't necessary to make. Danny was embarrassed about the whole affair, and around the office, jokes abounded about Friel wearing a dunce cap and sitting in the principal's office. Other jokes were directed at Dooley. "But who's watching Dooley while Danny's watching you?" I was asked. The police being the police, a good deal of betting was going on, too, as to whether Dooley or I would emerge as the winner. I never did find out the odds.

Meanwhile, communiques were flashing back and forth between the FBI, the Strike Force, and the Philadelphia Police. On the third day, Dooley said to me, "Get outta here. Go back where you belong."

So I went back to where I belonged.

John Hogan, the FBI boss, had done it. As I heard the story, he had called Commissioner Sambor and coolly informed him, "You can do what you want, Commissioner, but if you remove Friel, you end the Task Force. There will be no other homicide detectives coming over here, and you, Commissioner, explain to the press why this enormously successful Task Force has been terminated. We will have no comment other than to refer the press to you." He didn't have to spell it out any more than that. Sambor, media-beleaguered as he was because of the MOVE catastrophe and the corruption investigations, immediately rescinded his permission to have me removed.

A day or two later, to my surprise, I got a call from Captain Dooley asking me to arrange a meeting for him with Hogan's assistant Toland at which I was to be present. I remarked, "You didn't need me to make an appointment with Toland the last time; why now?" He said he wanted to apologize. I called Toland, advised him why Dooley wanted to see him, and he said, "Oh, yeah, I'll listen to that."

When Dooley arrived, I was sitting with Toland. It turned out Dooley had no personal apology in mind. Without an indication whatsoever of self-consciousness, he informed Toland he certainly regretted any inadvertent besmirching of my reputation, but that he was only acting on the Commissioner's orders. Somehow, he said, Sambor had gotten the wrong idea I was a loose cannon. Heaven forbid! On the contrary, he declared, I was the best detective in the history of the Philadelphia Police, and his admiration for me was boundless. After he left, Toland and I looked at each other. We shook our heads and got back to work.

That was the end of that problem in my attempt to reinvestigate the Meletis murders. It was not to be the last one.

24
Trying to Get the Truth out of Jerry Jordan

Once I became convinced that Raymond Martorano arranged the murder of Steve Booras at the Meletis, I immediately had a most likely suspect as the shooter: Frank Vadino, Martorano's chief lieutenant, who, according to Mario Riccobene, was to have helped Martorano murder Harry the Hunchback. Vadino had been convicted in 1982, along with Martorano, in the P2P case in which Raiton was the informant. He also had managed the Intermission Tavern for Martorano, where Martorano and Daidone had met with Moran to plot the

McCullough murder. Vadino weighed about 240 pounds, which was in accord with the most reliable description of the killer's size, and in his facial features looked rather like a powerful version of Neil Ferber.

I had Vadino transported from his Florida prison to meet with me at the Federal Building. He was visibly nervous as I outlined to him my knowledge of the case. He didn't confess, but I had rattled his cage, which was what I wanted to accomplish. I sat back to await further developments. They came in the form of a phone call from Vadino's lawyer. Vadino, he said, might be willing to make a deal if I could show him I had concrete evidence on his client. I didn't, but the contact from the lawyer convinced me I was right.

I was now ready for my next step: interviewing Jerry Jordan, the jailhouse snitch whose testimony had done the most to convict Neil Ferber.

When I first met him in the early fall of 1985, Jordan reminded me of a scared rabbit trying to cross a highway, ready to bolt at the first sign of an approaching car. He didn't look like a rabbit, however. He had ferrety features instead, set off by long, dark, greasy hair, and was a bit under average height. He had been an extraordinarily busy criminal. His adult rap sheet, which began in 1970 when he was 18 years old, showed twenty-one arrests and thirteen convictions. At the time he snitched on Ferber, he was awaiting sentence for a burglary on which he could have gotten 30 years when combined with revocations of probation in previous cases.

Almost immediately after he gave the statement on Ferber in July 1981, Jordan had been released from prison. In September, he was picked up on a retail theft charge, and in December, arrested for allegedly stabbing a man in the back in an alley brawl. Following his testimony against Ferber in

April 1982, he was taken before a judge, who was advised of his splendid cooperation. Jordan was then sentenced to time served on the burglary; the retail theft and stabbing charges were dismissed. (On the witness stand in the Ferber trial, Jordan had sworn he had been offered no sentencing deals in return for his testimony.)

Because I hadn't burned any bridges by mentioning my concerns about the eyewitness sketch, I was able to ask Danny Rosenstein to put me in touch with Jordan. Danny was aware of my doubts about Ferber's guilt, and always cooperated in my investigation; his embarrassment over his role in Dooley's putsch against me added, I think, to his desire to help. I could have located Jordan without him. However, Danny's role was vital in smoothing the way: Jordan was *his* snitch, which meant, in the symbiotic relationship that informants develop, Danny was *his* cop, the one he trusted, the one he believed would protect him. If Danny told him to talk to me, he would. And Danny did.

When I arrived at Jordan's house, his wife and daughter were present, so I limited myself to explaining I was looking for additional information about organized crime. Despite Danny's imprimatur, Jordan was, unsurprisingly, reluctant to open up to me, but after several more meetings in which I did him little favors—picked up his child from day care, lent him a few dollars, and listened sympathetically to his never-ending tales of woe about how badly life treated him—he agreed to come to police headquarters to answer my questions. By then, I'd told him I was interested in the content of Ferber's confession to him.

Arriving with wife and child—Danny Rosenstein obligingly took them off my hands—Jordan and I met alone in an office. I led him through the story he had originally told Danny and the other investigators, the story he had repeated (and had been believed in the telling of it) at trial.

From having read the police file, I was already familiar

with the content of his statement and the circumstances in which it had been made. The chronology began in June 1981, when Linda Egan's failure to identify Ferber at the lineup put the prosecution's case in disarray. Less than a week later, on June 29, Jordan and other inmates who shared the same cellblock with Ferber at the Detention Center were brought to the Police Administration Building for questioning. Jordan told Detective Checcia that Ferber "didn't say nothing about" why he had been arrested, save that "he was framed by the FBI." (Ferber believed the FBI was after him because of his alleged participation in DiPasquale's extortion schemes.)

Another inmate, George Reicherter, seemed, at one point in his questioning, to be saying that Ferber had made admissions to him. When working carefully through the garble of Reicherter's English, however, it became apparent he was actually describing what Ferber was saying the police claimed he had done. (The difficulty I had in following Reicherter's statement points up a problem in communications that all detectives encounter, from both suspects and witnesses. Ferber, while he was not nearly as bad as many, was typical in the maddening way he had of losing references as he went along: "This guy says this and that guy says that and then he says . . ."—who says? Because of an inability to express himself coherently, a suspect can appear to be lying when he isn't, can appear to be making an admission when he isn't; and similarly, a witness who is trying to be truthful may be misunderstood and lead an investigation awry. It is always assumed by the public that when detectives require subjects to repeat statements over and over again, they are trying to trip them up; that's true sometimes, but most often they are simply trying to understand them.)

Following the interrogations of June 29, the inmates were returned to the Detention Center where Reicherter—and probably Jordan—warned Ferber that the cops were trying to find someone to inform against him. (Jordan had already promised the detectives he would try to help them.) On July 9, Ferber made his $200,000 bail and was released. (In Pennsylvania, as in most states, a suspect can be freed on any crime upon posting 10 percent of the total amount set; Ferber's family had raised the $20,000 for him.) The day after Ferber's release, Jordan called the police, saying he had information to give. Again he was brought down to the Roundhouse, where he was interviewed by Rosenstein, detectives Mitsos and Perkis, and Pete Christ of the FBI.

Jordan told them that after he returned to prison on June 29, he and Ferber had talked daily about the murders. In one conversation, according to Jordan, Ferber "said that the lady who identified him coming out of the restaurant must be nuts because she described [him] as looking like a gorilla. Ferber laughed and said, 'I guess I would look like a gorilla—with shoulder pads on.' " Jordan went on: "He [Ferber] later told me, 'nobody knows about the shoulder pads.' "

Jordan further claimed that Ferber said he committed the murders with Mad Dog DiPasquale, and indicated that he, not The Dog, had fired the fatal bullets: "I asked him, 'Well, what did you get for the Booras thing?' Neil said, 'I got twenty thousand for the job.' " Jordan said, however, that Ferber didn't tell him who had hired him and The Dog.

Even had it not been for Frank Cryan's verdict that Jordan had failed his polygraph test, I would have been suspicious of several portions of his statement.

The $40,000 fee—$20,000 to Ferber, and presumably the same to the Dog—was way above any sum I'd ever heard of being paid for a mob hit. Martorano, Willard Moran told me, had surprised him by giving him a $5,000 "tip," for murdering McCullough, but that was highly unusual, and there is no reason to believe DeGregorio was offered anything close to the $20,000 he says he was offered to kill Harry Riccobene. Ordinarily, in a mob murder, no money changes hands; the gunmen do it because they're told to do it and have hopes their crime will stand them in good stead in the future.*

But there was another puzzling aspect to the $40,000 fee. When Jordan stated that Ferber told him he and DiPasquale were *paid* to make the hit, the investigators should have become aware that their theory of a robbery-murder plot by the two men was false. That theory, however, continued to be promulgated long after they heard from Jordan that the killing wasn't for robbery but for hire. Thus, the detectives either didn't believe Jordan on the money issue—and if not, why believe him on anything?—or else believed Ferber was lying to Jordan when he said he was paid. (The robbery-murder theory, of course, was incredible from the beginning, and only served the purpose of allowing the investigators to hold on to their original belief that the Meletis murders were not mob-related. Ferber and DiPasquale may not be criminal geniuses, but even they would have realized that the most stupid thing they could do was kill Booras in a restaurant and then—with the police hot on the case—march up to Booras's home and burgle it. Had they intended to rob and kill Booras, they would have done both crimes at one time, at Booras's house.)

The shoulder pad story made even less sense than the $40,000 murder fee. Hired killers may cover their faces, as the two Meletis gunmen had, but I have never heard of a disguise going beyond that. (The parkas would have been worn primarily to conceal the weapons they were carrying.) Besides, although football players, no doubt, learn to ma-

---

*I am referring here only to murders in which the victim is killed to carry out organized crime goals. Freelance hits are different. In the murder of the ex-Cuisinart executive, Jack Reese, which I solved, the person hiring the killers had no organized crime associations, and neither did the victim. The $65,000 paid to have the murder done was strictly a matter of how much the traffic would bear. With a little hard bargaining on the part of the woman who hired them, the killers, I have no doubt, would have agreed to do the job for half that amount, probably less.

neuver wearing shoulder pads, no hired killer is going to don them, for fear they will interfere with his freedom of movement when taking out the gun to do the shooting. Ferber's own version of the shoulder pad story, on the other hand, was entirely credible. He told me that one day in prison when he was discussing a newspaper story about the murder in which the killers were described as heavyset, he said to Jordan, "What did they think I did? Put on football shoulder pads?" When snitches are lying, they take innocent bits of conversation and twist them into their story.

But the timing of Ferber's supposed confession perhaps bothered me the most. Both in his interrogation of June 29 and his statement of July 10, Jordan said that prior to June 29, Ferber made no admissions to him. Thus, it's only *after* Ferber knew the police were looking for a snitch that he supposedly confessed to Jordan, who he knew was one of those asked to inform on him.

It could have happened, all of it. Jordan might have misconstrued Ferber's remarks about the shoulder pads. Ferber might have, for reasons best known to himself, bragged about getting paid and fingered DiPasquale. Ferber, for that matter, *might* have confessed because he was guilty. (Some murderers, in the rage of conscience, do confess to a cellmate even when they suspect the person to whom they are talking is an informant.)

Nevertheless, prior to meeting with Jordan, while thinking about the supposed confession—and thinking is the most important part of detective work—I realized I was back to the same constant that had been with me ever since I began to investigate Ferber's conviction. To believe him guilty, it was necessary to accept one unlikely event after another, whereas to believe him innocent, it was necessary only to accept one likely event after another.

I had still another reason for believing Jordan was lying about Ferber's confession. In September of 1981, a detective hired by Ferber's then-lawyer heard that Jordan had informed on Ferber. Soon after he was told that, Ferber left a message for Jordan to call him at a garage where Ferber had found employment while out on bail and awaiting trial. When Jordan returned the call, Ferber put a tape recorder to the mouthpiece. In the long and rambling conversation that followed, parts of it inaudible, Jordan denied he was the informant, in fact, put the blame on George Reicherter. The parts of that taped conversation that struck me as significant follow.

FERBER: Look, Jerry, you know, one thing I remember, you know, when you came back one day, you called me outside, you said you wanted to be a hit man. "How much do they get paid, $20,000, $25,000?" Do you remember that day?

JORDAN: Yeah.

FERBER: You remember that. You kept questioning me and questioning me. I said, "What are you talking about? Are you nuts or what?"

JORDAN: So what's that? That's just talking. You know? . . .

FERBER: . . . Let me ask you something: How could anyone nail me when I never made a statement in my life?

JORDAN: I don't know. Neil—Neil, I'm getting all the fucking blame for this shit and I'm tired of it, man. At first it was a fucking joke, ha ha ha. I've got the fucking hassle with Gail's ex-husband about this shit here. All right, it was over with. And now this shit—

FERBER: . . . You claim you're a friend of mine. And if I find out it's true, I'll help you all the way down . . . the line [but] I don't know, Jerry. They just come off—just certain things I remember, like you questioning me, "How much does a hit guy get? I'd love to be a hit man myself."

JORDAN: I would. What the hell? Twenty thousand a hit. I'd fucking love that kind of money.

FERBER: . . . I just hope you didn't make up any stories to people because I didn't think you were that kind of guy. I never told you anything, and you know it, just as well as I do . . .

JORDAN: . . . Neil, you ain't got nothing to worry about, man. I'm telling you.

FERBER: I don't have nothing to worry about because I never said nothing to nobody.

JORDAN: I know. I know.

FERBER: I mean, it's all lies.

JORDAN: You better start worrying about George Reicherter.

FERBER: I don't know what George can say because there's nothing I ever did. Tell me something.

JORDAN: What?

FERBER: Did I ever admit to doing anything like that?

JORDAN: Nyah.

FERBER: What did I tell you that Sunday, I was framed?

JORDAN: Yeah, framed by the FBI.

Ferber's taped conversation with Jordan was never used as evidence on his behalf at trial. I'm not sure of the reason, but when Cogan attempted to introduce the conversation at Ferber's posttrial hearing, he was warned by the DA's office that, under Pennsylvania law, he could be arrested for disseminating an illegally obtained recorded conversation. Cogan dared the DA to charge him—he wasn't—and entered the tape as evidence, but Judge Latrone rejected it, as he did all of Cogan's other new evidence, as insufficient grounds for granting a new trial.

After Jordan finished regaling me with his version of Ferber's confession, I asked him about the taped conversation. He sloughed off his statements to Ferber by explaining, "I was just going along with him."

He spoke in an oddly tight tone that contrasted with the content of his words, a manner I'd noticed before when he was describing his relations with Ferber. It wasn't so much the sense of prevarication I got, but rather of his holding something back. I tried to think what it might be. Taking an educated stab, I asked him, "Jerry, do you think Ferber killed those two people in the restaurant?"

He didn't hesitate. "Nah. He didn't do it."

I stared at him a moment. Then: "Did you ever say this to Danny, to the detectives?"

"No," he said.

I asked, "Why not?"

He said, "They never asked me. They just asked me what he said. They never asked me if I thought he did it. I don't think he did do it, and I don't think he could do it."

Ferber's entire confession, Jordan said he believed, was motivated by his wanting to have a prison reputation as a mob killer so that other inmates would be afraid of him and not attempt to assault or rape him.

I studied Jordan with some wonderment. "But didn't you ever feel you should have told those guys what you believe?"

"That was none of my business," he answered. "The cops just asked me what Neil had said, and I told 'em."

"And all through the trial," I went on, "you knew the significance of your testimony, and now you're telling me you're testifying against a guy and in effect putting him in the electric chair, and all the while you didn't believe he did it?"

"Yeah."

"Why? Why would you do that, Jerry?"

Jerry Jordan answered, "Why the fuck do you think? Because I was going to get out of jail."

By the conclusion of my interrogation of Jordan, it seemed possible to me he was now telling some approximation of the truth. Ferber, I knew, wouldn't be the first prisoner to claim he was a tough guy murderer in order to prevent being raped, and Jordan might have encouraged him to protect himself that way, perhaps even prior to the time Jordan was taken in for interrogation on June 29, with Jordan then waiting until after Ferber was released to inform on him, with elaborations like the shoulder pad story. If so, Jordan had failed the lie detector test not because Ferber hadn't confessed to him but because he believed the confession was a false one. Should that prove to be the case, the news for Ferber was grim. We'd never be able to get Jordan to admit he was lying, because he wasn't lying.

But I also had to consider that Jordan might not be telling any approximation of the truth. He struck me as the most unreliable of informants, the eager-to-please kind who is always trying to figure out what his police interrogator wants him to say, and then saying it. He might well have been doing that with me, if he sensed I didn't think Ferber was guilty, and if I didn't think that, why was I questioning him? He also had strong motivation not to give up on his story. He may have feared he could go to jail if he confessed that he lied, but I didn't think that was his most pressing concern. Rather, being labeled a perjurer would mean he'd never again be used as an informant by Danny or any other cop. That would take from him one way of bargaining himself out of trouble.

If he was still lying, the best way to find out was to have him take another polygraph, with better questions this time. But how to accomplish that? I had no legal grounds to force it on him. He had no reason to agree. I would have to find a way.

While driving Jordan home, I took the first step toward achieving that goal, the laying on of pressure. I told him I planned to call him before the grand jury investigating organized crime, because I wanted him to repeat under oath everything he'd said to me during our interview. I then planned to offer to take off the pressure by giving him immunity if he told the truth and proved it by passing a polygraph examination. He didn't seem happy at the prospect of testifying before the grand jury, but that much I could force him to do, and he knew it.

When I returned to police headquarters, I summarized my interview with Jordan to Danny Rosenstein, concluding by saying, "He doesn't think Ferber did it."

Danny immediately admitted he had never asked Jordan his opinion of Ferber's alleged confession, and seemed chagrined he hadn't. I didn't blame him for the omission. Even the most experienced detectives sometimes fail to ask obvious questions. (Including me: In a robbery investigation some years earlier, I had obtained a detailed description of the perpetrator from the victim which was then duly broadcast. The next day the victim called me to tell me that the perpetrator was, at the very moment, inside his house, and he called him by name. "You know his name?" I asked, astonished. "Why, yeah," he said. "Why didn't you tell me his name yesterday?" "You only asked me what the fuck he looked like. You didn't ask me his goddamn name," he answered.)

I studied Danny thoughtfully. So far, he had been able to push aside all the troubling aspects of the Meletis murders that I had been telling him about. I think that was because he didn't want to admit the case against Ferber had been put together by him and his squad with baling wire and chewing gum. It had collapsed when Mrs. Egan said Ferber was the wrong man at the lineup. After that, to push it back together, rather than question whether they were right about Ferber, they had gone hunting for a snitch—one they wanted to believe and didn't want to question too closely. (I didn't then know, and still don't, if Danny played any role in the creation of the eyewitness sketch; whatever occurred in the making of it could very well have taken place without his knowledge, and he has expressly denied to me in subsequent conversations that anything inappropriate took place.) Now, finally, Jordan's statement that he didn't think Ferber was involved in the murders appeared to have a pushing effect on Danny: "If this is all coming together," he said, "I think this guy should get a new trial. And I wouldn't be unhappy if he walked out."

25
What I Learned about the American Justice System

Although by the fall of 1985, Dooley's action against me over the Ferber case was behind me, it had been replaced by a new one, ugly and anonymous. My phone would ring, I'd pick it up, and a male voice (always a male voice but not always the same one) would tell me, "Back off the Ferber investigation," and hang up. Other callers were more explicit: "Drop the Ferber investigation," I was told, "or something could happen to you or your family." I received dozens of the calls, and two or three unsigned letters also of the "get out of the Ferber case" variety.

I had received threats in the past, but never of this intensity, frequency and single-mindedness. These were always couched in terms of Ferber, not the Meletis murders, not Booras, but Ferber. The source could have been Scarfo mobsters. I had to assume word was out on the street that I was looking into Ferber's conviction, but it seemed unlikely the mob would focus on that case and none of the others I was working, including the more recent Salvy Testa and Frankie Flowers murders. It was also true that at no time in the past had mobsters overtly threatened me, much less my family. That didn't mean it couldn't be happening now, but it seemed to me the likelihood was that the calls were internal, that is, coming from police officers who were angered by my investigation or else thought me disloyal to the policeman's code by going to bat for someone "we" had convicted of first-degree murder. I went ahead with what I was doing.

By October, when the threatening phone calls began coming in, a new development had taken place on the organized crime front that brought me back, as it were, to square one: the late John McCullough's Roofers Union. Following McCullough's death in December 1980, a power struggle had taken place in the union. Emerging victorious was one of its long-time officials, Steve Traitz, Jr. By the late summer of 1985, I was picking up information that Traitz had entered into an alliance with Nick Scarfo.

At 5′10″, square-jawed, muscular, with short-cropped hair and piercing eyes, Traitz, like McCullough, had a rough-and-ready charm. But, unlike that of Big John, Traitz's charm could be turned off in a second and replaced by anger and fists. Especially when he had his goons surrounding him, Traitz seemed to enjoy intimidating and beating people. As he remarked about himself to a Common Pleas Court judge: "If you hear Steve Traitz smacked somebody in the nose, believe it. That's all I do."

The FBI's Labor Squad had also been hearing about Traitz's burgeoning relationship with Scarfo. After we all discussed the problem, late on the night of September 26, 1985, FBI technicians arrived at Roofers headquarters, picked the locks and installed listening devices in the ceiling of the union's meeting room.

In the conversations picked up in this manner, Traitz frequently spoke of his relationship with the Little Guy. His tone was respectful, even wary—he warned his lieutenants how important it was to remain on Scarfo's good side—but he also bragged about the friendship. He apparently wanted it known at all levels of the union. As he told Scarfo, "If they know you're behind me, I'm unfuckingbeatable."

As part of his cooperation with Scarfo, Traitz provided men to help Scarfo collect on his street tax debts. At least on one occasion, Traitz himself did the persuading. In a recorded conversation, the man to whom Traitz was talking owed Scarfo $15,000. Explaining why he was speaking to him about the debt, Traitz said, "It comes from Nicky. I don't want you in no jam. . . . This guy is a bad guy. He's not like anybody else." The man paid up.

However, at times it was difficult for Traitz's lieutenants to appreciate the customs of mafiosos. At least, Traitz's right-hand man Michael "Nails" Mangini had a problem in that direction. The day after he accompanied Traitz to the Mafia's 1985 Christmas party at LaCucina (the restaurant in which Scarfo had held his party celebrating the murder of Salvy Testa in September of 1984), Mangini grumbled to Traitz, "I kissed more guys last night than I did in my whole life."

Traitz replied, "That's what you gotta do, brother. That's what they believe in so that's what we believe in."

Traitz did not appear to be aware that he had a tiger by the tail in his alliance with Scarfo—that Scarfo, if he followed the usual mob scenario, would gobble up ever-larger portions of the Roofers Health and Welfare Fund payments and other slush funds Traitz developed. One such scheme, which Traitz apparently put into effect about the time the listening devices were installed, called for each contractor or "working principal" to kick back to the union six cents for each hour worked, and a minimum of one hundred hours regardless of time on the job. (Roofing work is seasonal, and for many it is part-time.) Those who objected were brought into the meeting room and beaten. As one of Traitz's men explained to a recalcitrant roofer after he finished hitting him (the sounds of the blows are clear on the tapes), "I told you, it ain't no joke. You're lucky you're getting away with just a slap in the head. Next time it won't be as easy. It's just a turnover in the new regime; this is how we're working things from now on. You want to be with us, fine. If you don't, fine, too. But you'll wish you hadn't, OK?"

(Based on the wiretaps, Traitz and twelve of his henchmen were indicted on various racketeering charges, one of which was that the union had been used to extort money on behalf of Scarfo. All the defendants were convicted and sentenced to prison in November 1987 for terms ranging from 3 to 15 years. Traitz got the 15.)

But the electronic eavesdropping also picked up conversations that had nothing to do with extorting money for union purposes or to help Scarfo. Philadelphia judges were the subject of—and sometimes participants in—these conversations.

The union liked to be generous to judges in the most practical way it knew, with cash. Payments, in the form of "Christmas gifts," ranged between $200 and $500 and went to judges in a position to help out the union or who had already done so when members were arrested for whatever reason. Some judges were assiduously avoided. On one tape, Traitz warned against even approaching Judge Lynne Abraham, because she was too honest. Others, however, were warmly regarded. As Jimmy Brown, the courier who was to deliver the yuletide envelopes, said as they were going over their list, "Yeah . . . and Julian and, uh . . . Kenny are great guys, great guys," to which Traitz grandly replied, "They'll, they'll all get more than they ever got."

The favor expected in return was made clear by Traitz to a newly elected judge to whom he gave money at his union's Christmas party in 1985: "You'll hear from me once or twice a month," he said. "And . . . remember how I feel. You help me, fine. If you can't, that's all I ask . . . I won't embarrass. You'll never hear from me for drugs," just "smack-in-the-nose cases." Since, at that time, smacks in the nose were given to those from whom the Roofers were extorting money for themselves and for Scarfo, the cases Traitz was describing were not quite so minor as he was trying to indicate.

One new judge, Mario Driggs, after accepting his check, pointed out that he wouldn't always be in a position to give a not-guilty verdict, that the "break" would have to come at sentencing. Another new judge, Mary Rose Cunningham, after giving her thanks for the cash, remarked to Traitz—who controlled the union's PAC fund—how nice it would be if her husband could be elected a judge, too.

Altogether by 1986, seventeen judges were implicated in the gift receiving. The cases dragged on for the next three years. In January 1990, at the deadline for this book, the final decision had still not been made on one of them. By that time, two judges had been exonerated by the Judicial Inquiry and Review Board. One died before his case could be resolved. One was indicted but not convicted. Driggs was indicted, convicted and sentenced to prison. Mary Rose Cunningham wasn't. When confronted by the FBI with the evidence against her, she agreed to act as informant against her fellow judges, and went scurrying about City Hall with a tape recorder in her purse; she never turned up anything incriminating.

However, she and all the other judges who had taken the Roofer cash (except for the two exonerated judges and the one found not guilty at trial) were removed from the bench —including "Julian," Julian King. That was a deletion of about 15 percent of the Philadelphia judiciary.

Prompted by the Roofer tapes, the FBI investigation of the Philadelphia courts expanded. One of the two judges who had been exonerated was forced to leave the bench anyway in 1989 when he confessed to defrauding an insurance company. Three more judges were tried for case fixing. Probably the most flagrant in his activities was Kenneth Harris, the "Kenny" whom the yuletide cash courier Jimmy Brown referred to as a "great guy." He used his chambers next to his courtroom to demand and accept cash on the barrelhead in return for acquittals. All three judges were convicted and sent to prison, as were several of the lawyers involved in the bribes. (A fourth judge who was indicted had not yet been tried at the time of the writing of this book.)

As the criminal Roofers Union boss Traitz was sending his kind of Christmas cheer to his friendly judges in December 1985, and the murderer Scarfo was readying his joyous holiday celebration at LaCucina (for which the guest list included, in addition to Traitz and his boys, a Philadelphia city councilman, Leland Beloff), the innocent Neil Ferber continued to sit on death row.

By December, Ferber had been in his cell for fifteen months. While he was still probably years from execution (the appellate process in capital cases is a lengthy one) his mental condition had deteriorated sharply. The furniture salesman fantasies that had sustained him earlier had long since been played out. Now he spent hour after hour just curled up on his bunk staring blankly at the ceiling. He was having trouble with his memory, too; at times, he could no longer recall his home address or phone number. He was distancing himself from life. Suicidal thoughts occasionally shot like tracer bullets across the dark mass of fear his mind was becoming.

Cogan and I, with the help of our two lonely supporters, Guinther in the press and Homer, the radio talk-show man, might eventually be able to rescue Ferber, but unless it happened soon, I feared the saving would be of a shell, not a man.

In that sense, I knew we were running out of time. District Attorney Ed Rendell had only until January 3, 1986, to serve in office. If we didn't convince him before then to grant Ferber a new trial—in which, I had no doubt, Ferber, with Cogan representing him, would be found not guilty—we would have to start all over with whoever Rendell's successor turned out to be. Neither Cogan nor I could imagine the new DA moving quickly, if at all, on a case involving someone on death row in a mob hit. He'd be interested in compiling his own record, not scraping clean Rendell's.

But even if Rendell did act—and he'd promised me he'd reach a decision on Ferber before he left office—the best bet was (as had been true all along) that he'd permit the guilty verdict to stand. Let the appeals court handle it sometime in Ferber's perilous future, by which time Rendell hoped to be governor (a hope that was not to be fulfilled). Nevertheless, Rendell was keeping in touch with me, calling me more often than I did him, which I took as a good omen. (I was reduced to looking for omens by now.) The calls themselves, however, were as brief as the anonymous threats I was receiving. I don't think any conversation with him ever lasted more than thirty seconds, the maximum time he seemed to be able to spend on any subject. (I think many of his contacts with me resulted from Cogan's relentless pressure to keep in touch with me.) Because of the brevity of our conversations, I had no chance to do more than reiterate my certainty Ferber was innocent.

Despite Rendell's continuing interest—or his apparent awareness that the case could explode on him, maybe in the middle of his election campaign—nothing happened. September went by, October, November, with no discernible move toward a resolution. Then, in early December, I was called to Rendell's office.

* * *

In addition to Rendell, who seemed to have selected for himself the role of judge for the meeting, on hand were Steve Cooperstein, a young assistant DA who had been assigned by Rendell to read Ferber's case file; the bearded and intense Eric Henson, chief of the Appeals Division; and Arnie Gordon, the tough-minded head of the Homicide Division. He and I had disagreed over the Joey Pedulla sentencing deal, but otherwise, over the years, we had worked closely and, I thought, well together.

Rendell asked me to give my views. I started off by observing that Ferber never would have become a suspect in the murders if it hadn't been for a first wrong theory (that his associate Saltzburg was involved), and only remained a suspect because of a second wrong theory (that his associate DiPasquale was involved). I now had compelling evidence, strong enough to obtain an indictment, I said, that Long John Martorano had contracted out the hit, which meant he would have gone to his own people for shooters, a group that didn't include Saltzburg, DiPasquale or Ferber.

I next went over some of the other problematical areas. Why, for instance, if he was guilty, would Ferber, who had eleven days between the killings and his arrest to come up with an alibi, tell a story that required a single phone call to disprove?

For the most part, however, I concentrated my discussion on trial matters, principally the Egan identification and Ferber's alleged confession to Jordan.

I began by explaining how Mrs. Egan had said that Ferber was "most like" the killer out of seven mugshots she'd been shown, and turning to Gordon, I said, "Arnie, you and I know each other better than anybody in this room, and I trust you and I think you trust me. Now I want to ask you: If I, no matter how much you trust me, had come to you with an identification like that, as they did to the person who was in charge of Homicide then,* would you have given me a warrant based on what she said?''

The answer was obvious; Arnie knew it and he laughed, one of the few times I've seen him do that. Looking at the others, he said, "I have to admit, I think I'd have a problem with that."

But that wasn't the only problem, I said; the Egans were a problem every which way. John Egan's ability to identify Ferber occurred only after he'd seen his picture in a newspaper story that pronounced him guilty; but, even beyond that, I went on, based on all my experience as a detective, I was absolutely convinced the Egans' description of the killer was, no matter how sincerely intended, not worthy of belief. The group nodded sagely. Yes, the Egans did present a problem, they agreed.

Finally, I turned to Jordan, with whom, by now, I'd had a second meeting. After reminding them of Frank Cryan's evaluation of Jordan's polygraph, I told them how Jordan himself, in the first interview, said Ferber had confessed but that he didn't believe him, and in the second, in which he grew increasingly vague, that Ferber maybe hadn't actually confessed; he might have only been repeating the accusations against him. Your eyewitnesses aren't credible, I concluded, and your jailhouse informant can't tell the same story twice, and they're all you have.

Rendell had been listening patiently. Now he said, "Frank, it's not evidence," adding patronizingly, "It's a good closing speech to the jury for the defense, but it's not evidence for a new trial."

Rendell next went around the table. To my marked lack of surprise, young Cooperstein backed his boss, and Henson,

---

*It should be noted that prosecutor Arnie Gordon had the benefit of additional information that was known to him and me but that was not known to his predecessor.

a gung-ho type, stoutly maintained that "we can beat back any challenge on appeal." Then it was Arnie Gordon's turn. He turned to me and in a friendly, patient way explained the American justice system to me. I don't recall his exact words, but they went very much like this: "Frank, you just don't understand. This guy had a trial with a jury of his peers and the jury reached its verdict. Convictions are hard to come by, and we don't want to go upsetting this one. Now I can understand your doubt, just as everyone in this room can. But in our justice system, everybody does their job. Your job is to investigate the case and make an arrest, our job to prosecute the case, the judge's to preside over it to make sure the trial is fair, and the jury ultimately decides guilt or innocence. Everybody in this case has done their job. The system has spoken. It's not up to the DA and not up to the police, and it's not up to you to do anything more." As Dooley had said, it was my job to arrest, not unarrest.

Arnie turned to the subject of Dennis Cogan next. "And don't be misled by Dennis," he warned. "He'll do anything for a victory. The worst thing about Dennis is that unlike a lot of other lawyers, he's very bright."

I took a deep breath and, deciding to ignore the main lecture, I said, "Arnie, let me tell you about Dennis Cogan. At one point, he said to me, 'Will it be helpful to the case if I step out?' He had the feeling there was an animus from this office directed toward him personally and it was stopping you from looking at the facts of the case." Until this moment, I hadn't believed Cogan; now I did. "He anguished over that, because he believes in his case passionately. So do I, Arnie."

At that point, they sprang their little surprise on me. From the smooth way in which it was done, it struck me it had been worked out before the meeting and might well have been the sole purpose of the meeting. Everything that had gone on before was window dressing, and I had been wasting my time trying to convince them. I was there, rather, to be mollified. After all, I could cause them problems; I could go to the media and be listened to—the great terror.

Arnie was the one chosen to make the offer. As best I recall his words, he said, "What we'll agree to do is we'll drop our demand for the death penalty for Ferber. We'll concede there were some problems in the trial, and indicate to the appeals court that justice will be served if Ferber gets life in prison instead of the death penalty."

What could be more fair?

I looked from him over to Ed Rendell, who was leaning forward, looking eager. "You don't understand," I said. "Nobody here understands. This guy is innocent. He's innocent. What you're offering is no concession at all. What do you want me to do? Go back to Ferber and say I've got good news and bad news for you? The good news is you're not going to be executed for a murder you didn't commit, and the bad news is you're going to spend the rest of your life in prison for a murder you didn't commit?" I slapped my hands on my knees. I added, "He should go free, or at the least he should get a new trial."

A silence followed. The four lawyers stared at one another. No one tried to answer me. No one looked at me. Finally, Rendell said, "All right. We'll continue to work on it."

I left, figuring I had, indeed, learned something about the American justice system.

26
Neil Ferber Tries to Bathe Himself Clean

I still had one more card to play in the Neil Ferber case: the Jerry Jordan card. As I'd told Jerry I would, I had hauled him before the grand jury, where he reverted to the same story he told at Ferber's trial. His testimony there was utterly meaningless, my own piece of window dressing, its principal decoration the grant of immunity I had obtained for him, which was intended to give him the impression that he was now safe in saying anything and that once he was done with the grand jury, he could finally forget about the whole Ferber mess.

Within a day or two of the fiasco in Rendell's office, I brought him in again. I could see that, as I'd hoped, that scared him. It meant I was still after him like some hound of heaven. Patiently, quietly, as if I were genuinely puzzled myself, I went over the statements he had given at trial and now before the grand jury—both times under oath, I reminded him solemnly—and noted how utterly at variance they were with each of the versions of Ferber's supposed statements he'd given me. Finally, as if this were the only conclusion a reasonable person like him could draw, I said, "Jerry, you know we can solve all this once and for all, if you'll agree to take another polygraph test."

"Once and for all" was a useful phrase. I wanted to indicate to him by it, and apparently I did, that this was his one and only way to get rid of me. He agreed. I called Rendell, who seemed delighted by the news, as well he might have been. If Jordan passed the polygraph, Rendell could hang onto the conviction, and if he didn't, Rendell would have something to hang his hat on in moving for a new trial.

Rendell's choice for polygrapher—we both agreed it shouldn't be a cop—was Emily Wimberly. I had known her from years before when she was a Juvenile Aid Division officer. At some point, she had studied to become a polygrapher, was assigned to Rendell's office to carry out that function, and eventually moved on to become a chief of security at an Atlantic City casino. I knew her to be a person of absolute integrity, intelligent, femininely charming and, when the occasion called for it, stone-cold tough. I advised Cogan of the upcoming test; he also liked Emily, and his own polygrapher, Bill Anderson, held her in equally high regard. She was it.

The test was scheduled to take place on Wednesday, December 11, 1985. Confident as I was of Wimberly's abilities, I saw no need to be on hand, but Ed Rendell was present, as were two of his assistant DAs, as well as Cogan's polygrapher, Anderson. According to Wimberly, prior to the administering of the test, Rendell spent a lengthy period alone with Jordan. The two assistant DAs (whose names she doesn't recall) apparently were alarmed that the test was to take place at all, and held frequent conferences with Wimberly to point out that they didn't think Jordan was a suitable subject for polygraphing. Their announced reason, according to Anderson, was that Jordan had been on methadone, a synthetic substitute for heroin. Wimberly says she felt no "pressure" from the DAs to call off the test but was well aware of their "concerns."

When he was finally left alone with Wimberly and Anderson, Jordan appeared nervous, distracted, anxious to leave. During the pretest interview, Anderson, according to his notes, said to Jordan, "You seem like someone who wants to get something off your chest."

Jordan did. "I lied in the Ferber case," he told him. "Ferber only said to me that he ushered people out of the restaurant." The killers, in fact, ushered no one out of the restaurant, nor had Jordan ever previously claimed that Ferber said that to him. "And at trial, I said Ferber shot him."

It wasn't all his fault that he lied, Jordan explained to Anderson. Ferber's statements to him, he said, had been twisted by the detectives to make them maximally damaging. More than that: On the day of the trial, he said, he was told by detectives and someone from the DA's office that if he didn't testify that Ferber said he was the shooter, "all deals were off." (By that, he apparently meant the agreement that in return for his testimony he'd get time served on his convictions, and the charges on the two new cases, the retail theft and the stabbing, would be dropped. The agreement was carried out.)

I have no idea how many, if any, of Jordan's accusations were true (he also said he was supplied with drugs while still in prison), nor why he chose to make them then. He may have simply been thrashing about in his fear, and used them to distance himself from his own responsibility, the final truth installment that he was holding back.

Nevertheless, Jordan did receive one documented favor from the police. After giving his statement against Ferber in 1981 but before he was released on bail, he was permitted by police to visit his girlfriend. She testified at Ferber's posttrial hearing that she and Jordan had sex on that occasion. Danny Rosenstein, who brought Jordan to her house, had denied the lovemaking occurred when asked by Cogan about it also during Ferber's posttrial hearings.

Perhaps there was fear in the DA's office or among the police that Jordan might make accusations; whether true or false, such accusations could be highly damaging if they became public. This might explain their last-minute effort to abort the test but I have no way of knowing if that is why, and arguing against that theory is Rendell's eagerness to have the test proceed.

After the polygraph was given, Anderson read the charts as indicating deception. Wimberly felt they were inconclusive. Considering Jordan's emotional state, they decided a retest was called for.

Jordan, predictably, wanted nothing to do with a second go-around. I had to have another long conversation with him. In it, more so than I had in the first, I emphasized that his immunity grant meant that he couldn't be charged with perjury at the Ferber trial or before the grand jury even if the new polygraph showed he had been lying. All we wanted, I assured him, was the truth; we were not interested in him beyond that. For whatever reason, perhaps his safety from prosecution, but more likely, I think, his dread of what I might be able to do to him if he didn't agree (you don't want a police homicide lieutenant after you if you're a career criminal), he said, all right, let's do it.

The second test took place on Thursday, December 26, in a conference room in Rendell's office. Rendell was again present, as was Deputy DA Eric Henson (according to Wimberly's recollection) and Danny Rosenstein, who confided to Wimberly that he now thought Ferber was innocent.

As on the first occasion, only Emily Wimberly and Bill Anderson were present for the pretest interview. Again Jordan appeared nervous, preoccupied, spoke of having to get someplace, and seemed unwilling to focus on the subject at hand. Emily, however, warm and sympathetic, managed to get Jordan sufficiently calmed to begin the examination. In polygraphing, a key question is usually posed in different ways. Jordan's was asked four times, and in each reply he reverted to his original testimony:

> Q: Did you lie to me about Ferber's conversations to you about the Booras killing?
>
> A: No.
>
> Q: Did Ferber really tell you he participated in the Booras killing?
>
> A: Yes.
>
> Q: Did you lie about Ferber telling you he participated in the Booras killing?
>
> A: No.
>
> Q: Are you now being truthful about Ferber's admission to you he participated in the Booras killing?
>
> A: Yes.

After completing the test, Emily ripped the chart from the machine and took it off to read. Anderson joined her, but they did not confer on their interpretations. They then returned to Jordan. Emily wasn't being charming anymore. Giving Jordan a level look, with a shake of her head, she said, "Jerry? You're full of shit. You're lying and I'm tired of playing around with you."

The direct attack worked. Almost immediately, she recalled, Jordan mumbled, "All right, I'm lying."

She looked at him quizzically. "But why would you do that?" she asked.

"Because I was mad at my girlfriend," he answered.

She asked him to explain. "Well," he said, "every time I called my girl from prison, she was out, all the time she was out, and I knew the only way I could check on her was to be out of prison. The cops had already brought me down, and I knew what they wanted. . . ." So he decided to provide it: "I told Neil different things to help him keep other prisoners away from him, and one of them was to talk like a tough guy, talk like a killer. And some of the things I told him to say [I told to the police as if he had said them] and other things I just listened to what Neil was talking about . . ." (such as Ferber's description of the accusations against him, his joke about the shoulder pads); still other times, he put his own words into Ferber's mouth (such as those regarding the $20,000 hit fee). When to all that, he added everything he could learn about the murders, he had his package and delivered it.

Throughout his description of how he had entrapped Ferber, Emily recalled, he was as unconcerned as one "might be talking about a shopping bag in a supermarket." His main interest, even after he admitted he had been lying from the start, was that he get transportation home from this session: "Ed [Rendell] promised me a ride . . . Ed promised me a ride," he repeated.

Emily Wimberly isn't positive exactly when she related the results of the polygraph and Jordan's subsequent admission to Rendell. It may have been the same day, although Dennis Cogan's notes indicate that she wasn't able to catch up with Rendell until the following Monday. It was either that afternoon or the next that I got the news by phone from Rendell himself.

I'm sure he would have preferred that Jordan had tested

as truthful, but his only evident reaction, spoken in his usual upbeat way, was that he was glad we had finally reached an answer with Jordan. He was going to do the right thing, too, he told me, and he did. On Friday, his last day in office, a letter was transmitted to Judge Latrone. In it, Rendell stated: ''. . . I believe these test results when combined with other questions that have been raised by the work of law enforcement officials and considered in light of the obvious weight that Jordan's testimony had upon the jury, require . . . that given the standards this office has operated under for the past eight years we must recommend to you that the interests of justice require granting of a new trial.''

Rendell's call had come in the midst of a conversation I was having with an FBI agent in my office. When I hung up, I was aware that she was staring at me. ''What's happened, Lieutenant?'' she asked. ''You look so—so exhilarated.''

Perhaps exhilaration is a good word for what I was feeling, but coupled with it, acting in happy concert with it, was a sense of utter and total relaxation and relief, the kind that suffuses you when a source of tension is removed that has been part of you for such a long time that you are no longer consciously aware how much it has been draining you. It was this tension that had produced my sleepless nights: the tension brought about by facing, day after day, the very real possibility that at best, this man would spend the rest of his life locked up for a crime he hadn't committed. It was over. It was all over, I was positive. There would never be a second trial. They had nothing left. We had won.

It turned out I was right in my conjectures, but I came close to being wrong. When Dennis Cogan and Eric Henson, armed with Rendell's letter, went before Judge Latrone on that Friday afternoon—Rendell's last in office—Latrone, as Dennis recalled it, was unwilling to accept Rendell's recommendation. He opined there should be another hearing before he made a decision. At that, Dennis erupted with the pentup fury he had been developing toward the system over the past four years. Another hearing? he asked Latrone. That would mean another year, at best, before the new DA would be ready to act, and two years before there'd be that other hearing. And all that time an innocent man would remain on death row. You don't believe the district attorney about Jordan? Cogan asked. Then call Emily Wimberly.

Latrone agreed to call her. She was reached by phone and her answers were made part of the court record. When Latrone hung up from the call, he stared at Cogan for a moment and then said, "All right, all right. We'll give you a new trial."

Dennis pressed forward. "I want my client released immediately on the bail that's already posted, Judge," he said. (Looking forward to this day, Dennis had convinced the Ferber family to let the bail money stand rather than recovering it after the trial.)

Latrone replied, "You got it."

On the following morning, Saturday, January 4, 1986, a cold and sunlit day, Jay Ferber arrived at Graterford State Prison. A guard opened the door. Neil Ferber stepped out. He looked at his brother uncertainly and then fell into his embrace.

His arm around his older brother's shoulders, Jay led Neil to his car. Neil took short, uncertain steps, his features blank. Jay drove him from the prison and his sixteen-month home on its death row. They had gone about twenty minutes when Neil spotted a restaurant and asked if they could stop there. Thinking he wanted something to eat, Jay agreed. When they got inside, however, Neil excused himself to go to the bathroom, walking with the tiny steps that may have become habitual pacing his cell. At the counter, Jay waited for him. Five minutes went by, then ten, fifteen. Worried, Jay followed his brother to the men's room. He saw Neil stripped to the waist, covered with the pink suds from the soap dispenser, wiping at himself with paper towels. He turned to Jay. "I smell, I smell," he said. "I can't have my mother seeing me smelling like this." Gently, Jay cleaned him off, helped him get dressed, and they continued on home.

Almost another two months went by before the new DA's office reached the inevitable conclusion. On Friday, March 2, 1986, Neil Ferber, accompanied by his family and Dennis Cogan, appeared before Judge Charles Durham. Based on Arnie Gordon's recommendation, the new DA in charge of the Homicide Unit asked that all charges be dropped in the case of "this possibly innocent man."

That evening, one of the television stations tracked down Jerry Jordan. He was interviewed with his back to the camera. When asked if Neil Ferber had ever told him he killed Steve Booras, Jordan came up with his latest version: "Not in so many words," he said.

A few days later, Ferber admitted himself to a mental hospital, suffering from acute depression and bleeding ulcers; he remained there for several weeks. Over the next three-and-a-half years, he frequently called me, asking for my advice. Over and over again, he promised me he would remain straight. He held a number of jobs, had long periods of unemployment, was on welfare, had subsequent bouts of depression and ulcer attacks. He and his wife, who had suffered great emotional devastation from his death sentence, were not able to put their marriage back together. Late in 1988, Ferber's 21-year-old daughter, who, while still in high school, had undergone agonies of humiliation at the hands of her classmates when they taunted her for having a murderer as a father, died of a drug overdose.

After that tragedy, I heard from Neil less frequently. At one point, he was picked up for shoplifting. Although the charges were dropped, that was the signal he was drifting back to his loser's world. He found it again in the fall of 1989 when he was arrested on a felony charge involving the sale of P2P, set up for the bust by an undercover informant wearing a body wire.

Which sadly, but not unpredictably—if I were writing fiction, I could have told a happier tale—marked the end of the not-for-nothin' Victor DeLuca offered me back in the summer of 1984.

PART IV

Breaking the Mob

27
Del Talks and The Crow Negotiates

Ignoring the crucial role Dennis Cogan played in freeing Ferber from death row, District Attorney Rendell publicly bestowed the credit on me; modestly, he downplayed his own role, too, which, it occurred to me, meant that he figured if it turned out Ferber was guilty after all, he wouldn't have to take any of the blame. (Rendell has ever since maintained that he's still not sure Ferber wasn't involved in the Meletis murders.)

Ferber's release, rather surprisingly, also played well in the media for the Police Department. Apparently, we were willing to admit to our mistakes and attempt to rectify them. As good publicity, that praise came under the heading of a crumb, but a welcome one at a time when most of the headlines the Philadelphia police were garnering contained the word "corruption." Within the Department, I was treated as something of a hero rather than as a pariah who'd supposedly turned on his fellow police officers. As if by magic, the threatening phone calls ceased. But at no time did my superiors confer with me or make any other effort (of which I'm aware) to make sure another Ferber case could never happen.

In February 1986, an event entirely unrelated to Ferber occurred: I was promoted to captain. Several months earlier I had passed the necessary civil service test for the post, which I had never wanted—still didn't want—because it would take me from my beloved detective work and into administrative duties. Nevertheless, it had become clear to me it was a step I'd have to take. I had two reasons. One was purely practical. I had now been a cop for twenty-five years, my family financial obligations were mounting, and a captaincy not only paid more money but offered increased pension benefits as well. (I had become eligible for retirement after I finished my twentieth year.) My second motive arose from my experience with Captain Dooley. It brought home to me (as my long and happy relationship with my protector and mentor Jerry Kane had not) how vulnerable I was as a lieutenant in the police bureaucracy. I didn't want to have to fight through that kind of situation again.

Our new police commissioner, who had succeeded Sambor in December 1985, was Kevin M. Tucker, whom I had known as a highly able special agent in charge of the secret service in Philadelphia. Soon after taking office as commissioner, he issued a commendation to me for my work in the Ferber case. As part of his reorganization of the Department, Tucker put me in charge of a new intelligence unit that encompassed investigation not only of the Mafia but of other organized criminal gangs as well, including the Junior Black Mafia and the Jamaican Shower Posse, the latter a particularly violent assortment of cocaine dealers. I now had 70 officers reporting to me, and I no longer had the time to participate in the investigations of the Organized Crime Task Force, but I did retain supervisory input over its activities.

As part of my new job, I continued to work with various federal law enforcement agenies, among them the FBI in New Jersey, which for some time had been putting together a Racketeer Influenced Corrupt Organization (RICO) prosecution in which Scarfo and his lieutenants were to be named as defendants. For it, courtroom-admissible evidence had to be compiled that would satisfy a jury that the Scarfo organization had a history of carrying out crimes as part of a structured operation with its own rules, goals and financing mechanisms. It was a dull and unsatisfactory case to bring, but we still hadn't been able to get Scarfo (except on the Atlantic City gun charge in 1983), and the RICO indictment appeared to be the only way to go, much as, a half-century earlier, the government, not able to nail Al Capone as a murderer, had convicted him as an income tax evader.

However, the New Jersey RICO case in its existent form would soon become history itself. Something much better was about to come along to replace it.

That something was a Scarfo real estate shakedown attempt involving builder Willard Rouse. Members of Rouse's family had earlier become renowned for innovative real estate developments. The model city of Columbia, Maryland, was theirs, and they also were pioneers in the creation of indoor shopping malls. Willard Rouse's first major contribution to the Philadelphia economy came in the 1970s, when he created an industrial park near Valley Forge, which attracted a number of high-tech computer companies to the region. By the 1980s, he had expanded into the downtown area, where he constructed an architecturally striking new office building which the Philadelphia Stock Exchange, the nation's oldest, made its new headquarters.

By 1986, Rouse had turned his attention to Penn's Landing, an area that overlooked the Delaware River, just east of fashionable Society Hill. There, in 1682, William Penn had docked his little boat and stepped ashore to have his first look at the site on which he planned to build his City of Brotherly Love. Three hundred years later, the city was offering outdoor concerts on the historic site during the summer months, and occasional festivals, but despite many plans that had come and gone on the drawing boards, Penn's Landing had never been developed commercially. That, Rouse now proposed to do. He unveiled an ambitious and imaginative blueprint for a concentration of hotels and retail businesses. The media was excited, the mayor was excited; also excited were members of the City Council with, it seemed, only one exception, the tall, curly-haired, 43-year-old Leland Beloff. The scion of an old-time political family—his father was a judge—Beloff had just been elected to City Council following a tenure as a member of the state legislature.

Sitting on Beloff's desk, by the late spring of 1986, were several zoning variances that had to be passed before Rouse could put his new project into action. Had the bills gotten off Beloff's desk—he controlled them, since Penn's Landing was in his district—the Council members would have passed them immediately. But they didn't get off his desk, and neither he nor his trusted administrative assistant, Robert Rego, seemed in any hurry to have them do so.

The chubby and officious Rego spoke on behalf of Lee Beloff, as everyone around City Hall knew; he told them so. Despite his voluble personality, Rego, however, was not forthcoming about his background, and for good reason. He was a drug dealer, a member of the Riccobene gang, whom I had first heard about when his name appeared on Scarfo's death list. That he remained among the living was solely, we in law enforcement believed, because Beloff was a close associate of Scarfo's.

Rouse soon learned why his bills weren't moving off Beloff's desk. On June 2, 1986, Rego met with a Rouse employee, telling him that Beloff had indicated to him he'd like to support the Penn's Landing plans but that first he wanted a meeting with Rouse. Rouse immediately agreed, and the get-together was scheduled for June 10. However, on June 3, Beloff phoned Rouse, and when he couldn't get through to him, told his secretary there'd be no need for the meeting. When that word got back to Rouse—he'd been out of town because of a death in his family—he asked one of his executives, Peter Balitsaris, to contact Beloff to ascertain the reason for the cancellation. Rego took the call. "Ain't no reason for that meeting," said he.

The classic extortion scheme, the one that Angelo Bruno had worked on Philadelphia builders so many times in the past, was again about to unfold.

On June 4, at 4:30 p.m., Rego phoned Balitsaris and told him he wanted to meet him a half-hour later at Marabella's, a pricey restaurant a few blocks from City Hall, next to the Academy of Music. When Balitsaris arrived, he found Rego had a companion. "This is my close friend, Nick," said Rego, and then got up and left. Nick, who was "Nicky Crow" Caramandi, attempted, in his own inimitable gravelly-voiced, side-of-the-mouth way of speaking, to put Rouse's man at ease. "You don't got no problems," he assured him. He went on to say that Beloff honestly wanted to see the project go through, but this could be done "only if a deal could be arranged."

Taken aback, Balitsaris asked, "What?"

The Crow rubbed his fingers together suggestively. "We want one," he explained, holding up a finger.

"I assume," said Balitsaris, "there's some zeros behind that one."

With his usual rapier-like wit, The Crow responded, "As many as there is," by which he meant he wanted a million dollars.

Now eager to get out of there, Balitsaris advised The Crow that he himself wasn't in a position to make any such commitment and would have to take the demand back to Rouse. In parting, he did say he thought things could be worked out. On hearing the news, Rouse contacted a friend, lawyer Larry Hoyle, who'd had some experience of his own as a special prosecutor investigating corruption in Philadelphia. Hoyle brought Rouse to Ed Dennis, the U.S. attorney, who brought the FBI into the case. I was notified of the Caramandi scam, and a plan was worked out to counter it. I already had Caramandi under surveillance in a similar, if smaller-scale, shakedown attempt against real estate developers in the city's fashionable Society Hill area. The Task Force had infiltrated that operation with informant John Pastorella, whom I had first used for the "Cuddles" DiCaprio case involving the murder of Robert Hornickel. Now we had Caramandi sandwiched in two investigations simultaneously. He and his boss Scarfo were blissfully unaware of both.

The next step of the Rouse shakedown—and the first of the FBI's surveillance—took place on June 5 when Balitsaris called Rego and asked to set up another meeting, again at five o'clock, this time at DiLullo's, an elegant and even more expensive restaurant across the street from Marabella's. Rather than speaking—apparently worried that Balitsaris might be wired—Rego wrote a noted and handed it to him. It read: "We can put in or kill the ordinance. I talked to the Mayor and to Craig Schelter and he has a position at the Philadelphia Industrial Development Corp. and told them of our objections. See my friend for 15 minutes." Rego then took the note back, and instructed Balitsaris to cross the street and meet with Caramandi at Marabella's. The Crow, as advertised, was there waiting. Balitsaris informed him the deal was OK'd. Pleased, Caramandi told him the million was "necessary in four moves" of $250,000 each, and the first "move" was to be made the following morning. Balitsaris replied it would be impossible to put together that much cash that fast, and similarly balked when Caramandi immediately backed down to demand $100,000 up front. The affable Crow proved willing to compromise even further. "Then tell him," he advised, "to get whatever goddamn cash he has available. Between now and tomorrow morning, he should sell, hock or pawn his wife's goddamn jewelry." In parting, The Crow said he would be waiting in the lobby of the nearby Hershey Hotel for the payoff.

But the next day, Balitsaris didn't show up. Caramandi called him. Balitsaris advised him a problem had come up in putting the money together, but he wasn't to worry; everything would work out. Another meeting was scheduled, and it was postponed, as were several more over the next week. Same problem, Caramandi was told; same assurances. Finally, on June 12, Balitsaris kept an appointment at the hotel, accompanied by a man he introduced to Caramandi as Jim Vance, a colleague, who would be conducting the negotiations from then on. The Crow prided himself on being nobody's fool, and demanded that Vance show him a business card. Vance didn't provide that, but did give him something he liked even better: $10,000 in cash. After pocketing it, The Crow inquired how soon he could get the remaining $90,000 to fulfill the promised $100,000 down payment. Vance explained, "Rouse doesn't want to make any more payments until the legislation goes through."

Caramandi, who was not the world's best negotiator, again backed down. "All right, $45,000 when it's passed and $45,000 the day after," he offered.

Vance opined that sounded fair to him. The men then departed, and Vance—whose real name was Vaules and whose employer was not Rouse but the FBI—signaled surveillance officers to follow the diligent Crow, who then made his way over to City Hall, where he was seen meeting with Beloff.

That trip wasn't the only one the poor Crow had to make. The Little Guy in Atlantic City wanted to see to him too.

"Where's my money?" asked Scarfo.

"Well, uh, we don't have it," admitted The Crow.

"Why not?"

"Well, there's all these damn meetings, they get canceled and—"

"What kind of mobster are you?" Scarfo inquired. "Everybody agrees they're going to pay, yet you get shit."

But that wasn't all that was making The Crow's life a difficult one. Scarfo, while he was at it, had given him a new assignment. He wasn't just to chisel Rouse but Beloff as well, he learned, which may explain his trip to Beloff's office on the day after Vaules gave him the $10,000. The agreement between Scarfo and Beloff had been that they'd share the booty equally. Now The Crow had to advise Beloff that the split had changed to 60–40. On his next trip, The Crow had even worse news for Beloff. His cut was now down to 30 percent, with 20 percent looming on the horizon. I have no doubt Scarfo never intended for Beloff to get a penny. What was Beloff going to do about it? Call the cops?

As Nicky Crow had said in another context, being a criminal these days just wasn't any fun anymore. It was about to become even less so. Not until June 18 did he manage another meeting with Vaules, by which time the Little Guy was thoroughly displeased, which did not augur well for The Crow's longevity prospects. At this meeting, Vaules sadly informed The Crow that Rouse was having cash flow problems. Generously, however, he handed $1,000 to the Crow to tide him over; he was only $989,000 short now. As he gave him the money, Vaules casually asked him if he could help Rouse with some potential labor problems. The Crow immediately puffed. He sure could, he said, adding, "My power goes all the way to Atlantic City."

Vaules made a note of that remark. On June 23, he met with The Crow again. The news wasn't good this time either, he advised the by-now frantic Crow. Rouse, said Vaules, doesn't think he's dealing with Beloff at all and won't give out another dime unless Beloff assures him he is aware of the arrangement to accept money in return for passage of the zoning ordinances.

Caramandi immediately hurried off to see Beloff and his aide Rego, after which he called Vaules and told him he could meet with Beloff at his office the next day. When Vaules arrived, Beloff was nowhere about, and Rego shouted at him, "The bills are dead." Even as he spoke, however (apparently he was worried about a wiretap), he showed Vaules a note instructing him to meet "Nicky tomorrow at ten in the lobby of the Hershey Hotel."

When Vaules arrived, The Crow, reliable as ever, was on hand. Beloff, he informed Vaules, would arrive at one o'clock. Vaules departed, returning at the appointed hour. The Crow again met him and said the meeting site had been switched to Marabella's.

Beloff and Rego, he said, were already there. When he and Vaules arrived, The Crow explained, neither of them were to talk to the two public servants, but he, Caramandi, would give a signal and Beloff would give one in return, a wave followed by a hand to the breast pocket. On their arrival, The Crow waved. Beloff put his hand to his pocket.

That afternoon, Vaules informed Caramandi that Rouse wasn't going to pay a dime until the legislation went through. The following day, apparently to put the pressure back on Rouse, Beloff withdrew the bills.

The day after that was not a good one for Councilman Leland Beloff. He was arrested on extortion charges. It wasn't a good day for his drug-dealing administrative assistant Rego either. He was arrested on extortion charges, too. It was a doubly bad day for Nicky Crow. Not only was he charged in the Rouse case but also for the Society Hill developer extortions for which our informant Pastorella had provided the evidence.

We now had a bunch of Scarfo men dead to rights, but we still didn't have Scarfo. Beloff, whose political future depended upon being acquitted, wasn't about to turn state's witness, and neither was Rego, who was going to sink or swim with his boss. As for Caramandi, his boast that his connections went to Atlantic City meant nothing as evidence. Scarfo seemed to have escaped again. (He also escaped indictment when his lieutenant Saul Kane was arrested on the P2P importation charges. Kane and his associate, Gary Levitz, were convicted early in 1987, based largely on the testimony of Levitz's brother, Mark.)

Scarfo, however, was about to be arrested on an entirely different matter, a relatively minor one, but one that would suddenly blossom into the major case we had been looking for. The nucleus of the lesser case derived from the bug which the New Jersey State Police had maintained undetected for two years in Tommy DelGiorno's summer residence in Ocean City. From it, enough evidence was obtained to serve warrants on Scarfo, Del, Faffy Iannarella, Wayne Grande, Phil Leonetti (the new underboss) and Chuckie Merlino (the alcoholic ex-underboss), among others. Each defendant was charged with violations of New Jersey's RICO statute, specifically by operating a criminal enterprise dealing in gambling, loan-sharking and extortion. If everything went well for the prosecution at trial, Scarfo, as the kingpin, might be sentenced to 10 years and be back out in three or four.

Not having discovered a listening device in his own home for two years was not likely, Tommy Del realized, to make Scarfo happy with him. As it was, his day in the sun was already ending in the Scarfo empire, a fact of which he was all too aware. He'd made his crucial mistake, he figured,

when he tried to dissuade Scarfo from murdering Larry Merlino, the hard-drinking Chuckie Merlino's brother, by saying
it was a "crazy" idea. "Crazy" was a word about which the
Little Guy was quite sensitive. Soon after, Del was demoted
from capo to soldier, allegedly because he himself was drinking too much and having trouble controlling his crew. His
pals began to avoid him.

During the summer of 1986, the New Jersey troopers intercepted a conversation between Wayne Grande (the murderer of Salvy Testa) and Faffy (the murderer of Robert
Riccobene), who had replaced Tommy Del as capo: "I want
to tell you something about Tommy," Faffy said in the phone
conversation. "When we gotta talk business, Tommy ain't
supposed to be there," to which Wayne replied, "Ain't nothing going to happen to him—yet."

In a second intercepted conversation, this one between
Wayne and Joey Pungitore (Salvy's good friend who had set
him up for his murder), Del was referred to by the code name
"Rudy."

In the third tape, made nearly a year earlier, a drunken Del
is heard making a series of statements that implicate Scarfo
in crimes.

At the beginning of November 1986, immediately prior to
his arrest on the RICO charges, in order to heighten his fears
of Scarfo, New Jersey troopers Ed Johnson and Charley Cren-
deza paid a visit to Tommy Del's South Philadelphia home.
As Johnson recalled, when Del opened the door, "You could
see the fear in his eyes." Fear mounted to terror as Del
listened to the playing of the tapes. He knew the meaning of
the code name "Rudy" from having employed code names
himself. "We did that," he later said, "every time we were
going to kill someone." Del decided not to die. He decided
to talk. An informant had finally tumbled out of the very top
of the Scarfo tree.

That was the breakthrough toward which all our years of
effort had been aiming, all those months of trudging the streets

in South Philadelphia, collaring every mob hoodlum who came into sight, and telling him he could be next: "You know what Nicky's like." I remembered saying that to Del back in the fall of 1984 as he sat on the milk crate staring aghast at Salvy's grisly autopsy photo. I remembered the cushy sentencing deals I'd maneuvered for murderers, my belled sheep, ringing out their message of come-to-us (look around, look who's talking, look who might be talking about you)—we are going to get you if you don't get to us first. First in, first out.

That key Task Force strategy I'd implemented never would have worked when Angelo Bruno was alive. Had Del become a millionaire during the Bruno era, he would not have been happy about taking a fall on the RICO charge—he might have to do as much as 5 years—but he would have almost certainly done so in silence. He'd know that his businesses would be waiting for him when he got out, that his family would be taken care of while he was away, and he never would have had to fear with Bruno, as he did with Scarfo, that the payoff for his loyalty would be his own death. Not that Bruno wasn't capable of murder; we know of four killings he ordered, and he was probably directly involved in two others before he became don. But he didn't kill his lieutenants just because they made a mistake, because they greeted him when they shouldn't have or didn't greet him when they should have; he didn't kill someone because he fancied that person had taken his girl from him years before; and never did he kill solely because he "loved" it, as Scarfo did. The rules and regulations were known in Bruno's world, and as long as you lived up to them reasonably well, you did well and were safe. Thus, if we'd said, "You know what Bruno's like," they would have said, "Yes, we do," and remained loyal.

For that reason, had Bruno continued to live or been replaced by someone much like him—even the short-lived Phil Testa had some of Bruno's qualities—the Philadelphia/Atlantic City mob, I have no doubt, would still be largely in place and thriving. No Organized Crime Task Force would have been set in place to fight Bruno, and not because there shouldn't have been one. Six murders are six murders, and he and his men were heavy with evil; they were killers, narcotics dealers, extortionists, leg breakers, robbers and thieves, corrupters of business and unions and government. But in the application of violence, Bruno, crafty and cautious, never made the streets run with blood, and that was the difference between him and Scarfo. Scarfo's wholesale violence, impulsive and promiscuous, was the reason, the only reason, that the police and FBI were forced to lay aside the feuding they so delighted in and confront the Mafia instead of each other. Even then, Scarfo might have succeeded had not his own henchmen, dappled by the blood that spurted from within their ranks, begun to realize we were telling them the truth when we said, "You know what Nicky's like." They finally listened to the bell I had kept persistently ringing. Eventually, there would be five of them coming over to us.

I was immediately notified by Sergeant Mike McLaughlin of the New Jersey State Police that Del was talking. In the months ahead I would meet with him many times to question him about various crimes. At the moment, however, one crime interested me: the Meletis shooting. While Del had been a mob nobody when it occurred in 1981, it seemed probable to me he had heard the hit discussed during the course of his rise in the ranks. I contacted my colleagues in the New Jersey State Police with whom I'd worked closely since the days of the McCullough murder. The officers in charge of DelGiorno arranged to have him call me from the safe house in which they had him stored. When Del got on the phone, he sounded in a chipper mood, normal for him when he wasn't being surly. I quickly got to the point: "Tommy," I said, "I want to know about the Booras case. Do you know who the shooters are?"

"Yeah, sure," he said, as if offended I might think he

wouldn't. "Everybody knows Longy was behind it and the shooters were Frank Vadino"—that was no surprise—"and Cowboy."

That *was* a surprise. I'd never even heard a rumor in that direction. "Cowboy?" I asked. "Longy's son?"

"Yeah. Georgy."

He said he never heard the name of the getaway driver, nor which of the two gunmen put the bullets into Booras and Janette Curro. But that had to be Vadino. The Cowboy was built along Ferber's slender lines, which eliminated him as the big, burly shooter.

In naming Georgy as the second gunman, Del gave the answer to the one question in the Meletis murders that had continued to puzzle me. I had long since concluded that Martorano had brought his wife and her women friends along to the dinner solely to allay any suspicions Booras might have that he was being set up. Martorano also had to be absolutely certain that *both* killers, not just the one scheduled to do the shooting, were completely trustworthy. Too many things can go wrong on a hit, and it might become necessary for the backup man to do the job. Frank Vadino, who hero-worshipped Martorano, clearly fit the trustworthy qualification, but I had never been able to imagine who the second reliable killer could be. If Tommy Del was right—he had no firsthand knowledge—the answer had been in front of me all the time, like Poe's *Purloined Letter*: Long John's own son.

As I considered that, I visualized the sobbing Evelyn Martorano as she hovered over the body of her girlhood friend. Had she recognized Georgy? Had she recognized his voice when he yelled, "Don't nobody move!"? I remember how, when Evelyn Martorano left the witness stand after testifying at her husband's trial for murdering John McCullough, she had walked right by him without looking at him.

I had only discussed the Cowboy with his father on one occasion, shortly after Georgy had been convicted and sentenced to life on that vast array of narcotics charges. Said a disapproving Raymond, who, at the moment, was doing 10 years on his own narcotics conviction, "I told my kid to stay out of drugs, because we don't get involved in drugs."

I decided to bring Martorano Senior down. Despite his prison pallor, Longy looked dapper; his eyes had retained their familiar glitter. "Raymond," I said, "I now know all the pieces."

"What are you talking about?" he asked.

"I know who killed Booras," I said.

"Who?" he asked, with no apparent interest.

"Frank Vadino. And this guy."

I showed him a surveillance photo of his son. He glanced at it and, without a moment's hesitation, back up to me: "Who is this person?" he asked.

I smiled. "That's a great performance, Raymond. I wish I had an Oscar here handy for you."

"Why?" he asked.

"Because this is Cowboy. This is your son."

"That's not my son," he said.

By denying his son, he got his message across to me, just as I had gotten mine to him. By informing him I knew of Georgy's involvement, I was suggesting to him, in the shorthand we both understood, that if he confessed to the Booras murder—and gave me Scarfo—I'd be able to see to it that Georgy wouldn't face a death penalty. My appeal to his fatherly affection, however, did not work. Long John wasn't going to confess to killing anybody, no matter what it could mean for his boy.

It was Long John, however, who inadvertently handed us our second informant from the top of the Scarfo mob, Nicky Crow Caramandi. By late 1986, Caramandi, by then serving time on his conviction in the Rouse extortion case, was a worried man. He didn't think the Rouse mess was his fault; how could he have known that "Mr. Vance" was FBI? But might not Scarfo be blaming him? One day in prison, he encountered Long John. "How do I stand with the Little

Guy?'' he asked. Longy replied, ''No problem;'' but as he spoke, he made the sign of a gun with his forefinger and pointed it at The Crow, who walked away. Fast. He went to a phone. He dialed the Task Force. He reached FBI agent Jimmy Maher. ''I've had it,'' he said. ''I want out of here.''

28

The Scarfo Mob Trials

Nick Caramandi had made his debut as a government witness in Councilman Beloff's extortion trial. The information he provided had also permitted an indictment of Scarfo in the same case, but Scarfo was scheduled to be tried separately. Beloff was convicted and in July 1987, sentenced to 10 years in prison and fined $150,000. The bustling Bobby Rego was also convicted, and early the following year was found guilty on narcotics charges, too. His total sentence: 8 years.

Beloff was the fourth Philadelphia city councilman to be convicted of crimes of corruption in the 1980s. (One was the then-president of the City Council.) These four were just part of an assortment of individuals who had made the decade a time of shame for my city. During the same time period, judges had also been shown to be corrupt and the police were shown to be corrupt; state and federal legislators were shown to be corrupt: two congressmen from Philadelphia went to prison. The city had also caused eleven deaths, five of them children, along with wholesale destruction of people's homes, in the MOVE catastrophe, and then had managed, incredibly enough, to top matters off by hiring a crooked contractor to do the rebuilding. The first half of the 1980s had also been a time when, in South Philadelphia, it was worth an honest burgher's life to go out on the streets, not because of random crime—though that was also a factor—but because mobsters were using those same streets with apparent impunity to shoot one another while an incompetent police force and FBI both stood around wringing their hands and accomplishing nothing. These were the same mobsters who, some years earlier, had unleashed their own personal holocaust of death, crime and untold suffering when they ravaged the inner city neighborhoods, in which they never set foot, with their heroin and their methamphetamines. Nobody in law enforcement had stopped that either, nor, as far as I could ever observe tried to. On the contrary, six of the Police Department's crack narcotics team were convicted of stealing from the dealers and selling drugs themselves. It was a decade of shame.

At his trial on the Rouse real estate extortion case, which was held shortly after Beloff's, Scarfo—again with Nicky Crow's help—was convicted and received the first substantial prison sentence of his long criminal career, 14 years, of which he'd have to serve about a third. He was also fined $150,000, walking-around money for him.

Even before the Rouse prosecutions got under way, a turf battle had erupted among law enforcement agencies over who'd get the next crack at Scarfo. With Tommy Del and

The Crow on hand to offer evidence, the chances of winning loomed large. The prestige that would accrue to any prosecutor who brought down the little mobster on a murder charge could be a career-maker.

Since Del—the more important witness of the two because of his higher position in the mob—had confessed to New Jersey authorities, they had squatters' rights over him and thought their RICO case should be tried first, a view bolstered by the fact that Scarfo's home and principal headquarters were in Atlantic City.

The United States Justice Department urged with equal cogency that it should have primacy. Its own RICO case was prepared and could now be brought up to date, with Del's and The Crow's testimony, to include charges of conspiracy to commit murder. (Homicide, save in the sense that it is a violation of the victim's civil rights, is not a federal offense, but conspiring to commit murder is, and can be used as one of the two offenses that must be proved in order to convict under the RICO Act.) Rendell's successor as Philadelphia's DA, Ron Castille, however, had a powerful argument of his own to make. Of the more than thirty murders that had taken place, almost all occurred in Philadelphia. Local crimes, Castille pointed out, should be tried locally. The two he had in mind to try first were the Salvy Testa and Frankie Flowers homicides, on which our evidence was strongest.

New Jersey lost out entirely. It never did prosecute a single case against Scarfo, principally because its own RICO statute was much more narrowly gauged than the federal one. Ultimately, but only after a number of meetings, some of them acrimonious, everyone agreed that Philadelphia should take its shot on the Flowers and Testa homicides first, since they opened up the possibility of death sentences. (The maximum Scarfo faced under the federal RICO indictment was 55 years.) While there was every intention to prosecute the federal RICO case regardless of the outcomes of the murder trials—not all the same defendants were involved—it was also perceived as a fail-safe. Should the verdicts in the Testa and Flowers trials go against us, the RICO case, which was taking on mammoth proportions with hundreds of charges, could be wheeled into place next.

As much as having DelGiorno and Caramandi turn state's evidence improved our chances, we were fully aware the two men presented credibility problems as witnesses. Both had long records of lying about their participation in crimes, including many of those to which they were now confessing. Defense attorneys were certain to argue they were continuing to lie, this time to get lenient sentencing deals after the government had gotten the goods on them in other cases.

That this concern wasn't mere hypothesis, we learned when Caramandi and DelGiorno testified, also in 1987, in another federal RICO prosecution in which Cuddles DiCaprio was charged with participation in the Hornickel and Pat "the Cat" Spirito murders. The jury found him guilty in the Hornickel murder but not for Pat the Cat. The difference apparently was that in the Hornickel case, my investigation had developed evidence independent of DelGiorno and Caramandi—I spent hours on the stand outlining it—whereas for Spirito we had very little other than the two informants.

The result in the Spirito portion of the trial cast a pall, we thought, over our chances on the Frankie Flowers prosecution, where, although we had more of our own evidence than we did for Pat the Cat, we also had only DelGiorno to testify to the details of the murder plot; Caramandi had no involvement in that one. The DA's office, therefore, decided to try the Salvy Testa murder first. That one looked good. We had some supportive evidence of our own, plus both Del and Crow as witnesses.

Warrants against Scarfo and other defendants were issued simultaneously on the Testa and Flowers homicides. To avoid a crush of reporters and TV cameras, we arranged to have the bookings and interrogations take place in an out-of-the-way Pennsylvania State Police barracks. From there, the defendants would be shipped to the Police Administration Building—and the waiting media horde—for fingerprinting, photographs and arraignments.

The day at the barracks was a hectic one. Several defendants, including Scarfo, were already in custody, and we had to arrange to bring them from their various prisons. It was necessary to send teams out on the street to pick other defendants up. The barracks were bursting at the seams with law enforcement personnel—my men, the FBI, even the state troopers who belonged there. I handled a number of the interrogations, saving Scarfo for last. I had put him in a room by himself.

When I entered, he was sitting in a chair, looking lonely (as I'd intended) and resigned. The tan he had sported from cavorting on his yacht, *The Usual Suspects,* was now largely faded. I introduced myself. He looked up at me. "I'm glad to meet you, Captain," he said, "because, according to the papers, we're both leaders of organized crime, me of the organized crime LCN, and you of organized crime investigations."

I replied, "Nicky, you have no idea how happy I am meeting you under these circumstances. I've always passed on opportunities to arrest you previously because I knew one day I'd be standing here with a murder warrant in my hand, and that is why I'm here now, to inform you officially you are under arrest for the murders of Salvatore Testa and Frank D'Alfonso, also known as Frankie Flowers."

He shrugged. "I knew it was comin' because of them lyin' motherfuckers."

After reading him his rights, I introduced him to members of my squad who had spent years chasing him. I asked him how he was enjoying prison life, using my favorite line about the gray eggs. He laughed. "You eat anything that doesn't walk off the plate," he said, "but it takes a while to get used to it."

I supposed it might. I recalled the surveillance photos I'd seen of Scarfo and his men aboard Scarfo's yacht, living the good life as they sailed off the coast of Florida. No gray eggs then. I remembered pictures we'd obtained of them from our informants, arms around each other's shoulders, smiling into the camera, lolling about on the beach, the-fruits-of-crime pictures, as I'd thought of them. (One photograph shows Scarfo's son with him, the boy who later hung himself out of the shame of having Scarfo for a father.)

I studied Scarfo a moment longer. I then left him with several of my men and went back to processing other defendants onto the trucks to take them downtown. Scarfo was the last to go, and before he left, I returned to see him, the two of us alone. "At this time, ordinarily," I explained, "I'd be most interested and doing my persuasive best to try to get you to flip and testify on behalf of the prosecution, since I know you are an invaluable source of information. But, Nicky, I'm not going to waste either of our times with that, since as far as I am concerned you *are* organized crime. So, instead of offering you a deal, I'll only tell you that nothing would please me more than to be there when they strap you into Old Sparky."

I spoke calmly, quietly. He listened calmly, quietly. Then he laughed, a grunting "huh ha" laugh.

The next laugh was going to be his, too.

The Salvy Testa trial began in February 1988 and stretched into May. The defendants included, in addition to Scarfo, Joey Pungitore, the two Grande brothers, and the hoods involved in disposing of the body. I thought the government's case went well. Tommy Del was specific and credible as he recounted the details of the various plots that went awry and how the final one succeeded. Caramandi corroborated Del on several of the murder attempts, including a recounting of his own remarkable self-testing of the knockout drops. He told of his trip to New Jersey with Charlie White to buy the blanket in which they'd wrapped Salvy's body, and how they dumped it on the side of the road.

The defense, however, turned out to have one credible witness of its own: Captain Frank Friel of the Philadelphia Police.

The strutting, chain-smoking, bushy-haired Bobby Simone, who had been Scarfo's lawyer for years, called me to the stand. He made a point of focusing on organized crime cases I had solved. Next, deferentially—he sought to give the impression the sun rose and set on me—he led me through my investigation of the Salvy Testa murder. Yes, it was true, I said, we had information Salvy was killed on the evening of September 14, based on statements we had received from the police narcotics officer and the Girard Estates caretaker. From that information, yes, it was true I had obtained a search warrant to go through Testa's house. Simone then asked me if I hadn't searched the same house after Salvy's father was murdered in 1981. Yes, I had, I agreed. And wasn't it true, Simone inquired, that as a result of that earlier search I found a blanket and ropes similar to those in which Salvy's body was wrapped? I agreed that was true, too. By his questions and my responses, he raised the possibility that Salvy was still alive six hours after DelGiorno and Caramandi claimed was the time of his death, and that the blanket and ropes I'd discovered three years earlier could have been those used by a mystery killer who arrived after 6 p.m.

In his summary, Simone—I'm paraphrasing here—said that while the prosecution had many expert witnesses, and he had only one, the one he had, Frank Friel, was the most important. Friel, he said, was the most prestigious investigator of organized crime in the United States. (It's wonderful how much flattery you can get sometimes.) According to Simone, I felt that Testa was killed in his house, not where Caramandi and DelGiorno said he was. And here, Simone pointed out, was the paperwork to prove it. Now if this man, who represents the Commonwealth of Pennsylvania, and law enforcement felt that, so should you members of the jury, he concluded.

And the jury did. Scarfo and all the other defendants were found not guilty. They remained in prison because of earlier convictions or charges pending against them, but their families and friends had a lively and very liquid victory bash at the Four Seasons Hotel. As for me, I went home, reflecting on how I had now reached the pinnacle of my career: testifying for Scarfo and getting him off.

While the Testa trial was still going on, I had been kidded about my testimony. The defeat, however, left no room for joking. Along with others who had been involved in the prosecution, I participated in one gloomy postmortem after another. We asked ourselves if we had done our homework properly; might there not be some crucial lead we had missed that would have given us the evidence necessary to bolster DelGiorno's and Caramandi's testimony?

The Mafia, meanwhile, seemed to be on a winning streak. Scarfo and other defendants had earlier been found not guilty in a trial involving drug charges. (I was never familiar with the specifics of that prosecution, since it had been developed entirely separately from the Organized Crime Task Force.) More worrisome to us than the result in that case was the outcome of a highly publicized mob trial in Newark. While it didn't involve the Scarfo organization, the government had made use of criminals as witnesses, as we had in the Testa case. The prosecutor had lost there just as we had lost. The indication was that juries, confirming our worst fears, generally weren't believing mobsters turned informant.

To plan our next move, I met with Federal Strike Force attorney Al Wicks, with Joel Friedman, who was Al's boss, and with the FBI's Klaus Rohr, who had replaced Dennis O'Callaghan as codirector of the Organized Crime Task Force when Dennis was transferred to FBI headquarters in Washington. We decided to recommend that the DA's office hold back on the Frankie Flowers trial. If a Philadelphia jury hadn't believed Del and Crow together on the Testa case, the chances looked remote that they'd buy Del alone for Flowers. The best bet, rather, was to go immediately with our fail-safe RICO prosecution. If we won that, we just might shake out one of the convicted defendants to come over to our side in the Flowers case, strengthening it.

For the RICO case, we had all kinds of weapons that weren't available to us in the Testa trial. To begin with, while Del and Crow would still be our two principal Mafia witnesses, we also had Joseph Salerno, Jr., to testify to the Falcone murder, including Scarfo's disgusting, "I love it" comment when he peered down at Falcone's dead body, and which we figured wouldn't go down well with a jury. Moreover, we had recently flipped two lesser organized crime associates, Norman Lit and Michael Madgin, who could testify to numerous racketeering activities, although not any murders.

In the RICO prosecution, we had the further advantage of being able to introduce our vast hoard of surreptitiously gained evidence as part of our contention that an ongoing enterprise existed in which individuals associated for criminal purposes. We had numerous wiretap transcriptions (including the conversations recorded by the bug in Del's condo, about which he could offer amplifications), as well as 15,530 surveillance reports and more than 500 photographs of mobsters in each other's company that had been compiled by police and FBI.

All this patiently gathered material (the compilation of it had begun in the 1970s) would corroborate the principal testimony from Del and Crow in a way that would blunt the defense's best weapon—its attack on Del and Crow as "thieves, scum, drug dealers," whatever. When that happened, we could now happily reply, "Why, yes, they certainly are, but they're Nicky Scarfo's thieves, scum, drug dealers, and here are the tapes of the conversations and the pictures of him with them to prove it.''

There was still another great strength to the RICO case: sheer quantity. It didn't deal, as the Salvy Testa trial had and the Frankie Flowers would, with *a* murder, but with multiple murders, and a host of other crimes, creating a veritable cornucopia of homicidal violence, extortions and assaults. Thus, if I were called by the defense to testify again about Salvy's death, even if Simone were once more able to raise reasonable doubt—and we felt, having learned from experience, we'd be better able to counter him this time—he would not have the impact he had had when the jury had only that single crime to consider. (Retrying the Salvy Testa and Falcone murders, in which the defendants had been found not guilty, sounds like exposing them to double jeopardy, but the RICO law permits such prosecutions, since the accused are not technically being retried for murder but are being tried for participation in a conspiracy to commit murder.)

The decision to move the RICO case ahead of Flowers was agreed upon by everybody. Named as prosecutors were Strike Force attorneys Lou Pichini, David Fritchey, my friend Al Wicks, with whom I'd worked so closely on grand jury presentations, and Arnie Gordon, who had joined the Strike Force after leaving the DA's office, along with Joe Peters, representing the Pennsylvania State Attorney General.

Included in the RICO indictment, which was more than an inch thick, were charges of bookmaking, lottery running, narcotics dealing, extortions, with the feature items being the nine counts of murder and the four counts of attempted murder.

Scarfo himself was charged with the murder of Judge Helfant in 1978; of Falcone the following year; of Michael Cifelli, the drug dealer who probably was Salvy Testa's first hit; of John Calabrese; of Frank Narducci, Sr. (in which Salvy was also the gunman); of Salvy Testa; and of Robert Riccobene and Sammy Tamburrino, Mario Riccobene's friend and business partner. (Not enough evidence existed to charge him with the ninth murder listed in the indictment, Pat the Cat Spirito.) Scarfo further was charged with the attempted murders of Frank Martines, Harry Riccobene, Joseph Salerno, Sr., and Stephen Vento, Jr. (a 17-year-old boy whose father had turned informant). It was quite a lineup of murders and attempted murders for one person to be charged with, but it was only about a third of the total we believed him guilty of. (Scarfo was also included on the lesser charges.)

Also indicted and charged with murder, among other crimes, were:

Joseph "Chickie" Ciancaglini, for three murders, including Pat the Cat;

Crazy Phil Leonetti, Scarfo's underboss and nephew, accused of the Falcone, Tamburrino, Robert Riccobene and Salvy Testa murders, as well as the attempted murder of Martines;

Chuckie Merlino, who was to spend the trial sitting next to the man he knew had ordered him killed because of his drinking, charged with four murders and three attempted ones;

Larry "Yogi" Merlino, Chuckie's younger brother (who had also been marked for death by his codefendant Scarfo), on two murder charges;

Francis "Faffy" Iannarella, Jr., for the murders of Johnny Calabrese and Robert Riccobene and three attempted murders;

Charles "Charley White" Iannece, for four murders and three attempted;

Salvatore Wayne Grande, for one murder (Salvy Testa), and the attempted murder of Harry Riccobene in the phone booth;

Joseph Grande, for the Salvy Testa murder, and the attempted murders of Martines and Harry Riccobene (shooting him in his car);

Nicholas "Nick the Blade" Virgilio, for the murder of Judge
  Helfant (he was the shooter, Scarfo the get-away driver);
Philip Narducci, for two murders and two attempted murders;
Frank Narducci, Jr., for one murder and one attempted mur-
  der;
Eugene Milano, for one murder and one attempted murder;
Salvatore "Torry" Scafidi, for the Salvy Testa murder and
  the attempted murder of the 17-year-old Vento;
Anthony Pungitore, for one murder and two attempted mur-
  ders;
Joseph Pungitore, for three murders (including Salvy Testa)
  and two attempted murders.

The remaining defendant, and the only one not charged with
murder (but with two attempted murders) was Ralph "Junior"
Staino.

During the course of the trial, which began early in October
of 1988, I was called, as I expected, as a witness for the
defense by Simone. After taking me over the same ground
as in the Salvy Testa trial, Simone added something new.
Flattering as ever, he asked me (and again I'm paraphrasing)
if I wasn't the famous investigator who took on the system
when I learned that an innocent man, Neil Ferber, had been
convicted by the system and sentenced to death? Later, to
the jury, he suggested that the Ferber case proved that innocent people are convicted by the police, by the FBI, and
by the criminal justice system. Here, he noted, were more
innocent people being tried by these vicious prosecutors simply because they were Italians!

The chief prosecutor, Lou Pichini, who is of Italian heritage, took all this in with equanimity.

The jury began its deliberations on Thursday, the 17th of
November, 1988, and was still at it by Saturday evening when
I went out to dinner. During the course of their deliberations,
the jurors several times returned to the courtroom to ask the

judge questions. Each time that happened, we on the prosecution side huddled together, weighing the implications of their words and expressions as if we were so many Talmudic scholars or—perhaps more aptly—ancient Roman soothsayers reading goat entrails.

Some of the questions sounded good for our side—if they're asking *this*, they must be thinking *that*, mustn't they?—but others, which we interpreted as favorable to the defense, made us despondent.

Worrying us the most, however, was the length of time they were taking to reach a verdict. Trial folklore teaches that the longer it takes a jury to make up its mind, the better it is for the defense, and, gloomily, we bought into that wisdom. Just as we had after the Salvy Testa trial—only this time, in advance of the verdict—we asked ourselves where we had failed. Might we not have been better off trying each defendant separately? Wasn't it possible the jurors were intimidated by seeing that many reputed mobsters all at one time, staring at them, memorizing their faces? Might they not acquit them solely out of fear? Could all twelve be courageous enough to convict? If a few held out, that meant a hung jury and having to start all over again, with no greater likelihood of success the second time.

But even a hung jury would be better than an acquittal. An acquittal would mean six-and-a-half years of effort resulting in failure. There was no way I could rationalize my way around that fact. True, I could count the convictions we had gotten—Willard Moran, Raymond Martorano, Al Daidone, Harry Riccobene, Joseph Casdia, Ronald DiCaprio, Teddy Di Pretoro, Steve Traitz, among others; but with an acquittal, they'd only add up to one result: Scarfo had beaten us. The 14-year sentence he was serving on the Rouse extortion would be scant consolation; he could be out on the street in four years on that one. If we didn't get Scarfo, we hadn't gotten anybody. Failure.

Just as I was finishing my dinner at the restaurant that

Saturday evening, I got a message on my beeper from Al Wicks. I called him. The jury, he said, returned with its decision at 7:54 p.m. U.S. District Judge Franklin S. VanAntwerpen, referring to the first charge against Scarfo, asked, "What is your verdict—guilty or not guilty?"

The foreman, an accountant, replied, "Guilty."

Over the next forty minutes, Wicks said, the words "guilty" or "proved" was the answer to each question the judge asked. Every defendant had been convicted on every count.

As I put down the phone, I was surprised by my reaction to Wicks's good news: I didn't feel excited. Perhaps all the worrying I'd done while the deliberations were going on had chased away the possibility of excitement. Still—

Guilty . . . guilty . . . guilty . . . The words certainly had a pleasant sound. I wished I'd been there to hear them, felt I had cheated myself out of the pleasure of them by not staying in the courtroom a little longer that evening. If I had been there, I might have been excited, happier, but I'm not sure, because the feeling I did have, in place of excitement, was a strong and pervasive one, and it stayed with me for a long time after I heard the words of victory. It was a sense of objective satisfaction.

Proved . . . proved . . . proved . . . the jury had said, and that, in fact, was what we had done. We had proved our case. We had done good detective work. The FBI had, the Philadelphia Police had, the New Jersey State Police had, the detectives and agents had, I had. Good solid police work— and it had paved the way for Tommy Del and Nicky Crow to talk and for the good solid prosecutorial work that had followed. We had done what we were supposed to do. We had done what we were committed to do, as officers and as individuals.

I think it was this sense of having done my duty (although I can't say emotional exhaustion wasn't involved, too) that caused me not to have the same reaction of exhilaration that had overcome me when I learned that Neil Ferber was to go free. The Ferber case was different. It was about a system that had grabbed into its maw an innocent man and chewed him up, leaving him and his family emotionally scarred. For Ferber, the justice system hadn't worked, and I and a tiny handful of other people had had to battle it to save him from electrocution. Hence, the exhilaration when I succeeded. For Scarfo and his codefendants, the justice system—the one I'd always been a part of, proud and happy to be a part of—had worked, and from that I took a deep satisfaction.

But not completely. Guilty, guilty, guilty, and proved, proved, proved were all fine, but I wanted to hear them yet one more time. I wanted to hear them about the murderers of Frankie Flowers. To me, his death had been Scarfo's most loathesome achievement, the murder of a man because he was a nice guy, and I didn't want him to get away with that. Not that one, above all his crimes.

The Flowers trial began in Philadelphia's Common Pleas Court in April of 1989. Seven of the eight defendants were among those convicted of conspiracy to commit murder and other crimes in the RICO case the previous November.

The exception was 49-year-old Joseph Ligambi, who had pleaded guilty to gambling charges before the RICO trial began, and who, we believed, had finally made his bones as one of the two gunmen who shot Frankie. The second killer, according to our evidence, was Phil Narducci. Three other Young Executioners, Frank Narducci, Jr. (the getaway driver) and the two Milano brothers, Eugene (who, along with Salvy Testa, had brutally beaten Frankie in 1981) and Nick the Whip, were also charged with participating in the murder conspiracy, as were the Merlino brothers, Chuckie and Larry. Our final defendant was Scarfo.

The trial was barely underway when we gained our third defection from the top echelon of the Scarfo organization. It came about, as I'd expected it might, in the person of a refugee from the RICO conviction, the brutal Gene Milano. From the witness stand, he gave detailed evidence against the defendants, including his own brother. His description of the stalking of Frankie Flowers—it had required weeks before they had their opportunity—dovetailed with Del's earlier narration of how he recruited Milano and the others for the murder crew and carried out the deed.

The jury listened to the case for nearly three weeks but needed only three-and-a-half hours to reach a verdict. All defendants were found guilty on all counts.

Scarfo had just become the first don in the history of organized crime in America to be convicted of first-degree murder.

As the verdict was announced, Adeline Narducci, mother of defendants Philip and Frank, Jr., screamed at the jurors. "Youse all oughta die! Youse all oughta die! Youse all oughta die!"

Gina D'Alfonso, the younger sister of Martina who had sobbed over her father's dying body, having at last found justice, shouted back at Mrs. Narducci: "Like my father died!" at which the murderer Ligambi turned from his seat at the defense table and snarled at Frankie Flowers' grieving daughter: "Fuck your father."

I thought his comment aptly summarized the real code of the Men of Honor.

The Flowers defendants were sentenced almost immediately. Having been convicted of first-degree murder, they were going to get either the death penalty or life imprisonment, the only two sentences available for that crime under Pennsylvania law. We were hoping the jury would make the legally binding recommendation of capital punishment—certainly for Scarfo, Ligambi and Phil Narducci—but the trial judge removed the sentencing decision from the jury, stating we didn't have sufficient evidence of "aggravated" circumstances. (We would have if he had allowed us to use the

RICO convictions against the defendants, but on a technicality, that wasn't permitted.) As a result, all eight got life.

One Flowers defendant, however, Larry Merlino, won't serve life. He became our fourth defector. It may well have been the prospect of spending his remaining years behind bars that caused him to talk. However, he also by now knew that Scarfo had, at one point, ordered him killed, which, I think, was the deciding reason for him to break the code of silence. His decision to cooperate was significant in terms of future prosecutions, not just against Scarfo but against the New York crime families as well, which had hitherto remained untouched in their Atlantic City activities. Through his associations with Bayshore Rebar and Scarf, Inc., Larry possessed information about the awarding of contracts to mob-controlled companies for casino construction as well as those let out by the Atlantic City municipal government. Further, he was in a position to provide evidence concerning infiltration and extortionate control of the Atlantic City casino unions by various criminal organizations, and about their relationships with management.

During the course of his debriefing, Larry also related what he knew about the Meletis murders. Raymond Martorano, he said, had told him that he set up the Booras hit with Scarfo's approval, and that the two gunmen were Frank Vadino and George Martorano. Larry's testimony was admissible in court as Del's wasn't, since Del had his information only secondhand.

Despite the strong case I had compiled against Martorano (motive, opportunity, Moran's statements, and Martorano's admission to Mario Riccobene, now seconded by Larry), at the publication deadline for this book neither Long John nor his son nor Vadino nor Scarfo had been charged with the Meletis murders by the Philadelphia DA's office.

I believe, however, the prosecution will be forthcoming, even though it entails some embarrassment for the district attorney; making new arrests in the case means a public avowal will have to be made that the first time around a wrong man was convicted and sentenced to death. Until now, that admission has not been made. When the charges were dropped against Ferber, it was solely on the basis that no prosecutable evidence remained against this "possibly innocent" person. Ferber recognized that the cloud still remained over him. He believed, and I think he was right, that the fact that he hadn't been exonerated was the reason he never got employment in the furniture business, the only field of honest work he knew. In the furniture trade, rumors were rife that he'd gotten off on a technicality. "What I'd like," he said to me, "what I want is an apology from them. If they'd just say for the record I had nothing to do with it, I think I'd really feel better. You know, I just wish they'd do that for me." They didn't, and it was shortly after he said that to me that he was arrested on the P2P charge.

29
Scorecard

The defendants in the RICO case weren't sentenced until May of 1989, nearly five months after the trial, and a couple of weeks after the Frankie Flowers trial was completed and its defendants sentenced. The reason for the delay was the need to do pre-sentence reports. These are carried out by the probation department and have as their purpose to balance the severity of the offense with the criminal's prior record, and his probable propensity for committing future crimes (based on psychological evaluations). The results are often meaningless, misleading or both, and it can take an enormous amount of time to reach them. (There'd be no need for pre-sentence reports after the Flowers trial, since, once the death penalty was ruled out, life sentences were mandatory.)

On the eve of the RICO sentencings, a fifth Scarfo mobster came over to the government's side. This time it was literally a Scarfo, Nick's nephew and underboss, Phil Leonetti. More murderous and violent than Larry Merlino, the handsome Phil not only provided corroboration for Larry's statements but was in a position to add to them meaningfully. Unlike Larry, Phil was constantly with Scarfo and was perhaps the one person Scarfo trusted completely. And, most importantly for making cases beyond Scarfo, he was also privy to Scarfo's dealings with the New York mafiosos, most notably John Gotti, the boss of the Gambino family.

With the conclusion of the Flowers trial and the RICO sentencings, the cooperating law enforcement agencies had completed their mandate to solve the organized crime hom-icides. While we didn't convict every murderer for every murder he committed, all of the surviving killers in the Scarfo organization were convicted of at least one. Scarfo himself was found guilty of eight of them in the RICO trial, and the Frankie Flowers trial made nine. As I noted in the Preface, it is my belief and that of other law enforcement officials that he either committed, authorized or was otherwise involved in the commission of at least twenty-six killings (including those who got in the way when a target victim was murdered). His homicidal career began with the unknown person whose death made him eligible for Mafia membership sometime prior to 1963, the year he fatally stabbed the longshoreman Dugan in the Oregon Diner. The other deaths are those of Judge Helfant, Pepe Leva, Vincent Falcone, Michael Cifelli, Tippy Panetta, Rochelle Podraza, Pete Inzarella, Dominick "Mickey Diamond" DeVito, John McCullough, Frank Nar-ducci, Sr., Rocco Marinucci, Robert Hornickel, Johnny Cal-abrese, Pat the Cat Spirito, Sammy Tamburrino, Frank Forline, Salvatore Sollena, Matteo Sollena, Michael Micali,

Robert Riccobene, Salvatore Testa, Frankie Flowers D'Alfonso, Steve Booras and Janette Curro.

When the sentencings in the RICO convictions were completed, law enforcement's scorecard on the significant Mafia members and criminal associates had been filled out this way:*

Leland Beloff, 10 years for the attempted extortion of a million dollars from Willard Rouse

Nicholas Caramandi, 8 years for murder and other crimes (government witness)

Joseph Casdia, life for the murder of Frank Monte

Joseph Ciancaglini, 45 years on the RICO convictions, including three murders

Albert Daidone, life for the murder of John McCullough

Thomas DelGiorno, 5 years for guilty pleas to nine murders (government witness)

Victor DeLuca, 17½ to 25 years for the shooting of Salvatore Testa, concurrent sentence for the Monte murder (government witness)

Ronald DiCaprio, 20 years for conspiracy to murder Robert Hornickel

Teddy Di Pretoro, two concurrent life sentences for the murders of Philip Testa and Edward Bianculli

Joseph Grande, 40 years on the RICO convictions, including one murder

Salvatore Wayne Grande, 38 years on the RICO convictions, including one murder

Francis Iannarella, Jr., 45 years on the RICO convictions, including two murders

Charles Iannece, 40 years on the RICO convictions, including four murders

---

*Criminals convicted in more than one trial are serving consecutive sentences unless otherwise noted. All life sentences were imposed under Pennsylvania law, which rarely permits parole. For some of the defendants, appeals were still pending at the time of the deadline for this book.

Vincent Isabella, 20 years for third-degree murder in the killing of Frank Monte

Saul Kane, 25 years for drug trafficking, illegal importation and sale of P2P

Phil Leonetti, 45 years on the RICO convictions, including four murders, probably to be reduced to 10 years as government witness

Joseph Ligambi, life for the Flowers murder, 3½ years on a guilty plea to RICO gambling charges

Raymond Martorano, life for the murder of John McCullough

Michael Matthews, 15 years on corruption charges

Larry Merlino, not yet sentenced; guilty of Flowers murder; guilty on RICO charges, including two murders (government witness)

Salvatore Merlino, life on the Flowers murder, 45 years on the RICO convictions, including four murders

Eugene Milano, not yet sentenced; guilty plea to Flowers murder, guilty on RICO charges including one other murder (government witness)

Nicholas Milano, life on the Flowers murder

Willard Moran, Jr., death for murder of John McCullough, reduction of sentence to life pending (government witness)

Frank Narducci, Jr., life for the Flowers murder, 35 years on the RICO convictions, including one other murder

Philip Narducci, life for the Flowers murder, 40 years on the RICO convictions, including two other murders

Joseph Pedulla, four years, pleaded guilty to Salvatore Testa shooting and Monte murder (government witness)

Anthony Pungitore, 30 years on the RICO convictions, including one murder

Joseph Pungitore, 40 years on the RICO convictions, including three murders

Robert Rego, 8 years for extortion and for narcotics conviction

Harry Riccobene, life for the murder of Frank Monte

Mario Riccobene, 4 years, pleaded guilty to various offenses (government witness)

Salvatore Scafidi, 40 years on the RICO convictions, including one murder

Ralph Staino, Jr., 33 years on the RICO conviction

Steve Traitz, Jr., 15 years for extortion, assault

Nicholas Virgilio, 40 years on the RICO convictions, including one murder

Nicodemo Scarfo, 14 years on the Rouse extortion conviction; 55 years on the RICO charges; life on the Flowers murder. (Immediately after sentencing, the 60-year-old Scarfo was transported to the federal government's maximum security prison in Marion, Illinois, which houses the most violent and dangerous of offenders. Marion is the definition of "doing hard time.")

That was law enforcement's scorecard. My personal one had an additional listing: one innocent man convicted of two mob murders and subsequently exonerated.

Epilogue: Some Lessons I Have Learned

The Organized Crime Task Force, launched in Philadelphia in 1982, proved to be the single most successful tool ever devised to fight La Cosa Nostra. More than sixty convictions, almost all of them for major felonies, resulted from our efforts, and an organization which had thrived, virtually unmolested, for sixty years was destroyed. Beyond doubt, the remnants of the Philadelphia/Atlantic City mob will attempt to resuscitate their gang, but it will be years before they can even begin to exercise their former influence over the political and business infrastructure of the two cities in which they centered their efforts. With some vigilance, we can make sure they won't succeed in doing that at all.

Even though the dismantling of the Scarfo organization did not destroy New York LCN influence in the New Jersey casino industry, significant progress had been made against the New York families even before the emergence of Phil Leonetti and Larry Merlino as government witnesses. Major indictments and convictions have resulted there from a joint police and FBI Organized Crime Task Force patterned on the pioneering one we established in Philadelphia to investigate mob homicides.

The success of the Task Force concept evolved out of two key decisions. Had they not been made, I believe, the squad would have failed to carry out its mandate, regardless of the abilities of detectives and agents, regardless of funding, regardless of other investigative resources. The first decision was to permit free and full sharing of information between the police and FBI components of the Task Force. The second was the establishment of two-man teams consisting of one police officer and one FBI agent.

The second decision was the more important of the two. Sharing information would have soon ceased if parallel investigations—cops on theirs, FBI on theirs—had been permitted, and we would have reinforced the long-standing mistrust between the two forces.

The Philadelphia Task Force and the slightly different one in New York City, which has separate squads for each of the five New York LCN families, provide models that should be replicated nationally. By that I mean not only in pursuit of the Mafia—as important as that effort is—but in combating the Colombian and associated cocaine cartels with whom the Mafia, as I have noted, has only a peripheral involvement.

The cooperative effort to fight cocaine is fraught with more difficulties than those we had to resolve in taking on the Scarfo mob. Essentially, all we had to do to fight Scarfo was get two agencies, the police and FBI, to work together. (Once we succeeded in doing that, showed we were serious and began to break some cases, other law enforcement agencies that had no particular reason to work with either of us in the past joined with us, and in the case of the New Jersey State Police, made an enormous contribution.) In the cocaine enforcement nexus, however, the agencies are multitudinous. Among them are local police, state police, FBI, DEA, customs agents, Coast Guard, Treasury Department agents, to say nothing of various prosecutorial arms—local, state, federal—which all have their own disgraceful history of fighting turf battles for individual glory that well matches that of police and FBI.

As the first crucial step, we must recognize that unless interagency rivalries, no matter how psychologically rewarding they are to the participants, are subdued, and cooperation enforced, no meaningful progress will ever be made to cut off the cocaine supply. What I am suggesting can be done, too. That's one of the virtues of law enforcement's quasi-military discipline: commanding officers can force their people to cooperate, just as Dennis O'Callaghan and I did with our men.

We have, however, yet to make even a start in that direction. Neither the President nor his drug czar nor heads of the rival agencies have even admitted the existence of the rivalries, although everyone in law enforcement, if not the public, is fully aware of them. The result has been a frustrating and unsuccessful scattershot approach, marked by parallel investigations and withholding of information, a bust here and a bust there that allow crowing but no significant consequences, just as was true of law enforcement's losing war against the Mafia until 1982.

The widespread addiction to narcotics in the United States represents a sociological problem, rooted in economic conditions, that is of monumental proportions. Thus, cutting off substantially the flow of cocaine does not mean a replacement epidemic won't break out, maybe heroin again, or quite possibly meth usage, which seems to be sharply on the rise nationally. Law enforcement's duty, however, is not to fight causes but their consequences, and in order to do that, the lesson to be learned from the Task Force is a simple and ineluctable one: Organized crime, in all its forms, succeeds to the extent that its opponents are disorganized.

The lessons of cooperation and common sense that were applied to our Task Force also suggest how to improve the quality of crime fighting of all kinds by our police departments.

The operational problems I am about to describe are not, in my judgment, frivolous or nit-picking, and neither are they limited to Philadelphia. They are found, to greater or lesser degree, in all our metropolitan police forces. Because of them, police are hampered in their work, the streets are less safe for our citizens than they should be, and crimes—often very serious crimes—that could be solved are not.

Ineffective use of time is probably the most obvious and prevalent deterrent to effective police work. I doubt there is a cop in the country who isn't aware of and doesn't deplore the vast waste of work hours, and yet nothing is ever done about it. As I noted in the Preface, in Philadelphia, the statistic for detectives is 70 percent—that is, a detective spends about 70 percent of his or her work time typing up reports on crimes and only 30 percent of the time out in the field trying to solve them. Thus, if you have a detective force in your city of no more than 100 officers each of whom works no more than 40 hours a week, in a single year, based on the Philadelphia figure, you as citizens are paying for 145,600 hours of typing and only 62,400 hours of work to solve crimes and catch criminals. (The typing problem is less critical among uniformed patrol officers, but is hardly absent there, either.)

The most irritating aspect of all this waste is how readily it could be eliminated. Detectives and uniformed officers could be trained to do their arrest reports by dictaphone, often while in their cars, with secretaries transcribing them with a speed and accuracy which (as anyone who has read police reports knows) is almost always sorely wanting when the cop has a go at a typewriter or word processor. At present, the entire Philadelphia Homicide Bureau has *one* secretary; if that number were only quadrupled, the effect minimally would be to reverse the present statistics to 70 percent investigative and 30 percent paperwork.

If a meaningful paperwork reform were instituted in police departments, a rich opportunity would present itself to improve the quality of policing, since, presumably, the more time available to solve a crime, the more crimes are solved. That will happen, I think, even with no other improvements in police work. However, that doesn't mean 70 percent more policing will lead to 70 percent more arrests. On the contrary, for a large and intractable mass of criminal activity, the chances of arrest will always range between small and nil. For most—but by no means all—crimes, unless the perpetrator is caught in the act or fleeing the scene, apprehension is unlikely. A salient quality of the good cop is the ability to know which cases stand a realistic chance of being solved. It's for those cases that greater time availability will pay the biggest dividend, and not just in the sense of clearing the crime under investigation. Most criminals are repeat offenders, so that by solving a "good" case, one will also frequently clear old "bad" ones as well. For instance, a study of prisoners in Ohio found them *admitting* to an average of six crimes each in the twelve months prior to the offense for which they were finally apprehended.

Providing for better use of police time should also permit the opportunity to improve exchanges of information. At present, and here we get to one of the weaknesses of a military structure, only vertical communication occurs in any regularized way: The patrol officer reports to the sergeant, the sergeant to the lieutenant, the lieutenant to the captain, the captain to the inspector, the inspector to the commissioner or deputy commissioner. Information goes up; orders come down. Except for officers assigned to the same case, lateral exchanges of information at the field level ordinarily only occur by happenstance, as when a couple of cops are talking shop. Even when these lateral exchanges aren't officially discouraged, no formal protocols exist to permit or encourage them, principally because the police bureaucracy is attuned to thinking only in vertical terms.

As an illustration of the kind of police failure that regularly occurs without lateral communication—and can be avoided when it is present—imagine two investigations in two parts of the city, supervised by two teams that ordinarily never see one another, much less speak to one another. Let us say that in one case we are looking for a man who wears a green hat, and in the other for someone who drives a yellow car, and that an informant tells a green-hat detective about noticing a man in a yellow car. That tip means nothing to the detective because all he is interested in is a green hat. If, however, he attends meetings such as ones I initiated, he learns that the other detective team is looking for a yellow car, and so he will say, "Hey, I have a snitch I think can help you with that." Which is how you solve crimes through lateral communication that don't get solved vertically.

Recognizing how counterproductive and dangerous to public safety the absence of lateral communication can be, when I became captain of the Organized Crime Unit in 1986, I regularly brought my detectives, sergeants and lieutenants together for round-table discussions of *all* major cases in which we were involved. My officers, I found, were pleased to have input on investigations to which they hadn't been assigned; it added to their sense of self-worth, and the practical results were often excellent.

Like reforms to get rid of the paper-chase problem, the round-table reform I instituted sounds like an obvious solution to an obvious problem, and it is. But in my experience it had not been tried in the Philadelphia Police Department before, and it is, I believe, hardly commonplace elsewhere.

The quality of police work can also be improved—significantly, in my judgment—if steps are taken to reduce the interdepartmental frictions between detectives and uniformed officers. In my experience, the antagonisms frequently lead to faulty police work, which is to the disadvantage of the public and the considerable advantage of the criminal.

The enforced cooperation that Dennis O'Callaghan and I applied to the Task Force should, I believe, be inaugurated within police departments. Detectives should be required to go out on patrol with uniformed officers on a regular basis (as becomes feasible when time is saved by cutting down on the paperwork). A weekday midnight-to-8 a.m. shift, when work is ordinarily light, is probably the best time. This reimmersion into life on the streets, which the detective may have forgotten (or wanted to forget) or of which he may have had only limited knowledge, depending on where he was stationed before he became a detective, forces both detectives and uniforms into sharing their experiences, breaks down the barriers of elitism, jealousy and competition. They will become more aware, on both sides, as they cruise or answer calls—just as our Task Force detectives and agents did—that they are fighting crime together, not as rivals, and the beneficiaries of that realization will be the tax payers who pay their salaries.

Sharing duties in this fashion is a form of continuing education. The validity of this concept is widely recognized in the business world and within the medical and legal professions, but not nearly sufficiently so among police. While it was not their instigating purpose, my round-table discussions had continuing education values, as detectives exchanged information.

Sometimes training for a new assignment can be a problem, too. In Philadelphia, detectives receive a two-week course in their duties, which is about average, I think, throughout the country, and that is fine. However, the training is ordinarily not given by detectives who have field experience and understand the practical difficulties that the new detectives are going to encounter. The instruction, rather, comes largely from commanders, most of whom never were detectives, even though they are now in charge of a detective unit.* In my case, I never received any detection training, because I was a lieutenant; my rank presumably gave me expertise in something I knew nothing about. The result is that detectives are educated by non-detectives. When they begin their new jobs, they frequently are serving under captains and lieutenants who have no knowledge about the components of a good investigation, who therefore can't judge when it is being done properly, and who don't know when the plug should be pulled on a losing investigation, thereby freeing their staff for more productive work. Some commanders learn by doing, as I think I did. Some don't.

In addition to the structural and personnel training reforms I have suggested, I believe the quality of detective work can be substantially improved, and the likelihood of error lessened, when certain ground rules are followed.

First, investigators must be protected from outside influences. High profile cases like the Meletis murders can create extraordinary pressures. Headlines are generated by them. The public is horrified. The police commissioner wants results. The district attorney wants results. The assigned detectives realize that by breaking such a case, their careers can be furthered; they'll be written up in the papers, maybe interviewed on television; and their commanding officer is fully cognizant of the same ego-gratifying possibilities. The temptation in this kind of situation is, therefore, to proceed with undue haste, to make an arrest to get the pressure off and the good publicity on. There is probably no single way to get worse results.

The commanding officer of a detective squad has no more important job than to fight these influences, both on his of-

---

*Instruction by detectives was introduced in Philadelphia in January 1990.

ficers and on himself; human psychology being what it is, he may be tempted to share the glory a quick arrest will bring in a hot case. Required, therefore, are both support and vigilance from the police administration. Too often that has not occurred. Too often, high-ranking officers themselves rush to the press conference, their main concern that someone in the lower echelons is getting the credit they crave. Thus, ultimately the responsibility to demand professionalism in all investigations falls on the police commissioner. Good ones try to assure it as a first order of business. Bad ones don't.

Second, don't make assumptions. The Meletis murders provide an example of the bad things that can happen when this rule isn't obeyed. The assigned detectives learned almost immediately of the murder of the other Greek gangster that had occurred 48 hours earlier. Rather than hypothesizing that there *might* be a connection between the two crimes, the detectives *assumed* the connection. Because they did, they ignored entirely the correct line of inquiry they otherwise would have hit upon, namely, Booras's associations with Philadelphia Mafia figures, including Raymond Martorano, who was on hand to witness the murder. Detectives should never assume they know the answer to a crime until and unless they have supporting evidence—they had none for their assumption in the Meletis murders—and then only if there is no reputable contradictory evidence, and other possible motives for the crime have been checked out and found wanting.

Third, do not target someone for arrest because that person is believed to have gotten away with previous crimes. Every cop and every prosecutor knows of "bad" people— walking time bombs, as DA Ed Rendell called them—who are a constant danger to the public safety. Not infrequently, such persons have been prime suspects in major felonies that the investigators were positive they committed, yet their guilt could never be proved. As I found out in organized crime cases, nothing can be more frustrating for a law enforcement officer. That is why I still recall so vividly Rocco Marinucci's contemptuous grin when he realized I knew he had murdered Phil Testa and that I didn't have a shred of evidence on which to arrest him.

At times, it becomes possible to charge a "bad" person with a crime he didn't commit, solely to make up for ones he got away with in the past. Getting the necessary evidence is not as difficult as it might seem. An informant, who may himself be facing serious charges, will be quick to understand, when questioned by detectives about a certain case, who is wanted, and will be glad to provide the desired information in return for having charges against him dropped or mitigated. That type of help can come in the form of a jailhouse confession, as it did with Jerry Jordan; it can come when the informant helpfully places the "bad" person near the crime scene or recalls how the "bad" person once "threatened" the victim. The possibilities are nearly endless.

Two "bad" persons were involved in the Meletis investigation. The original suspect, Barry Saltzburg, was believed to have gotten away with numerous violent crimes. The police wanted to get him. The second "bad" person was Mad Dog DiPasquale, who had earlier been found not guilty of a murder that police believed he had committed. Ferber was implicated because he knew Saltzburg, and when Saltzburg had to be dropped as a suspect—not a shred of evidence against him —Ferber's other "bad" friend, DiPasquale, took Saltzburg's place. A new theory was developed by the detectives that DiPasquale and Ferber wanted to rob Booras and decided to kill him first. It was as if, not being able to get the one "bad" guy, they decided subconsciously to settle for the other one. Jerry Jordan, guessing or told of the detectives' needs, helpfully supplied them with Ferber's supposed implication of DiPasquale in the killings. I am not suggesting that the detectives, at some point, didn't genuinely believe DiPasquale was the shooter, but rather that they had gotten onto him not with any evidence, but with a *desire* for him to be the shooter.

To understand the implication of the "bad" person syndrome, assume that an innocent but desperate Ferber named DiPasquale (as he once offered to do for me) as his confederate, and made up a story to fit the facts—"tell me what you want me to say." Assume further that DiPasquale had gotten away with murder previously and now was tried and convicted for the murder he didn't commit. In that event, an argument could be made that DiPasquale finally got what was coming to him. However, even if one agrees with that conclusion (and I don't), the inevitable corollary is that by going after the "bad" person, rather than going after the crime, one lets the actual perpetrator walk free.

Fourth, recognize when the case is weak. People want to succeed in life, and detectives are no exception. After putting long and exhausting hours into an investigation, and after deciding, sometimes in desperation, on a suspect, their natural human inclination is to go ahead and "clear" the case by making an arrest. At that point, they are likely to see only the strength of their evidence and ignore the weaknesses that had previously made them hesitate. The job of their commanding officer is never to have an emotional stake in the outcome, and always to confront the problems that the detectives no longer want to look at.

In the Meletis investigation, that didn't happen. No one said, "Hey, wait a minute, fellas. What do we really have on this guy Ferber? Two eyewitnesses who not only don't agree with each other but keep changing their own identifications; that's it. Maybe he is the guy, but it's not good enough. Let's go back and take another look at this thing. We might have missed an angle. Like, who benefits by Boor-as's death?"

Those were the right questions; they weren't asked, because nobody recognized or wanted to recognize how weak the case was.

Fifth, never try to shore up a weak arrest. A week after Mrs. Egan withdrew her identification of Ferber, police and

FBI were bringing down Ferber's cellmates for questioning. The admission they required to bolster their disintegrating case was quickly and predictably forthcoming. It proved vital, too. Following the trial, several jurors told prosecutor Sciolla that Jordan's testimony was the main reason they found Ferber guilty.

The fact is, guilty persons often do confess their crimes. They feel a compulsion to explain why they did what they did. While these confessions most often occur during the course of police interrogation, they can also be made to a fellow prisoner.

Nevertheless, as I learned from the Hornickel homicide, no matter how convincing a jailhouse confession appears to be when heard from the lips of the person to whom it was allegedly made, it must always be treated with the highest degree of suspicion. Not only should it not be used unless the informant passes the lie detector test ("inconclusive" isn't good enough), but as a general rule, it should never be used unless there is other substantial evidence linking the suspect to the crime.

However, even if the informant passes the polygraph, the detective must realize that doesn't necessarily prove the confession is valid. To illustrate, suppose that Ferber, although innocent, did confess to Jordan to get a tough-guy reputation so he wouldn't be raped by other inmates. In that event, Jordan presumably would have passed the polygraph, but the confession remains invalid.

If a detective has the inclination, the falsity of a confession, whether it comes from the informant lying or the confessing party lying, can usually be sniffed out, as in Ferber's alleged confession, which contained at least two red flags of warning: The shoulder pad story made no sense, and the $40,000 murder fee was simply unbelievable.

The difficulties with Ferber's supposed confession, however, were ignored because at that point, the detectives, while they still, we will assume, believed him guilty, were in desperate need of new evidence. They couldn't bring themselves to admit they might be wrong. Because Jordan shored up their weak case for them, they didn't challenge the patent inconsistencies in his story.

Finally, don't let mistakes stand. When Captain Dooley told me my job was to arrest people, not "unarrest" them, he was wrong. When Arnie Gordon, whom I like and whose prosecutorial skills I admire, told me that the "system has spoken" in the Ferber case and I, therefore, had no reason to try to help the man, he was wrong, too. Because, if either were right, then the cop has no duty to enforce the law (for should not enforcement of the law be applied to the innocent as well as the guilty?); no duty to preserve the public order (for how is preserving order worthwhile if the ultimate disorder of putting an innocent person to death is not protested?); and no duty to serve justice (for how does one serve justice if one does not attempt to do justice?).

Selected List Of Characters

Anastasia, Albert. Head of Murder, Incorporated; murdered.

Beloff, Leland. Philadelphia city councilman; Scarfo associate.

Berkery, John. Member of Pottsville burglary gang; drug dealer; associate of Raymond Martorano.

Booras, Steve. Drug dealer; head of the Greek Mob; murdered at the Meletis Restaurant in May 1981.

Bruno, Angelo ("The Gentle Don," "Angie"). Don of the Philadelphia Mafia, 1959–1980; murdered.

Calabrese, Johnny. Gambler and drug dealer; member of Bruno organization; murdered.

Caponigro, Antonio. New Jersey gangster; consigliere to Angelo Bruno; murdered.

Caramandi, Nicholas ("Nicky Crow," "The Crow"). Extortionist and murderer for Scarfo organization.

Casdia, Joseph. Member of Riccobene gang.

Casella, Peter. Underboss to Phil Testa, whose murder he ordered.

Ciancaglini, Joseph ("Chickie"). Member in Scarfo organization.

Cifelli, Michael ("Coco"). Drug dealer; murdered.

Daidone, Albert. Vice president of Bartenders Union in New Jersey; organizer of Hotel Workers Union in Atlantic City; associate of Raymond Martorano.

D'Alfonso, Frank ("Frankie Flowers"). Gambler; longtime associate of Angelo Bruno; later a member of Riccobene gang; murdered.

DeGregorio, James. Leader of Pagan motorcycle gang.

DelGiorno, Thomas ("Del," "Tommy Del"). Capo in Scarfo gang; participated in nine murders.

DeLuca, Victor. Enforcer and extortionist; member of Riccobene gang.

DeVito, Dominick ("Mickey Diamond"). Gambler; murdered.

DiCaprio, Ronald ("Cuddles"). Bartender at Cous' Little Italy Restaurant.

DiPasquale, Anthony ("Mad Dog," "The Dog"). Independent muscleman and extortionist; enemy of Scarfo; suspect in Booras murder.

Di Pretoro, Theodore ("Teddy," "Choirboy Killer"). Associate of Rocco Marinucci in murder of Phil Testa.

Falcone, Vincent. Scarfo associate; murdered.

Forline, Frank. Associate of Chickie Ciancaglini; murdered.

Gambino, Carlo. Boss of bosses of organized crime in the

United States from early 1960s until his death in 1976; protector of Philadelphia don Angelo Bruno.

Genovese, Vito. Don of New York City organized crime family; murderer of Albert Anastasia (head of Murder, Incorporated); died 1969.

Gotti, John. Boss of the Gambino organized crime family in New York City; associate of Nick Scarfo.

Grande, Joseph. Associate of Salvatore Testa.

Grande, Salvatore Wayne ("Wayne"). Associate of Salvatore Testa.

Hornickel, Robert. Drug dealer; murdered.

Iannarella, Francis ("Faffy"). Member of Scarfo organization.

Iannece, Charles ("Charley White"). Member of Scarfo organization.

Inadi, Joseph ("Joey Eye"). Ex-Philadelphia cop; bodyguard to Greek Mob leader Steve Booras.

Isabella, Vincent. Member of Riccobene gang.

Kane, Saul. Adviser to Nick Scarfo.

Lentino, Frank. Teamsters Union organizer; adviser in Atlantic City to Nick Scarfo.

Leonetti, Philip ("Crazy Phil"). Nick Scarfo's nephew; murderer; succeeded Chuckie Merlino as underboss.

Leva, Pepe. Low-level gangster; murdered.

Levitz, Gary. Associate of Saul Kane.

Ligambi, Joseph. Member of Scarfo organization.

Luciano, Salvatore ("Lucky"). Organized crime boss in New York City; created the National Commission of crime families.

Marinucci, Rocco. Driver for Phil Testa's underboss Peter Casella; murderer of Phil Testa; murdered.

Martorano, George ("Cowboy"). Son of Raymond Martorano.

Martorano, Raymond ("Long John," "Longy"). Adviser to dons Angelo Bruno, Phil Testa and Nicky Scarfo; employed Bruno as a "salesman" for his John's Vending Company.

Matthews, Michael. Mayor of Atlantic City; controlled by Scarfo.

McCullough, John ("Big John"). Business agent for Roofers Union Local 30B; extortionist; close ally of Angelo Bruno; murdered.

Merlino, Larry ("Yogi"). Younger brother of Salvatore "Chuckie" Merlino; member of Scarfo organization.

Merlino, Salvatore ("Chuckie"). Underboss to Nick Scarfo.

Micali, Michael. Drug dealer; murdered.

Milano, Eugene ("Gino"). Associate of Salvatore Testa.

Milano, Nicholas ("Nicky Whip"). Associate of Salvatore Testa.

Monte, Frank. Consigliere to Nicky Scarfo; murdered.

Moran, Willard, Jr. ("Junior"). Gunman and drug dealer hired to murder John McCullough.

Narducci, Frank, Jr. Associate of Salvatore Testa.

Narducci, Frank, Sr. ("Chickie"). Long-time lieutenant to Angelo Bruno; ally of Peter Casella in the murder of Phil Testa; murdered.

Narducci, Philip. Associate of Salvatore Testa.

Panetta, Vincent ("Tippy"). Numbers writer and gambler; murdered.

Pedulla, Joseph ("Joey"). Bookmaker; gunman; member of Riccobene gang.

Peetros, Harry. Greek Mob member; associate of Steve Booras; murdered.

Piccolo, Nicholas ("Nicky Buck"). Uncle of Nicky Scarfo and alleged successor to Frank Monte as consigliere.

Pollina, Antonio Dominick. Don of Philadelphia organized crime family, 1958–1959; Angelo Bruno's predecessor.

Pungitore, Joseph ("Joey Punge"). Salvy Testa's closest friend.

Raiton, Ronald. Cornered the market in P2P, the chemical necessary for making illegal methamphetamines; government informant.

Rego, Robert ("Bobby"). Administrative assistant to Philadelphia City Councilman Leland Beloff.

Riccobene, Enrico. Member of Riccobene gang; son of Mario Riccobene and owner of Enrico's, a jewelry store.

Riccobene, Harry ("The Hunchback"). Member of Mafia since 1929; fought Scarfo for control of the Philadelphia/Atlantic City mob.

Riccobene, Mario. Younger half-brother of Harry "The Hunchback" Riccobene.

Riccobene, Robert. Member of Riccobene gang; half-brother to Harry Riccobene; younger full brother of Mario Riccobene.

Sabella, Salvatore. Founder of the Philadelphia Mafia.

Salerno, Alfred. Brother-in-law and driver for Antonio Caponigro; murdered.

Saltzburg, Barry. Associate of Neil Ferber; suspect in murders of Harry Peetros and Steve Booras.

Scafidi, Salvatore ("Torry"). Associate of Salvatore Testa.

Scarfo, Nicodemo ("Nicky," "Little Nicky," "The Little Guy"). Don of Philadelphia/Atlantic City mob, 1981–1989.

Simone, John. Cousin to Angelo Bruno and capo in his New Jersey organization; murdered.

Sindone, Frank. Enforcer for Angelo Bruno; murdered.

Spirito, Pasquale ("Pat the Cat"). Gambler; murdered.

Staino, Ralph ("Junior"). Member of Scarfo organization.

Stanfa, John. Driver for Angelo Bruno on night Bruno was murdered.

Stillitano, Frankie. Low-level Mafia enforcer whose murder was the first organized crime killing investigated by Frank Friel.

Tamburrino, Samuel. Member of Riccobene gang; best friend and business partner of Mario Riccobene; murdered.

Testa, Philip ("Chicken Man"). Underboss to Angelo

Index